My 20
MIRACLE PRAYERS
FOR A WIFE

"Then the Lord said, Look, I am setting a
plumb line among My people." —*Amos 7:8 NIV*

CRAIG L. SNYDER

WESTBOW
PRESS®
A DIVISION OF THOMAS NELSON
& ZONDERVAN

WestBow Press books may be ordered through booksellers or by contacting:

WestBow Press
A Division of Thomas Nelson & Zondervan
1663 Liberty Drive
Bloomington, IN 47403
www.westbowpress.com
844-714-3454

Because of the dynamic nature of the Internet, any web addresses or links contained in this book may have changed since publication and may no longer be valid. The views expressed in this work are solely those of the author and do not necessarily reflect the views of the publisher, and the publisher hereby disclaims any responsibility for them.

Any people depicted in stock imagery provided by Getty Images are models, and such images are being used for illustrative purposes only.
Certain stock imagery © Getty Images.

ISBN: 978-1-6642-9450-9 (sc)
ISBN: 978-1-6642-9451-6 (e)

Library of Congress Control Number: 2023904537

Print information available on the last page.

WestBow Press rev. date: 04/19/2024

My 20 Miracle Prayers For a Wife

[14] *"If ye shall ask anything in My name, I will do it."* John14:14. KJV.

Today is November 11th 2022 and I was watching a fun romantic Hallmark movie in my living room **by myself** as usual when the Lord gave me a thought about the romance I missed in real life and then I started thinking back 15 years ago to 2007 before my first cruise liner trip to the Bahamas' Sun. That's when my once in a life time repetitious 20 miracles occurred within a few months all directing me toward the Lord's goal to answer my many years of prayers asking my heavenly Father to find me a godly wife. Back then I had been praying daily for a soulmate who would love the Lord as much as I do when all these miracles actually started occurring one right after the other and all of them were directing me to a specific single woman who had never been married before and who I didn't even know. So while watching this love-chasing Hallmark movie, part of an old love song entered my romantic but lonely mind as I heard the Lord's thought singing, ♩ **"My heart is saying that it's time again"** ♩ . Intrigued by this God induced love lyric I went to You Tube to punch in those exact lyrics and hear the entire song as I discovered that nostalgia love-longing line that God placed in my mind. It came from an old song 36 years ago released on March 22nd 1986 that was sung back then by Patti LaBelle and Michael McDonald, entitled **On My Own** as God was starting His Mission of Love. Remember the verse, [17] *". . . He will joy over thee with singing."*? Zephaniah 3:17. NKJV. Those love lyrics in that song God spoke to my romantic mind were stirring up my love hungry heart I missed back then about what had happened 15 years ago. Lyrics like, ♪ "<u>Why</u> <u>did it</u> <u>end</u> this way<u>?</u>" "**This <u>wasn't how it was</u> <u>supposed to end</u>**." "**I've got to find <u>where I belong</u> again**." And then the line God stirred me up with, "**My heart is saying that <u>it's time</u> again**". And lastly, "**And <u>I</u>, <u>have</u> <u>faith</u> that <u>I will</u> <u>shine</u> <u>again</u>**" ♪ . These song lyrics reflected my past trip to the Bahamas <u>perfectly</u> as the Lord was <u>restarting my prayers</u> back up by stirring my romantic heart after all these many years. For those of us who have romantic hearts and you might wonder where you got them. Just remember, God is Love, [8] "*Whoever does not love does not know God, because <u>God is love</u>*". 1 John 4:8. NIV. He created us to <u>love like He does</u>; so why shouldn't He speak love songs to us we already know. [17] ". . . *He will joy over thee with singing*." Zephaniah 3:17. NKJV. So I was wondering, "Does God, knowing <u>our</u> romantic heart<u>s</u>, answer our prayers <u>we</u> Christians have <u>given up</u> on even 15 years ago? Hmmm. And if so, <u>what triggered this start</u>? Is God trying to complete <u>what **He** started</u> in 2007 because the <u>spiritual door</u> has become opened again <u>somehow</u>? **Philipp<u>ians 1:6.</u>**

v4 Your love longing heart I still See,
and I have not forgotten Thee. ♥☺☺♥
v5 Remaining lonely is not your Fate,
good things come to <u>those who Wait</u>.
v6 I know you're still longing for a Date,
and so I'm sending you a sweet Soulmate.
Dad 1:4-6

God Speaks the Continuation of <u>His Original</u> Plan

Right after the Lord gave me that thought and that song, <u>**On My Own**</u> by Patti LaBelle and Michael McDonald another thought came into my mind. "Why don't you write about your 20 miracles you had; I'm sure lots of people would like to hear about that." So I thought about that idea and with my recorded romantic Hallmark movie on TV still on pause, I went to the computer started it up and with the Lord inspiring me I opened up a new folder and started typed out the <u>title</u> of this new book from my God

My 20 Miracle Prayers For a Wife and my very last thoughts.

Those last thoughts would be the pinnacle of this book in a question form because my diehard unfulfilled romantic heart still <u>just wouldn't die</u>. But it was very late around bed time that night when I got that God-induced idea, and so I said to my God, "Yeah, Lord, that's a good idea. I'll start writing those thoughts out tomorrow when I'm fresh and not now when it's late and I'm tired.

However, the next morning came at 62 degrees and I found myself shivering under my covers as I discovered the hard way the furnace just quit working in the middle of the night. But that delay of fixing the furnace cost me four long cold days but in the process of this irritating interruption I had managed to forget all about writing this book idea. But the Lord trying diligently to complete our prayers reminded me again to write this book and so I thought, "Oh that's right I forgot, Father; I'll start that good idea in the morning since it's late at night now." But like dejavu or a dastardly driven demon the furnace stopped working a second time in the middle of the night as I woke up freezing all over again.

So after the enemy's eight day delay was finally over and the furnace was completely fixed <u>I was totally discouraged</u> and decided to <u>skip this whole book writing idea</u>. But my Lord trying to complete <u>our</u> prayers reminded me again right before bed time with <u>two other songs</u> urging me to start writing my many miracles I had 15 years ago as I just turned on the TV and saw the end of this old 1960 movie from Turner Classic Movies. That song spoke directly to my past 20 miracles and the missed love relationship I had in 2008 as I'll save that song till the end of this book. These song lyrics were so unusual and had such strange lyrics I decided to look them up on line and when I did my Lord gave me a <u>third</u> song that really connected to my past with this single lady I met on a cruise liner ship. So after the enemy's eight day delay was finally over on November 19, 2022 we are now going to journey back to the start of these many miracles God did in my life to begin the amazing process to finally introduce me to a woman who sings worship songs on stage that I never knew or even saw before.

V12 If what you're doing doesn't bother the enemy, that enemy won't bother you.

"The chief priests and the whole Sanhedrin were <u>looking for</u> false evidence against Jesus <u>so that they could put Him to death</u>."
Matthew 26:59.

V13 But if Satan hates what God is doing in your <u>Life</u>, he'll <u>Disrupt</u> or <u>Stop</u> anything,

1 Kings 19:1, 2. * Mark 14:55-59, 65 * 2 Corinthians 11:23-28 * **2 Timothy 3:12**

even meeting your <u>Wife</u>.

Dad 1:12, 13

My Original Plan for Sweet Love

I had been praying for a godly wife so I could lavish all my love on her and maybe then she might even reflect all that lavished love I give her back on me for the Majestic Marriage of Oneness I have always longed for my whole life. As you may or may not know, men or husbands should be like flash lights shining their love on their wives and wives were designed by God to typically be like mirrors reflecting back to their husbands what he gives to her daily. Now back in 2005 I bought my first computer because I wanted to write out my romantic thoughts in a book of romance I hoped my future wife would read thinking maybe she might want the same romance I wrote about and then seek out the author so we might finally meet and so possibly live happily ever after. But little did I know there was a godly woman somewhere else in this love-starved sin-loving world who was also praying for a godly man so she could lavish all her stored up sweet love on him and be loved back deeply by that same righteous husband she had been praying for. The only thing wrong with my plan for love is that it wasn't God's plan; and when you pray to God, He always has a much better plan than you do. However, God getting His plan across to me was not going to be easy for Him as I was sure my plan would work, but then after all, that's why He's God Almighty, because He can get through to anyone, even someone like me with my own **stubborn** plan. I'm not sure who had the harder job; me trying to make my own romantic plan work to get some sweet lady, or God trying to get His thoughts and plan across to me with my blind **Stubborn Love** thinking as I thought I had this soulmate thing all figured out. But the battle plans for finding sweet love of Oneness were started and may the best planner win.

God Starts <u>His</u> Incredible Plan to Show me my Future Wife

So as I can recall 15 years ago, it was a Sunday morning about July or August 2007 right after the church service was over and I was still in the Church building walking through the corridor on my way to the exit door to go home when the Lord spoke a thought to my mind. "Check out the library and see if there is anything you might find interesting." But I answered the Lord quickly in my mind, "I never go in the library. I have 66 books <u>You wrote</u> to read and study and that might take a lifetime so I'm happy just reading my Bible." 📖 After that quick answer I kept right on walking toward the exit door. But the Lord was persistent (James 1:12 * Luke 11:5-13) and repeated, "There might be something in there you find interesting; you should take a look." I stopped walking to consider His prompting as a second thought on the same subject is not that common and after I considered it I replied, "No, I'm not interested in reading someone else's book when I have the Holy Word of God I could be reading to direct my life."

<u>Side Note</u>: When Jesus told the disciples to throw their nets on the opposite side of the boat in John 21:4-12 and they did, they caught 153 fish. "*. . . It was full of large fish, 153, but even with so many the net was not torn*." John 21:11. When new Christians read the Bible, they don't **<u>DIG</u>** in very deep, but read like a <u>motor boat</u> speeding across the water like they were reading a newspaper. But every detail in the Bible is there for a reason and if you study <u>deeper</u> and <u>slower</u> like a <u>submarine</u> (Psalm 107:24) you will find God's hidden golden nuggets of deeper truths for those of us who are hungry for more of God's truth. Colossians 1:10 * 2 Peter 2:1 * 3:18.

Now you ask. "So what's so significance about 153 fish? Very few Christians study Hebrew but some of you know that every Hebrew letter has a corresponding number. And the God-chasing Hebrews used their alphabet as a numbering system as well. The number <u>153</u> is the numerical total for the Hebrew words "<u>Ani Elohim</u>"; when translated into our English those Hebrew words are, <u>**I AM GOD.**</u> So when Jesus caused the disciples to catch exactly 153 fish, He was doing more than just making them money for their upcoming <u>people catching</u> ministry, or feeding the Jewish community, He was also declaring to His disciples that not only is He the <u>Son of God</u>, but that <u>He is God Himself</u>. So as you can see, I will need to study a lifetime to understand all His hidden truths.

A		1				
n	+	50	=	51		
i	+	10	=	61		
E	+	1	=	62		
l	+	30	=	92		
o	+	6	=	98		
h	+	5	=	103		
i	+	10	=	113		
m	+	40	=	153	=	<u>**I AM GOD.**</u>

Now back to my testimony 15 years ago. And with everything considered I proceeded toward the exit door again. But the Lord was not going to give up on answering those prayers we both had prayed many times <u>with a fervent heart</u> and so He reiterated <u>a third time</u> impressing me, "You should check out the library and see if there isn't anything you might find interesting." I stopped again and this time I'm thinking, "There must be something He wants me to check out in this library or He wouldn't have prompted me three different times." So now after being at this church for <u>five years</u> and <u>not once did I ever go into the library for any reason</u>, I am now going into the church library for the very first time out of curiosity to see what the Lord wanted me to, "check out".

Now being a typical logical male I started this God-prompted endeavor <u>I didn't even want to do</u> at the top of the first row looking at books, CDs, cassette tape series, study guides, teaching CD booklets et cetera. Scanning from top to bottom I went along down each row very systematically considering everything I saw and weather this godly material would interest me <u>more than the God written Bible</u> I was already reading and happily enjoying while thinking. "Do I really want to commit my time and energy to this teaching series instead of reading my own Bible that I enjoy every day? Hmmm. Nothing really jumped out at me and so I just kept scanning quickly to finish this thought the Lord had of, "Checking out the library to see if there was anything I might find interesting." When I finished looking through all the rows and still found nothing, the librarian noticed I didn't find anything yet so she asked, "Did you find what you were looking for?" I answered, "I'm really not sure what I'm looking for." She then points to a back hallway with metal shelves on either side and boxes of old teaching materials on those shelves from the floor to the top over my head in this poorly lit darkened hallway as she says, "We have a back hallway here with shelves of old technology we're eventually going to get rid of; you might try looking there."

So, not having any real thing in mind I entered this unlit back hallway with low lighting and older teaching paraphernalia just thrown in a box and not displayed neatly like the new technology stuff was in the well-lit library. The lower shelves were easier to look down into the dark boxes in this lower lit hallway and so I considered them first but did not dig down very deep at all because this whole endeavor was not really my idea.

Then looking up I saw only the bottom of brown cardboard boxes which told me absolutely nothing. Now not wanting to turn this whole frustrating hunt into a dark attic box shuffling sweaty day workout I finally said with frustration, "Lord, there's nothing here, I'm going home;" and that's when I gave up. Have any of you ever given up on anything? How many know when we Christians give up, that's when God begins His behind the scene planning to steer us in His direction. But the Lord was waiting for me to be right under a certain big cardboard box and as I was looking up at the bottom of that brown box He said, "What's in that box?" Feeling like I was intruding on somebody's privet stuff I said in my mind, "I don't know." The Lord encouraged me, "Well, pull the box down and take a look."

So now I'm thinking to myself, "Okay, the dark attic reshuffling sweaty box day has now begun. But when I looked into the big box I saw Dr. Gary Smalley's VHS tapes (old technology) on The DNA of Relationships and how to have a great marriage which I actually saw before and enjoyed very much. Since my only marriage to an unsaved woman ended in 2001, this time (2 Cor. 13:11) I wanted to be the best husband I could possibly be. So suddenly my eyes lit up with joy and excitement and I now saw the reason the Lord wanted me to enter the library and find something I would be interested in learning. The librarian said I could only take out one VHS tape at a time. But I was excited and wanted them all and she could see the enthusiasm on my face and so with persuasion she finally allowed me to check out all of them at once. Now with this entire big box in my hands, and a happy smile on my face, I went home with my new treasure to start watching and learning how to be the best possible husband for my new sweet wife I believed Lord Jesus would pick out for me soon.

My Vow to the Lord

Father's Day June 18th 1995 the Brownsville Pensacola Revival started with Holy Ghost power featuring evangelist Steve Hill. [3] "*When You did awesome things for which we did not look, You came down; the mountains shook at your presence.* [4] *For since the beginning of the world men have not heard nor has the eye seen any God besides You, who acts for the one who waits for Him.*" Isaiah 64:3, 4. NKJV. Have you ever waited on the Lord? "*But those who wait on the LORD Shall renew their strength; They shall mount up with wings as eagles, They shall run and not be weary, They shall walk and not faint.*" Isaiah 40:31. KJV. Is this His perfect timing for you? Back during the 1995 Brownsville Pensacola Revival I was in another church building in Grove City at 145 South Broad Street called Solid Rock. We had just bought an old shoe store and were in the process of converting it into our new church building.

This being my third time of converting a prior building into a new church building I reminded my current church staff that back in 1991 and 1992 I was at a different church building where we had bought a big telephone company building in Cranberry at 2710 Rochester road and a master plumber, a painter and I the carpenter, converted it over after many months into our new church building. There was a lot of demolition work to be done as those old walls needed to be ripped down for our new sanctuary to be constructed. At first there were lots of us good Christian volunteers willing to help with the manual labor of converting this old telephone building over into our new Church building. Dumpsters were brought in the parking lot as many volunteers helped rip down and carry out the old tattered pieces to the large dumpster. However after the <u>basic manual labor</u> work was done, those willing to help <u>construct</u> and actually <u>build</u> the new sanctuary thinned down considerably to only a master plumber, a painter and I the carpenter as those volunteers lacked the talent and skills to build with any kind of precisions. Interesting to note: This is where I got <u>my very first job in construction</u> as <u>building and creating</u> just came naturel to me while remodeling the old building.

So I constructed a 30 by 24 foot stage two feet high with 33 precision made trap doors for accessing electrical panels, break away plumbing pipe panels and other large doors for hiding tables in the stage to <u>feed the poor</u> when the time came. Constructing quick set-up (no tools required) collapsible six by six foot wing stages on both ends of the main stage with removable stairs to the floor when needed as the main stage, both wing stages and stairs all had to be covered with commercial grade carpet. Four huge speakers also needed to be sunk into the curved corner of this same <u>quarter round</u> stage. The large baptismal was complete with running water for the growth of the new converts to God's people. With laser level I also had to construct a 6,000 foot drop ceiling over the sanctuary and two higher levels over the stage and again higher yet over the baptismal with wooden framework and drywall bulkheads between the three different ceiling heights. Building just came natural to me as this was one of my God given gifts. 🎁 After I installed the 3,500 square foot entry and bathrooms with commercial grade VCT tile with my professional **Gundlach** floor cutter tool the Church building was finished and ready to occupy.

But years later at this shoe store building we were now converting it into our new church building and I warned the young Pastor John Lesley we will need to get a permit from the City Building in Grove City. They will want an engineer to look over all of our plans in a blue print form which we have not done yet. I sternly warned them these city officials take a very dim view of new owners who do their own thing and leave them out of all their authority planning; there could be fines if we don't include them. But my experienced words and past knowledge of warning them all fell on deaf ears as their excitement got the better of them.

So I submitted my building skills to the Church authorities and did as they instructed me. "So I cut away the first floor sheeting where they indicated and then saw where to support the basement rafters with a stairwell supporting wall. After removing those rafters I installed a stairwell with landings from the basement to the first floor continuing up to the ceiling to the second floor supporting it with walls and then removing the rafters to install the stairwell to the second floor. All of this was done with proper landings and continuous railings obeying the Building Code Book right <u>where the church staff wanted it</u>." They also instructed me to, "Take out these old shoe store walls and put new church walls where they wanted using metal studs where the Building Code demanded them at the entrance." It all looked good until the city officials got wind of our own decisions as it was shut down by the city officials just like I said it would happen. So the church staff was then educated by the city officials and so we got a building permit from the city and hired an engineer to look over all of our brand new blue prints we had to have drafted up by an architect.

But months later after we were all finished with the church building and when we were having our church services there was a serious Christian woman who said she was going to leave Grove City and go down to the Pensacola Revival in Florida to sit under their tutelage. I was very impressed with just that statement alone, but then I later found out she didn't even watch TV at all as she didn't want to become calloused or even tainted from this wicked world with Satan's sinful system. When I overheard her say that in church I stopped as I was stunned while my mouth hung open and I just stared a hole through that godly woman because she was so dedicated to God and His holiness. Later in 2001 I heard of another woman who didn't watch TV either and I stopped again in utter amazement and this time I said to myself back then, "If those two women can walk that close to God, then so can I." It was then that I made a **vow** to my Lord, "<u>NO MORE TV FOR ME</u>".

But then I had a conflict with that vow as I had my own business as I was an A to Z construction man who did all kinds of remodeling and home repairs on houses but 60% of my main business was roofing where you had to watch the weather very closely so it wouldn't rain in on the customer's living room when replacing their roofs. So I had to make this one exception to my God promised vow of not watching the TV back then as I had to watch channel 25 for <u>one minute</u> to catch the local weather to see what day was dry to schedule my next roofing job and then call up my workers to inform them what day we were working. Thus every ten minutes this weather channel would do what they called, "Local on the eights". Therefore, <u>8</u>, 1<u>8</u>, 2<u>8</u>, 3<u>8</u>, 4<u>8</u>, 5<u>8</u>, minutes after every hour you could catch the local weather every ten minutes and this was perfect for me and my regular roofing jobs I needed to schedule back then in 2007.

But as you know, Satan is the god of this worldly sad sinful system. 2 Corinthians 4:4. So right before the local on the eights, where our enemy knew the public was sure to see, that evil system placed a commercial with this mermaid swimming under water who was covered with as little seaweed as legally possible and only in curtain key places. THEN, after the devil got everyone to view his sin of lust, channel 25 would then show the local weather on the eights that I needed to see for my roofing business. It's like you can't win in Satan's world; he's going to shove his sin in your face so you have to see it. No matter how holy you try to be or how godly you try to walk before your Lord, Satan was working just as hard to corrupt God's children so that holiness just can't be done without his sinful system trying to corrupt you every step of the way in **his** wicked world. I was furious; I'm a single Christian guy trying to live for God and I don't need any temptations to lead me into sin I wasn't even thinking about. But always remember . .

v9 If we play with Sin, the demons will surly get In!
". . . you are slaves to the one whom you obey . . ." Romans 6:16.

v10 If we embrace Hell, our wisdom will Fail!
Isaiah 6:9, 10 * Matt 13:14-15 * Mark 4:12 * Luke 8:10 * Acts 28:26-27.

v11 Always guard your Heart, or you'll give Satan his Start.
"Jesus replied, 'I tell you the truth, everyone who sins is <u>a slave to sin</u>."
John 8:34.
Dad 1:9-11

Now, I said all of that to set the stage for the Lord's next <u>set of miracles</u> as you have to know what God knows to see and understand these next set of miracles all in rapid succession. Rare as it is to get even one miracle in your entire life time, but to get a set of them all happening in the same 15 minutes is really rare and almost impossible; so here we go with the hand of God in my life.

Always Keep Your Vow To The Lord

So now I had my old technology VHS tapes of Dr. Gary Smalley on the DNA of Relationships that I was excited to watch. I wanted to learn how to have the best marriage as I was trying to be the best husband that I could possibly be and so I think the current date was late July or August of 2007 some six years after I left my <u>unsaved wife in 2001</u>. But even if you've suffered greatly in the past, if you just spend <u>lots of time</u> before the Lord in worship before His throne, He can heal all of your past emotional hurts and <u>make you brand new again</u>; thank You Lord Jesus. Now this next part is where my vow and God's plan come head to head. The very thing I vowed to God <u>back then</u> was to "Never sit in front of a TV". Yet that was the very thing I now wanted to do with these Dr. Gary Smalley VHS tapes. But I reasoned, this material is godly and will make me a better Christian so it was okay to watch them on the TV. Now I brought my big cardboard box of Dr. Gary Smalley tapes out to dad's 1980 TV in the living room at my parent's house as I left my own house I remodeled in 2001.

Now I'm looking at my parent's old 1980 consult TV with mom and dad's new DVD player my sister Chris and her husband Louis got them for Christmas and mom still had her old VHS tape recorder which I needed for these old VHS tapes of Dr. Gary Smalley. But staring at three different remotes with over 40 buttons each, one for the TV, another one for the new DVD player and yet even another one for the old VHS tapes she still kept in her end table drawers to watch some of her old 1970s movie she taped years ago. All this new and old technology mixed together and the knowledge to push which button first and turn what knob next on the TV and I had no idea what went first or what to do second. Then on top of all that, not watching TV for six years now, I forgot the proper procedure needed to make this plan work as I really didn't know how to set it all up so I could just simply push play and pause to learn my treasured tapes I got from the church library. So I went back the long hallway in my parent's home to get mother in her master bedroom where she always watched her soap operas on TV and have her set this all up as she still had all of her faculties back then and so she pushed all the right buttons for me to simply watch. Mom said, "There you are, all you need to do is push play on this remote and right there is your pause button. So I thanked her for fixing the confusion and pushed play seeing Gary Smalley teaching and so I was happy to learn my desired subject of how to be the best husband and having the best marriage."

Now I put all three of these confusing TV remotes on the couch cushion beside me and happily watched my desired subject. But I always have an ongoing habit of talking to my Heavenly <u>Father</u> (1 Thess. 5:16- 18) when I do anything. [23] "*And in that day* (our future) *ye shall ask Me* (Jesus) <u>*nothing*</u>. *Verily, verily, I say unto you, Whatsoever ye shall <u>ask the Father</u> in My name, He will give it you.*" John 16:23. KJV. So I hit the pause button and started sharing some of my ideas with the Father to get His valued input. As you may know these conversations with God can linger on for hours if you give them a chance. But little did I know, the pause button only stays on pause for a minute or two and then it jumps off the VHS tape you were watching and on to the <u>real TV</u>'s last channel "**someone**" was watching prior to me being in the living room. Now God begins His hand of direction and starts pointing me toward His goal for us praying Christians to create our meeting on the TV to start. So those few minutes passed by quickly and the pause button jumped off the VHS tape and on to the real TV <u>I vowed to God I would not watch</u>. When this happened I panicked for two reasons. One: I remembered the scantily clad mermaid trying to draw me into the sin of lust from the weather channel before, and so I didn't want to see any more commercials like that. And two: There was my **vow** I made to the Lord. [4] "*When you make a vow to God, do not delay in fulfilling it, because He takes no pleasure in fools.* **Fulfill** *your vow*. [5] *It is better not to vow than to make a vow and not fulfill it . . .*" Ecclesiastes 5:4, 5. NIV. So there I am suddenly looking at the real TV and <u>breaking my vow to the Lord</u> and to my right there are three remotes and over a hundred buttons to push in the right sequential order and so I'm now fumbling through these buttons with panic and what to do first and what comes second. While the TV is on right in front of me I finally figure out the right combination of buttons and there is Dr. Gary Smalley talking again on the TV screen as I hit the pause button again and so I could finally start to relax after that panicky situation. I then said to the Lord, "Boy, that was close." But the Lord spoke a quick thought to my mind, "Why the panic? Did you not see the Life Today ministry with James and Betty Robison? You've seen them before, it's a Christian program." But I defended my panicky actions and replied, "Well I know how crafty that devil is with his sinful commercials, plus it's not good to make vows to the Lord and then not keep them. So where were we Lord before all this commotion happened? Oh yes, we were discussing my ideas about how I could be the best husband." I no sooner got back into my conversation with my Lord when this whole panicky situation happened all over again. Suddenly there I was breaking my vow to the Lord again and you can't be too careful when dealing with the sneaky devil and all of his controlling sins. And so I panicked like before fumbling through the many remotes and all those numerous buttons. Finally I saw Gary Smalley on the TV and so I hit the pause button again and then started to relax having gone through this alarming routine twice. But once again God questioned me, "Why the panic? Life Today with James and Betty Robison is a Christian program. You could watch these Gary Smalley tapes at any time." I responded in my mind, "Well, that's true. But right now I'm watching Gary Smalley. And besides, I want to be the best husband I can be so <u>when You introduce me to my future wife</u> someday I'll be ready to meet <u>her</u>." I thought I had successfully made my point with the Lord and so I started up our conversation again. But now for the third time those few minutes went by quickly and there I was watching the real TV again. It never occurred to me God might be trying to introduce me to <u>my new future wife</u> **right now** and that she might just be on the very TV I was trying so hard to avoid watching. So I panicked the third time and started pushing buttons quicker this time as I was beginning to learn the proper sequence of which buttons to push first and witch one was second. But every second I was looking for the next button to push and waiting for this old technology to slowly kick-in and respond, the Lord was stating in my mind, "Its James and Betty Robison. They're a Christian program. You don't have to panic. You could watch them now and learn your Gary Smalley tapes at any time." The Lord had a plan for us praying Christians to meet on TV and He was only using the Gary Smalley VHS tapes from the church library <u>as a reason to sit me in front of the TV</u> I vowed to God I would not watch so He could introduce me to my new future soulmate. I may be slow to catch on to the Lord's leading, but I think the Lord is trying to tell me something. It seems He wants me to watch this James and Betty

Robison show now. So here I am in my mind breaking my vow I made to the Lord and pushing the stop button **on purpose** and actually watching the TV I vowed to God I wouldn't watch.

Now I'm watching James Robison talking to his guest; "**some Italian woman**" I never saw before. Near as I can remember 15 years ago I think she got up to sing a worship song and then did a little teaching from her latest DVD lesson after that. Once I finished watching the rest of this show the Lord wanted me to watch, I decided I liked her worship song and enjoyed her teaching. Then James and "**this woman**" showed the viewers on the TV screen how to get her worship CD and also this DVD teaching I just saw a snippet of for a certain price. I said inside my mind talking to the Lord as I usually do, (1 Thessalonians 5:17), "You know Father I'd like to have both the worship music and the biblical teaching DVDs as well." He responded a thought in my mind indicating there's the phone number on the TV screen right now; why not write it down and call and get them both. I thought, "I've never bought anything off the TV before in my entire life." The Lord responded, "There's really nothing to it. You just call the number that's on the screen. They'll answer, and then you tell them what you want." I just barely wrote down the last two numbers before the program went off the air. And when I called in they still answered the phone anyway and I made both purchases and thanked the Lord for helping me get these Christian tools off the TV for the very first time in my life. Keep in mind the Lord does not speak to us Christians word for word in plain English like we humans have to do to each other limited by our fleshly lips but He can speak a thought in our mind conveying an enter concept and then as a Christian you understand that thought He's speaking to steer you in His direction or communicate with you His will.

The Lord's Inner Workings

So now let's take a look at the nuts and bolts of the Lord's plan from His point of view and what He needed to do to make just one of these two praying Christians who don't know one another to meet on just the TV alone. Lord Jesus, the Master Matchmaker, can't introduce Craig's future wife to him on TV if Craig won't even sit down and watch the TV at all because he's trying to set himself aside for Holiness to the Lord so God will honor his efforts and find him a soulmate someday. Both of my brothers are just as biblically dedicated to God as well as it runs in the family. My parents raised in the 1929 depression learned diligences as all of their six kids were dedicated workers. So God had to devise a plan of precision to get around Craig's devoted **vow** to Him to be willing just to sit in front of a TV as then God can have him "accidently" see **this woman** that He picked out for him. So the Master Matchmaker starts His strategy off by having me walk into a church library that I didn't even want to enter as the Lord had to talk me into it several times. Neither was I in that Church library before in all the five years I've been going to that Church building. So one day out of five years, those odds are one out of 1,826 if you include the leap year in 2004. So was this long shot possibility a simple coincidence that just happened to occur; or is there a God in Heaven who hears and answers prayer for His praying Christians? Psalm 116:1, 2. And what about finding the Dr. Gary Smalley VHS tapes in the back dark hallway library in some upper card board box I couldn't even see into that I was never going to look in; was that also a simple coincidence that just happened to occur? Certainly not as I wanted to go home and was never going to look in that upper box without God's ongoing prodding. Or was this

God's amazing impossible method to get Craig <u>to want to sit in</u> <u>front of the TV</u> so He could start this process of introducing me to my new future wife someday if she's even willing to have me? Then after searching up and down every row and finding nothing, I was then ready to give up on <u>God's idea</u> of finding some Christian material I might find interesting more than the Bible I was already reading. But God having the master plan directed me to find the only Christian teaching material in the whole library that I actually <u>saw before</u> and would be exceedingly excited about seeing again and would finally be willing to watch <u>on the forbidden TV</u> I vowed not to watch back then. Then out of the hundreds of books, CDs, and teaching materials available, maybe 1,000 to choose from, what are the odds of me finding the one and only teaching material I would actually watch in some card board box over my head in a dark leftover hallway on some upper shelf I couldn't even see into; would those odds be **100,000 to one**? God also had to pick the <u>perfect time of day</u> when that Christian program Life Today with James and Betty Robison would actually be <u>starting</u> on the TV with me willingly watching a TV that just a day ago I vowed absolutely I would not even sit in front of. And how often was **"this woman"** on that program as a guest; <u>once every six months</u>? I don't know. Times those 182 days by the 24 hours in every day that I could have sat in front of that TV and that alone comes to 4,368 hours and Craig who doesn't even watch TV just happened to see that one particular hour on that one day on that one channel that she just happened to be on? And remember I missed almost 15 minutes of that show do to not wanting to watch the real TV and all those pause button jumps took up time from the one hour show. The chances of all these long shot miracles all occurring at the same time synergistically together is some astronomical number to say the least and we are still just getting started with the Master Matchmaker's intervening. God also had to work through the perfect timing of this back and forth or the on and off process with the pause buttons and the three remotes, the VHS player, the connection with the real TV and Craig's ability to figure out the right sequence of buttons plus my stubborn will of not willing to watch the TV at all as I was <u>wrestling with God's</u> (Genesis 32:24) <u>will</u> trying to keep my vow to the Lord. So God had to factor all that time in as well and not miss when **"this woman"** would be on that show for me to actually see. That process took time from the show where James was talking to the TV audience and so I missed all that time when I assume <u>she was not on for me to see</u> anyway. That would increase the odds of 4,368 hours into 6,552 hours making the chances of seeing her all the more impossible. Then when I did finally concede to watching the TV, **"<u>this woman</u>"** I didn't know and never saw before in my life had to be on where I could finally see her for the very first time ever and she needed to be talking about a subject that I would be actually interested in hearing, like relationships that I was already studying to be the best husband. But God never told me she was anyone special to me so I simply saw her as some guest James Robison had on his Christian program and so I figured God only wanted me to order her teaching material and grow spiritually and so that's all I did and understood at that time. Then God had to talk me into buying something off the TV I never did before in my entire life with a bank card I only got a few days ago; otherwise this whole purchase of her material would never have happened. The long shot timing and multiple miracles just keep adding up and all these numerous things needed to all line up or this whole amazing phenomenon occurring in 15 minutes would have never happened at all.

Split Second Timing

But there's another complicated piece to this impossible puzzle we must consider to understand how God's inner workings actually worked for us both praying Christians. Watch the ancient technology my parents still had of the past which God understood and I certainly did not. The old TV also had to be put on channel three first or you can't use the other devices like the DVD player or the old VHS tapes mom taped off the TV and stored in her end table drawers from the 70s like, The Sons of Katie Elder rerun that originally came out in 1965. Then the Christian program God wants me to **"accidently"** watch to see this **"singer/teacher woman"** on channel 40 the only Christian channel at that time had to be selected by **"someone"** at the TV before I got there. But how did the TV get to the only Christian channel 40 (Cornerstone), out of all the channels available or **"who"** selected that particular channel? This is where it really gets down to split-second timing.

Watch carefully how precise God is while making this whole amazing miracle work as just the right split second had to be chosen. When I entered my parent's living room wanting to watch TV for the first time in six years with my Dr. Gary Smalley VHS tapes, the living room I needed that day was conveniently empty. Normally my dad would be sitting in his wheelchair at that time watching that same TV since he was not able to walk anymore after his stroke. Normally he went downstairs in his "man cave" he built back in the late 60s in the finished basement and watched his desired big square ☐ TV. So out of the four TVs my parents had, the only one that had the VHS tapes recorder I needed for these old technology VHS tapes was the living room TV that my dad normally watched seven days a week and all day long from 9:00 in the morning to his bed time at 9:00 pm. But at this time when I needed it, my dad had a doctor's appointment at the same time I just happened to want to watch these tapes. So the living room TV I needed after all these years of not watching was conveniently available that particular day as God was setting the stage for all the right people to make these multi-miracles work synergistically. Working with the doctor office to scheduling my dad's appointment the same day I needed the living room TV, God alone knew I would need that day after six years of not watching. Now the magic of the pause button flipping back to the real TV could only have been done with an old TV as that 1980 TV needed to be put on channel three first so this old technology VHS player would work that someone should have upgraded and gotten rid of years ago. That combination in 2007 would be very rare as just about everyone else in my dad's age group had moved on except my parents who were very old. The VHS tapes mother was still hanging on to in her end table drawers would probably not even play being recorded from the 1970s. The singer/teacher lady had to be scheduled weeks in advanced on that program so I could see her at that precise moment. A lot of things had to be set up for everything to go just right that one day after the six years of deciding not to watch the TV. So were all those necessary people, items, places, old technology, timed perfectly by mere chance as it all just happened to fall into place at that precise time, or do you see all the many pieces coming together by the hand of God to answer His children's heartfelt ongoing prayers they prayed for years? But my earthly father, who was a wonderful father by the way, was at age 82 where he had Alzheimer's disease and so his mind was not all together there. Therefore, his sad understanding was highly crippled and so he would **channel surf** **all day long** for his own simple amusement. Back at that time if you still had an old TV you could still "channel surf quickly" as you would look for your preferred programs fast by clicking the up or down channel button rapidly to find your favorite TV shows. As the technology was evolving on our modern TVs if you click the up or down channel button it will take two to three seconds per click to register and then slowly click over to the next up or down channel; a very slow process that stopped this channel surfing quick method in the past. But back then my dad was still using this old method of channel surfing on this very old 1980 TV and so he could click as fast as he wanted to and this old quick method was his simple amusement all day long until he got up to channel 71. After that the higher channels would turn all white with static as no one was broadcasting from those channels yet and those all-white screen static channels were called "snow" by the people in the 60s and 70s when I was growing up. So I educated my dad on not going beyond channel 71 but to start back down the channels toward channel two which was the lowest channel and then back up again to channel 71; this is what my dad did all day long as his understanding was highly limited. Then at the end of every day while dad was still clicking his remote up or down for his amusement, my mother, the R.N. nurse, who took care of him, would come out from the master bed room to the living room while her TV was on a long commercial break at 9:00 pm. She would then quickly yank the remote out of dad's hand and throw it on the couch to wheel him back into his bed room so she could hurry back and not miss her next TV show before the commercial break was over. Then in the morning she would pick up that same remote off the couch where she threw it the night before and place it right back in dad's hand so he could do the same simple activity all day long as this was my dad's daily routine at that time.

But as you can see, there were 70 channels to choose from, channel two up to channel 71 and the only Christian channel at that time was channel 40; Cornerstone. So while my dad was selecting the next channel, one click per second up or down, while clicking from 39 up to channel 40, at that precise split second, mom totally unaware of God's split second timing plan, yanking the remote out of dad's hand. That fast action by mom, "accidently" chose channel 40 the cornerstone Christian channel while throwing that remote she yanked on the couch like always to put dad to bed and hurry back then to see her next TV show which was on a long commercial break at 9:00 while dad never did get to click up to the next channel 41. So the Lord had this all timed out perfectly within that same split-second between two people who had no idea about God's plan to have these two praying Christians meet just on TV alone the next day when I entered the living room to watch a TV I hadn't watched in six years. Do you see the long shot odds?

There were 70 channels and so the odds of just that one channel being selected for me to "accidently" default to by this old technology every time the pause button let go while watching the Dr. Gary Smalley VHS tape the following day was **one out of 70** just on the channels alone. However you also must factor in this technical phenomenon happening the very night before Craig watches the TV the following day for the first time in six long years or 2,191 days if you include leap year in 2004! So now when you apply all those incredible long odds to the astronomical odds already mentioned before, those combined astronomical odds would be multiplied by 70 times for all the channels; and then that huge exorbitant number multiplied by the 2,191 days that must also be factored in as well just to get these two praying Christians to meet and only on the TV just to start our relationship. That way when the pause button jumps off the Dr. Gary Smalley VHS tape, it would then end up at channel 40 every time where my mom and dad with God's amazing calculating help left it the night before in a single split-second while dad innocently was clicking the remote.

God also had to calculate the time of me not wanting to watch the real TV and that back and forth pause button flip I went through. So when this singer/teacher lady was ready to sing a worship song I just happened to like and teach from her DVD that I just happened to enjoy, that timing had to be all calculated down to a precise short moment or I would have missed her completely. So God found a way passed Craig's **stubborn vow** and the devil's sin of lust trying to corrupt the public with a scantily clad mermaid commercial and through all those astronomical odds as I was now finally willing to relax and just watch the TV calmly and see this singer/teacher woman God was trying to show me who I didn't even know for the very first time. I cannot factor in all these large numbers exact and astronomical odds like God can and all the numerous probabilities of hit and miss ratio that God can calculate perfectly in order to make these incredible multi-miracles all work synergistically in those complicated decisive moments.

Listen to what God was up against and just how impossible it was for God to have Craig "accidently" hear or see this woman even by long-shot astronomical chances. I never watched TV in those past six years so it was absolutely impossible for God to have me accidently see this woman teaching anything on TV not even by long-shot miracle chance. I also would not even listen to the singing on any radio either Christian or secular but would only listen to godly biblical teachers in the morning on my way to my work site on 101.5 WORD FM like Dr. David Jeremiah or John MacArthur or Charles Stanley; at that time. So even the long shot chances of hearing her music was not even possible by radio either at this time; yet God found a way to make these impossible multi miracles happen just to start His plan of boy meets girl. Also in all my years I never saw this woman before, nor did I ever hear her singing in the past, neither did I even hear her name mentioned in conversation before; she was in fact a complete stranger to me. Do you see God's incredible impossible challenge? And yet all of these impossibilities and incredible long shot astronomical chances came together all simultaneously at the same split-second.

All this occurred just so Lord Jesus could start phase one and begin this ongoing process of placing these two praying Christians together just to answer their many years of prayers for a godly spouse? I found out many years later the woman James had as a guest on his show, whose name I will not mention out of respect for her privacy, had been praying for a spouse for many years just like I also had been doing for years. So you tell me, did all these things just fall into place all by themselves by some sheer long shot exorbitant coincidence; or is there an Almighty God who lives in Heaven who does indeed answer prayers for His beloved children who love Him (Matthew 7:11) and put Him first. Matthew 6:33. 12 *"For the eyes of the Lord are on the righteous, and His ears are inclined to their prayer."* 1 Peter 3:12a. AMP. Remember, God loves to lavish gifts and grand blessings on His children because He is the God of Love. 8 *"Whoever does not love does not know God, because God is love."* 1 John 4:8. NIV. Now if these multi-miracles we just saw are impressive, wait till you see the rest of them coming up. I have to tell you, I was so into my own plan for sweet love that I missed God's plan completely again and again.

Still Working My Own Plan

So what has God accomplished with His plan so far on Earth at this point of introducing that singer/teacher lady to me? I may have seen His choice for my future wife on TV chosen by God Himself, but I haven't understood who she was to me yet nor His matchmaking plan of boy meets girl and so I didn't make any of these marital connections in my own mind at this point. So as far as I knew, that whole exercise with the pause button and me watching the real TV for the first time in six years for 45 minutes was done so I could buy a worship CD and learn some spiritual knowledge (Proverbs 1:7) from that woman's teaching DVDs that was still coming in the mail and so I thought that was all the Lord wanted me to accomplish in that Life Today Christian program. But as you remember back in 2005 I bought my first computer because I was longing to write a book about romance in hopes that my future wife would read it and maybe seek out the author and possibly we would meet some day in the future and then live happily ever after. Now in September 2007 or there about I was still oblivious to God's matchmaking plan and so I was still working on my own plan or my first novel which started out with a romantic theme just as I had planned in hopes to catch the romantic heart of my future bride someday. However, me being the daily Bible hound that I am and talking to God every day about spiritual questions I longed to know, I wanted to know how do all these many spiritual laws work synergistically between the angels, the demons, and us humans saved and unsaved? So then the book novel I started turned more biblical with godly insight rather than romantic like I started as I got into spiritual matters all the more about guardian angels and how they interact with their human

Christians they protect and our sins we Christians get into and how that affects our lives. Also I learned extensively about demons and fallen angels how they both get into our homes and what it takes for them to enter our lives and I discovered they are not the same; but that is a rather lengthily teaching I will have to teach another time. More importantly I also learned how to get these unwanted thorny things out of our homes and out of our lives so we're not oppressed continually as they can lead us Christians astray and into greater sins. Since I was saved back on June 1980, my biblical hungry mind took over the novel I was writing and so my first book began turning more spiritual and biblical instead of romantic as I was learning daily about the spiritual rules while the Lord revealed them to my mind. Therefore, I had two powerful themes in just one long book and ended up with over 1,200 pages and so I realized this one dictionary-size book needed to be divided up into several smaller novel-size books with sequels to the first novel. Since my God was my ". . . *first love* . . ." (Revelation 2:4), I put God's spiritual rules first in my first novel and so the romance novel I started out writing for my future wife came in second place and ended up as a sequel to my first novel about spiritual rules.

Anyway, I was happy using my KJV Strong's Exhaustive Concordance and my NIV Strongest Exhaustive Concordance and of course my KJV Bible and my NIV Bible as well. I was hearing from the Holy Spirit every day as He led most of my thinking and so I was happy believing if I kept God first in my life, someday my future princess will come. sw? But at this time while writing my book, I never thought in a million years God was trying to connect me to some singer/teacher lady on TV. I guess I should give this singer/teacher lady a pseudonym name to protect her identity so I'll just call her "Kay". Now since all five of my siblings moved out of my parent's house years ago, I turned the back bedroom, which originally used to be mine growing up, into a computer room so I could type up my book. I was having the time of my life typing up <u>biblical principles</u> in my novel and learning God's spiritual rules to teach others in my first book on how to deal with demons in these fictional characters I had in their lives that most Christians do not know they were asking in through their <u>ongoing</u> <u>sins</u>. Since <u>teaching</u> and <u>creativity</u> were two of the gifts God gave me, life just couldn't get any better as I was deep into my biblical books and typing up God's spiritual rules I was learning from Him every day at that time as fast as my Lord would reveal them.

One day my mother who always went out and got the mail, and who was also glad I was there back at her house since my dad's mind checked out a while back leaving no forwarding address, opened my computer room door, and said, "You have a package here"; as she held it up waving it to get my attention. Mother learned shortly after me being back at the house, if you want to break Craig's concentration from his typing <u>while he's in</u> <u>the spiritual zone</u> listening to God speak to get his attention you might have to drop a grenade first, then tell him its supper time. In the midst of writing my book and all the fun I was having, I barely took my eyes off the print in my computer I was still typing out as I was trying to complete my current spiritual thoughts and so I responded to mother quickly, "Just put it on the book case in the living room and I'll get to it." That package was the singer/teacher lady "Kay's" material I ordered off the TV for the first time in my life. Days went by and I never touched Kay's material because I was enjoying God's gift of creativity and so I just loved spending time with my God listening to Him and creating in my novel with His biblical principles. So while I was having fun typing out my book listening to the smartest guy I know, <u>God</u>; I was making no effort to further God's plan of watching Kay's materials.

Days later while I was typing up my book believing God would bless "<u>my plan</u>" for sweet love, He reminded me while trying to get His own plan moving. "The worship music and teaching material you ordered from Kay is still sitting out there on the book case." I heard the prompting in my mind but was having too much fun with typing up my own plan in my first book. I had planned on getting to that material but the book I was writing, or my plan for sweet romance, kept getting in the way and so I forgot all about Kay's material <u>again</u> as I was so engrossed in <u>learning every day God's spiritual rules about the spirit world and all the rules of how they all work together</u>. A few more days went by and again I heard the same thought prompting me again, "The worship music and teaching material <u>YOU PAID FOR</u> is still sitting out there on the book case." Hearing this prompting again I finally decided if I'm ever going to get to Kay's biblical stuff I'll just have to interrupt my typing which will probably go on for years if I don't and start her material now. That way I can finish it quickly and then get right back to **MY PLAN** so I can <u>discover who my future wife is</u> some day and how soon I could start loving her.

Can you believe this guy, avoiding God's plan with <u>the right woman</u>, while he chases his own idea which by the way never did pan out as <u>my first book was stopped by the enemy's interference and eventually by my decision for various reasons</u>? So while God is trying to introduce me to my future wife, I'm so busy with my own "<u>perfect</u>" plan that I'm missing God's plan completely. So I finally started Kay's worship CD (Draw me close) to worship God first every morning and fell in love with the first seven songs before going to work each morning and continued worshiping God seven days a week every morning to those same first seven songs for the next two years while praying for my connection to my wife someday. [18] *"yet I will rejoice in the Lord, I will be joyful in God my Savior"* Habakkuk 3:18. NIV * Psalm 138:1, 2.

The incredible irony in this perplexing paradox scenario as this soul searching man is constantly staring at God's blatant choice for his wife and yet the deeply focused man chasing his own "perfect" plan can't see the forest because the trees keep getting in the way is utterly astonishing; is it not? Every day after that worship and prayer time to get close to my loving God, I would read the number one best seller of all time, my Bible for further insight into the Core of God's Heart and then I could not wait to get right into writing my beloved book if I was not working that day as I hoped my novel would get the attention of my future wife. Shortly after I started worshiping with the worship music from Kay, I also started watching Kay's teaching on her DVDs. You know I tried to find that DVD teaching today after I moved for the third time and I just can't find it anywhere. But as my visual remember can recall, it was the one on the cover where Kay was throwing autumn leaves up into the air. Somewhere in the many moves I had to make, that DVD teaching was lost but I do remember it was very good and I'm pretty sure it was about relationships the very thing I was hungry to learn about back then. Anyway I finished all the DVDs and I thanked the Lord for steering me into that godly material that day on the living room couch watching that Christian program with James and Betty Robison. But missing again the Lord's pick for me I then happily went back to typing up my romantic book so maybe my future wife and I could "finally" meet some day and live happily ever after whenever God finally thought I was ready someday. Incredible.

Asleep at the Wheel

Now when you get a new computer its set up that your incoming emails hit these three musical cords every time one comes in. But I didn't get this computer so I could waste half the day reading silly ads from countless emails to make some merchant rich on my hard earned roofing money. So when I heard those three musical notes I just learned to ignore them like always and kept right on writing my fun novel I was enjoying. One day while writing, I heard those same three musical notes and the Lord spoke in my mind, "You should look at your emails." Still typing and not even slowing down to respond I replied in my mind, "Lord, it's just those pesky silly ads in those emails" and so I kept right on typing. But five to ten minutes later I heard those same three musicale cords again and the Lord prompted me a second time in my mind, "Take a look at your emails." I have to confess I did get irritated as I responded, "Lord, it's just those senseless pesky emails. A bunch of ads and worthless things nobody ever needs" as I kept right on typing with my latest spiritual concept.

Isn't it amazing how we Christians ask God in prayer for lots of things, but should He ever try to answer our many prayers we basically tell God to, "Buzz off! I'm busy?" This is why He speaks to us saved sinners in a still small voice. So when we respond poorly to the Lord of the Universe, He doesn't just blast us off the face of the Earth with a lightning bolt. It's a good thing He's not as impatient or as rude as we are. 1 Corinthians 13:4-7. But a few minutes later those same three cords ding ding dinged again and even though one of these two praying Christians seeking a godly soul-mate was asleep at the wheel, the Lord was still patient and persistent (Luke 11:8) with His own plan and spoke with a still small "kind" voice prompted me for the third time; "Take a look in your e-mails." Right in the middle of trying to complete one of my thoughts I was frustrated I had to stop **my plan** for chasing after sweet love to answer these pesky emails and so I said with a huff, "What is it with these emails? Okay, Lord, **"I'll show You**.""

Have you ever tried to show or educate the Lord on something before? Matthew 6:8. Thank God He's patient with us "brilliant" sinners. So I marked ":::" where I was in my book so I could find it again and then off I went to those pesky emails. Opening up the first emails I started in with my "tone"; "All were going to find here Lord are a lot of worthless ads I don't buy and silly senseless things I never use and don't need anyway." I might have been irritated and not very kind to our loving Lord's promptings, but at least I went. Matthew 21:28-32. So now with my "tone" I'm "educating the Lord" saying, "See Lord, a lot of worthless ads I don't buy. And look here, "more senseless silly things I never use"; "I told You Lord . . . . . . Oh, ... wow, what's this? It's that singer/teacher lady again, Kay. Look Lord, she seems to be going on one of those cruise liners. . . . . and to the Bahamas no less. . . . . . I see here it's her 10th anniversary. Ha . . . . Oh, and look here Lord, she's inviting her many fans to go with her on this tropical trip to have fun in the Sun.

Is this what you wanted me to see? Father, I'd love to go to the Bahamas, dig my toes into the warm white sand and look at all that clear teal/blue water and that sure does sound like fun but we both know that's out of the $ financial $ question." "Here I'm still trying to find a way to pay for this year's taxes coming on April 15th and now I'm supposed to add to that mounting financial burden an expensive trip to the Bahamas?" God knows children love water and so He creates fun by the moon on the ocean waves.

The ocean is
where our Father goes
to play with His children;
among the rolling waves.

Dad 2:4

"Deep calls to deep in the roar of your waterfalls; all your waves and breakers have swept over me" Psalm 42:7. NIV.

I continued explaining to the Lord, "Father You know how I hate going anywhere romantic **by myself**. It just emphasizes the fact that I'm all alone and then I get depressed because I don't have anyone." But despite how I felt, the Lord impressed upon me that I should go down on this tropical trip and see this Italian lady for **some** reason? So I started thinking about all the multiple finances I would need to make this incredible journey happen, but without seeing God's helping Holy hand at work. So I missed His willingness to help financially, and so I did not see the whole wife connection thing He was trying to show me because my own plan was blinding me to His perfect plot and so I went right back to writing my plan in my own novel. So thinking it was only a simple vacation for just me **by myself**, I dismissed the whole lonely idea as I'll just be there watching other loving couples together and probably just get depressed not having a love of my own on this tropical trip to love or lavish on and enjoy.

Vacations in my opinion should always be done with someone you love which is one of God's ways of true happiness that comes while you see her happy heart on her face and watch her eyes light up with elation as this is where I get a lot of my reflective fun <u>watching her happy heart light up and show up in her smile</u>. But I didn't have a sweet someone in my life and so I had no one to go on this trip and love. So I said, "How boring would that trip be Lord without "someone" I love to share that romantic atmosphere with? Therefore, I came to the conclusion that this whole trip to the Bahamas was completely out of the question and said. "Okay Lord I considered this expensive trip <u>where I might just happen to long-shot meet somebody</u> and since I don't have the money to pay for this expensive "hunt for love" game, let's just get back to <u>my believable plan</u> of getting a wife in my loveless life."

So while living in the naturel world and **napping on the spiritual dashboard** while dreaming of a method to get a future wife **on my own**, I was <u>not seeing</u> God plan and so I was blazing my own trail right through the Lord's grand idea of showing me <u>His pick</u> for my sweet romance I prayed for years to get. Then I simply went right back to **my "perfect" plan** of finding <u>a</u> love of my ow<u>n</u> so <u>I</u> can hear music, sweet sweet musi<u>c</u> as I was sure my way would work. But here's how you can tell if it's God's plan. His plan will always include <u>faith</u> and trusting Him. Just seeing God's plan requires **FAITH** followed by **TRUST** living in total **BELIEF** in our Lord and I was being blinded by my own **safe plan** being afraid to <u>step out in faith</u> and trust the Lord to confront this beautiful face of Kay's <u>up close</u>.

V14 Faith is how you Pray as you wait all Day.

Daniel prayed 3 times a day 6:10 * David prayed 7 times a day Psalm 119:164

V15 Expect God's Plan,

"*Commit your work to the Lord, and your plans will be established.*"

while you're **trusting** all you Can, then you'll be God's Man.

Dad 1:14, 15

Isn't it good the Lord is patient with us <u>who don't look for His answers</u> when we pray for them over many years? And isn't it beneficial for those with "wise" <u>attitudes</u> that God is persistent and doesn't get impatient with our quick "<u>tone</u>" of voice and our own "<u>brilliant</u>" methods <u>we trust in</u> while ignoring His perfect plan were totally oblivious to because as you know, we humans always think we know best, don't we? And we always "trust" <u>in ourselves</u> rather than trusting in our loving Lord who is always trying to work everything out for our own good. Romans 8:28. *"The LORD is gracious and compassionate, slow to anger and rich in love."* Psalm 145:8. NIV. If there is one thing I have learned in all my walking with God these many 43 years, it's that "<u>Humble is always your best friend</u> and humble is always the best way to live your entire life trusting your Lord when you see nothing in front of you and trusting our Savior even through <u>the dark years</u>"; (Jeremiah 29:11) never forget that." Believe me I'm preaching to myself as I have made plenty of miss-steps along the way. I only wished I would have learned all I know now back then when God's hand was so strong upon me to find my sweetheart <u>I still miss and long for</u>. Remember, even king David, *a man after God's own heart* (1 Samuel 13:14 KJV * Acts 13:22 KJV) wasn't perfect; (2.Samuel 11:1-27) so please cut me some slack while God is still educating me. Matthew 7:2 * Romans 2:1. So after that email experience, as usual I went right back to the typing in my book because I believed in **my own plan** for sweet love which kept me blind to God's perfect plan.

The Lord Rebukes the "Worthless" Man

So [9] "... *according to the custom* ..." of Craig (Luke 1:9 NIV)
I was sitting at my computer again working hard trying to create
my own plan for sweet love in my life when the Lord said, "Why
not look at Kay's teaching CDs again, you'll get more out of it the
second time?" I thought about the Lord's prompting and said
within my mind, "Yeah, that's true. The first time people hear a
message they grasp about 30 to 50% and the second time they
understand about 50 to 75% of that message." I think the Lord
waited till I was at a place in my book where it was convenient for
me to stop and so I said, "Okay, I need a break anyway, I've been
typing up this book all morning." So since my dad was not at the
doctor's office he was using the upstairs 1980 TV as this was his
norm in the living room, so I went down stairs in his 2004 TV
"man cave" and used the big "square" ☐ TV that only had a
DVD player. Half way through Kay's teaching I had a thought✒
I wanted to discuss with my Lord so I put the DVD on pause.

Now this pause button in the downstairs den was newer
technology and did not have a VHS recorder so you did not have
to put this newer TV on channel three first but simply put in the
DVD and hit play on the DVD remote; something my non-tech TV
mind could handle. Kay was teaching again and about half way
through I put her on pause to talk to my Lord like usual about
relationships as I wanted His valuable input. Now sometimes
when you hit the pause button the person in this still picture on TV
is in the middle of a blink at half way making them look like
they're sleepy or on drugs with maybe their mouth in an odd
position as they then look weird or strange. But Kay's still picture

was at the <u>perfect look for viewing</u>. Her eyes were open and her eye lashes were beautiful. When I hit the pause button her smile was at just the right look for snapping a photo as if "**someOne**" had planned that split second pause I had no control over. So now the Lord and I were discussing my thoughts about relationships and meeting my future wife someday when He indicated quite plainly and clearly, "What about her?"

Dad's chair I was sitting in was directly facing the TV and so I said inside my mind where this conversation was taking place, "You mean Kay, the singer/teacher lady?" When I first heard that thought I was absolutely <u>elated</u>; that paused picture had her looking like an angel from Heaven. I blurted out in my mind, "Wow! She's the most beautiful woman in the whole wide world." But then the enemy started casting doubts in my thinking as my next thoughts were, "No way. Why would someone that beautiful want anything to do with an average nobody like me? I'm not famous; I don't sing and put out albums like she does. As many churches as I've ever been in and even built, I've never once taught any Christian classes like she does all the time. No, this is just another pipe dream the enemy is trying to trick me into; I'll just end up getting my heart <u>broke again</u> believing in wild ideas"

Talking to the Lord as always I reasoned, "Besides, think about it Lord; have I ever met anyone on TV before in real life? No! I've seen Andy Griffith a million times on TV and Barney Fife, Opie Taylor and Aunt Bee and everyone else on that show, but I've never seen any of them in real life. I grew up watching Lucille Ball for decades, but I never met her in real life either. No Lord, you just don't meet people on TV in real life; it just doesn't happen." So once again <u>I had it all figured out</u> and with that "<u>mistake</u>" <u>fixed</u>, I dismissed that "<u>trick</u>" <u>from the enemy</u> because inwardly I couldn't handle facing Kay's stunning beauty up close. But the Lord doesn't give up on His plan like we earthlings who wear flesh do. So walking upstairs after the lesson with Kay I got another thought in my mind, "This is why I wanted you to see those emails so you would see Kay's email with her going on that cruise liner ship to the Bahamas; that's where you belong, and that's where you will actually meet her in person in real life." Again I heard the Lord speak to me and I believed every stunning thing He spoke to my mind as I began to get nervous again.

But shortly after that thought from God the enemy came again bringing fear to my soul. Matthew 13:4. And so I was then scared to meet her as I reasoned back to the Lord, "Lord she sings to thousands of people on stage and maybe even millions through her music CDs. I'm not worthy of her personal intimate company." But the Lord encouraged me. "Lots of famous people have non-famous spouses and they don't sing or sell teaching DVDs either." But the enemy used his chief weapon of **fear** to lead me in another rebuttal to the Lord's encouragement and so I reasoned back. "But Lord, ". . . *who am I . . .*"? Exodus 3:11. I'm just a common carpenter in a small town making much less money than her; surely she deserves better than that." 1 Corinthians 1:27. But another thought came to my mind, ". . .*Am I not sending you*?" Judges 6:14. NIV. And besides did I not choose Peter, James and John for my bride and how many other regular people for my future wife in Heaven!?" Revelation 19:6-9. The Lord's rebuke continued.

"And you need to stop seeing yourself as unworthy and not good enough. You project to others exactly how you believe you are. If you see yourself as unworthy, others will pick up on your own sad opinion of yourself by how you act and speak and they will copy your own sad unworthy opinion that you are projecting.

Then they'll start to see you <u>as the enemy has convinced you you</u> <u>are</u> rather than the bold godly man I see when you're quoting My scriptures fearlessly to your many business customers. I see you courageously and audaciously standing up for Me and <u>holding out</u> <u>My truth</u> you believe in as y<u>ou fear absolutely no one</u> (Daniel 6:10) while witnessing to them about your salvation in the midst of true haters of My gospel. I've also seen you fearlessly place your very life on the line many times explaining all the shocking facts you've learned about the secret evil organizations corrupting this world today. 1 Samuel 14:6-14. How these evil organizations are systematically dismantling My godly biblical world into Satan's secret ranking sinful system. How the kingdom of darkness is using certain key global controlling people to steer this world into Satan's evil and bring about the <u>end time</u> <u>New World Order</u> for the <u>one world government</u> that My Bible talks about in Revelations 18:1-24 and how this <u>New World Order</u> is coming very soon."

I knew the Lord was right about those statements but then the real reason behind my rebuttals were, I was <u>just plain scared to</u> <u>meet and speak face to face to this incredibly beautiful woman</u> and so I said, "But Lord, I'm not the only one who knows about these end-time evil things; there must be others willing to speak the truth placing their lives on the line; so why only me?" Deuteronomy 7:7.

Then other thoughts in great abundance came to my mind one right after the other as I heard, "I've also seen the other side of you like your compassion (Colossians 3:12) you had for that crippled man as you bought him that expensive Thai-go health drink so he would be well and I saw how you risked your very life trying to finish his roof, soffit, fascia and gutters for him. Then I also saw how that same crippled man you made a good and friendly relationship with during that month long job <u>stiffed you</u> on the balance $5,000 on the hardest job in your entire life as you almost fell off that slippery metal roof several times just trying to finish that incredibly difficult deadly job for your new "<u>friend</u>". Then when your new "friend" didn't paid you, I watch carefully as you felt betrayed by this new "friend" and ripped off but you chose not to get physically violent with that crippled man and demand your money as you could have easily over powered him (Proverbs 1:10) but remained <u>shocked but peaceful</u> with his blatant thievery." [9]*"Blessed are the peacemakers, for they will be called the sons of God."* Matthew 5:9. NIV. The Lord continued, "I then saw you use the biblical thankful principle you learned in My Word, [18] *"give thanks in <u>all</u> circumstances; for <u>this is God's will</u> for you in Christ Jesus."* 1Thessalonians 5:18. And so you didn't argue but let him have the money and never took him to court (1 Corinthians 6:6, 7) when you had the moral and legal right to do so. *"Blessed are the meek: for they will inherit the Earth."* Matthew 5:5. NIV. And when I gave you that verse in Matthew 5:44 NIV. [44] *"Love your enemies, bless them that curse you, do good to them that hate you, and <u>pray for them that despitefully use you</u>, and persecute you"*; on your way home right after his bold-face statement, "<u>You are rich, and I am poor, so I'm not going to pay you the balance $5,000</u>." I saw you struggle a bit while driving home to pray for his well-being but you ended up doing the biblical principles and prayed for that crippled man's good health despite his <u>communist</u> Obama statement he spoke ripping you off while communist call it "<u>Spreading the Wealth</u>." *"Bear with each other and forgive whatever grievances you may have against one another. <u>Forgive as the Lord forgave you</u>."* Colossians 3:13. NIV. *"Wisdom is supreme; therefore get wisdom.* **Though it <u>cost all</u> you have**, *get understanding."* Proverbs 4:7. NIV.

I also saw the other young man who you treated like a dear adopted son helping him all through the bleak winter months finding him jobs and lavishing every good thing on him like he was your own beloved son. Then in the summer months when he asked to barrow (Matthew 5:42) your tools for one of his big jobs to make money for himself, he ended up keeping and stealing all your tools (Proverbs 17:13) he borrowed from you and you followed the biblical principles that time as well. [30] "*Give to everyone who asks you, and if anyone takes what belongs to you, do not demand it back*." Luke 6:30. NIV. Others thought you were foolish for letting him get away with that, but most people who read My Holy Word don't follow it closely when reality hits hard as you did. "*Bless those who persecute you; bless and do not curse*." Romans 12:14. NIV.

Then I saw the $5,000 you barrowed from your own mother to replace those stolen tools that young man stole as it took you years to pay her back. And what about the unscrupulous man who committed insurance fraud by lying to Eire Insurance and he cost you $9,000 for that lie he told the insurance company. You simply wanted peace between you and him and the endless arguing to stop as he pushed relentlessly for his highly coveted money. That's when I tested you and gave you that verse, [7] "*Why not rather be wronged, why not rather be cheated*." 1 Corinthians 6:7. NIV. So rather than argue with him any farther about the money, you simply said, "Let him have the money; God will make it up to me some day for choosing peace over earthly money." ". . . *doing what is right and just and fair*." Proverbs 1:3b. NIV. ". . . *whoever listens to Me will live in safety and be at ease, without fear of harm*." Proverbs 1:33. NIV. And what about the compassion you showed to even your ex-wife despite all the pain in your past unequally yoked marriage and all those suicidal thoughts you had at the end of the 18 years (Proverbs 4:23) and yet out of compassion for the poor and hurting you still gave her $4,000 cash to put toward a new car because hers was literally and completely falling apart? *"Be kind and compassionate to one another, forgiving each other, **just as** in Christ God forgave you."* Ephesians 4:32. NIV. And what about the poor people's leaky roofs pouring in on their living rooms you replaced entirely for free because you wanted to show them the love of God as they had no money and needed help badly? *"He who is gracious and lends a hand to the poor lends to the LORD, and the LORD will repay him for his good deed."* Proverbs 19:17. Amp. Craig, your compassion in Heaven has not gone unnoticed and the list for loving people first over earthly money is long in your life! Do you know how rare it is for Me to find someone like that? You think this is normal Christianity and every good Christian is living this way, but I tell you this is just not so.

The enemy tells you daily you're **worthless** and you'll never amount to anything, just to keep you down and oppressed with a poor crippled persona so My ability to work through you is greatly hindered, but those ongoing lies he tells you are just not true! **Don't listen to the enemy running you down anymore**! When you hear the dark kingdom calling you **worthless**, just remember my name for you is, Precious! Genesis 32:28. You're my beloved son and you need to [12] *". . . rejoice and be exceedingly glad for great is your reward in Heaven!"* Matthew 5:12. KJV. Why do you think the enemy attacks you like he does? The dark kingdom hates you're bold witnessing to your customers in your business. This is why I chose you for Kay over all the thousands of other men I could have chosen. **Now trust My judgment!** I know the future! Besides, I was just a simple carpenter from a small town Myself as you are and I made a lot less money than you do now."

Satan must see something in the spirit realm that he doesn't like in me because he has been condemning me for <u>decades</u> since my youth stating "y<u>ou're worthless</u>"! I remember my dad telling me that same lie in the basement after kickball in the back yard while I was standing inside by the washing machine getting a cool drink of water from the green hose when I was only 10 or 11 years old. My dad said in an angry loud tone as the enemy prompted him to speak, **"You'll never amount to anything! You'll just be a ditch digger all the days of your life! And you're ugly!"** The enemy was simply trying to cut me down and using my unsaved dear dad at that time to do it as Satan is always trying to <u>divide relationships</u> and destroy people while they're still young, vulnerable and willing to receive his negative crushing input. To make those terrible statements much worse, <u>my dad was always my hero</u> as I'm sure that's why the enemy chose him to try and destroy me. When I was growing up that generation in the 60s had super heroes every Saturday morning with cartoons; and in real life my dad was my super hero that I still love today despite the fact he said all those terrible things led by the enemy when I was growing up and now I still miss my dear friend as he died back on April 29th 2010. But God went out of His way to prove those destructive words false as I became an A to Z man building additions, remolding Churches and repairing just about anything and everything in and on homes today. But as far as the "ugly" statement my dad said, you'll just have to take my word for it, that statement was a lie as well.

I felt the Lord's rebuke and His encouragement at the same time as I considered all of the Lord's words and decided to stop arguing with my loving Lord for two reasons. One, I knew He was right about me thinking so lowly about myself that I projected the enemy's lies to others I heard all my life that I was **worthless** as I have done this <u>self-destructive thing</u> before many times in the past decades. And two, I really did want to believe this very beautiful woman was going to be mine to have and to hold in sickness and in health, for better for worst, till death do us part; what a great honor the Lord has picked out and bestowed on me.

Now I need to explain to the non-Christians how the Lord speaks to us Christians in our minds. He does not speak word for word like we humans do to each other or even face to face like He did with Moses. Exodus 33:11. So when I say, "God told me thus and so, it's not like I heard those exact words verbatim; I simply heard a quick thought conveying <u>an entire concept</u> and then as a Christian you know His complete idea. But I can't communicate to you in a book just like He communicates in my mind. So you and I will just have to continue reading black ink words on white paper to catch our thoughts. Now after I heard all that the Lord spoke about me being right for Kay these astounding thoughts were rolling through my mind as I went up to my computer room to see Kay's email about going to the Bahama's and actually seeing my new future wife He picked out for me for the first time in real life if she'll have me. God finally established His plan in my mind for sweet love **His way** and my **stubborn love** was now starting to melt into **His pleasant plan** of boy meets girl.

So now for the first time my dream since I was nine years old was finally coming true. I guess I didn't explain that thought to you yet, did I? Oddly enough, when I was only nine years old, my parents were getting along well as I saw them interacting in kindness and love for each other. Seeing this harmonizing love displayed before me I said to myself on a sunny day out in the back yard by the driveway, "That's what I want God when I grow up, **a great loving marriage** someday with kindness and love like mom and dad have." And I didn't even get saved until I was 23 and I was at the end of my rope physically with these terrible drugs I did for <u>two years</u>. People very close to me were doing these drugs and so I got caught up in them. After I got saved in June 1980, I destroyed all my Rock 'n' Roll vinyl albums by scratching them with my keys and bending them out of shape so no one else could play them because my secular friends, who thought I was foolish for destroying them, were saying, "If you don't want them anymore give them to me." But I learned early on in my Christian life you can't sell or give sin away. Acts 19:18, 19. Then I further burned over a hundred album covers I cherished like <u>gods</u> in our back yard fire pit as I decided to dedicate my life to God Almighty. But what kid at age nine is thinking about "marriage" of all things? Yet that's what I remember saying to myself as that's what I truly wanting at the very tender age of nine. I wonder if God is still trying to complete that unsaved prayer I made at age nine back then? Hmmm. But as for being afraid of Kay's beauty . . .

v7 If beauty didn't have so much Power, women wouldn't chase it every Hour.
"How beautiful you are, my darling! Oh, how beautiful!" Song of Solomon 1:15.

v8 If beauty didn't make me Cower, I would live in confident Power.

v9 If beauty didn't make me so Shy, I wouldn't be such a shy Guy. But beauty sure is fun to look at.
Dad 5:7-9

The Enemy Came in Like a Flood
Isaiah 59:19

Now the time line at this point is about September or October of 2007 and God has finally gotten through to me that Kay is not just a godly singer/teacher lady that God wanted me to buy worship CDs from and then worship Him every morning for the next two years, or purchase teaching DVDs from for my own spiritual relationship with Him. So now I started to seriously see myself going down to Fort Lauderdale Florida where the ocean liner would depart on this week long ocean voyage, boarding one of those enormous titanic ocean liner ships and staying there a week away from my normal familiar surroundings. Then at some point while in this unfamiliar environment, where my confidence would be the weakest, I needed to somehow gathering up enough courage to actually meet and carry on a loving conversation with this incredibly beautiful, famous and God-gifted singer. But the truth still was, I was still just plain scared to talk to anyone that beautiful and famous; and she was a singer on stage as well, so while I was feeling highly intimidated I just put that fear off for the moment because I didn't have to face that intimidating concept right then. But the enemy who is always looking to Disrupt or Stop this whole God generated love connection Lord Jesus the universal Master Matchmaker was trying to set up before it even gets started on February 25th 2008 saw his chance to do what he does which is to Disrupt or Stop whatever God is doing.

Listen to my past and see into my inner weaknesses. So I remember back in 1991 and 1992 I was selling carpet at Prezant's Carpet at 172 Point Plaza Butler before my 25 years as a contractor started. We had just gotten in a new sales lady with better than average looks and the day she arrived early she just wanted to meet and talk with the other salespeople she would be working with. Yet despite me being the number one salesperson at the Butler store and known for my speaking skills, I struggled that day just to carry on a simple conversation and look her in the face while she was smiling and speaking to me way to close.   With the dark kingdom telling me repeatedly how **worthless** I am all my life and my hero dad repeating those same destructive words, my self-image at that time was still fairly weak as talking to girls was never my strong point and so I was nervous just to see her that close.   So as you can see, Kay's lofty level of overwhelming beaming beauty was definitely going to be a major struggle for me to just relax and have a casual conversation like she wasn't anyone special or my future wife God told me she would someday be.

V10 Longing for love, as she looked so Fine.
V11 A sweet loving heart, I hope will be Mine.
V12 Then wait on Me, as you will Shine.
V13 If only my confidence, would get in Line.
Dad 5:10-13

So when I thought about that face to face moment of looking at Kay's incredible beauty and knowing she was looking back at just me and not some audience of 1,000, I was very intimidated and so I just procrastinated that fear for another day. Therefore, sitting at my computer I was thinking about all of those $financial$ realities I had to come up with and the enemy was still looking for a way to Disrupt or Stop this whole relationship of love he didn't like, so he started "helping me" think. I thought all about this long list of logistics I would need money for and so with the enemy's "help" I now started to protest back to the Lord in fear of facing her, "How can I go down there and do all those things if I'm still looking for a way to pay off my own pressing taxes that are due by April 15th in 2008?" The enemy continued to sow doubt in my mind (Matthew 4:3, 6 * 14:31 * Mark 9:21-**24**) and supply me with more impossible reasons to convince me to give up this whole notion of going down there to see and face Kay's beauty.

Yielding to fear the enemy's thoughts came to my mind in many questions. "And what about getting through this upcoming winter bills when all of my outside work comes to a screaming halt because of the winter snow? I also don't have money for a ticket on this cruise ship or plane fair to get down there and back again. I'll also have to get a hotel room for one night before I board the ship early the next morning and I'll need a cab ride from the airport to get to this hotel and then another cab ride in the morning from the hotel to the dock where I will board the ship. And then I'll need another cab ride to get back to the airport from the cruise liner when this adventure is all over. I don't even have proper clothing to wear for a week on the beach in the Bahama Sun; and then I'll need nice new dress cloths for the evening shows for a week; after all Lord she's a classes lady, I can't go see her in my regular roofing tattered garb. Lord, I don't even have luggage to travel with on this spur of the moment trip. What is all this going to cost me? And what about food on this journey in the airports or anywhere else I might need to buy food; how much will I need for that? You know Lord how much these places love to fleece the customers when they know you can't buy food anyplace else. And what about another $500 for emergency money just in case anything goes wrong along the way; I don't want to be stranded in the rain in a strange place far from home if there's a problem? I had worked myself right out of all that the Lord had just accomplished moments ago; or maybe I had the enemy's "help"?

Lord, there're a million and one reasons why I can't go and why this whole idea is just an impossible pipe dream that will quickly turn into a nasty nightmare for me. No Lord, this whole plan is just a bad idea I never should have started believing in at all. Now that the enemy has my feet sitting in wet cement waiting for it to dry and harden rock solid, I said to the Lord in my mind, "All I'll get by dreaming about this beautiful lady and this far-fetched deception is another broken heart and I'll spend all my hard earned roofing money on things that will accomplish nothing but heartaches and bad crushing memories for me. And when the enemy was done "helping" me think, I started building a lifetime of walls. The enemy convinced me to play it safe and guard your heart. So I stopped taking a chance on love and decided to guard my heart this time and not let my feeling flow. Then I quickly withdrew my loving heart that God said **was** ready for love, and put it back on the shelf where I could wise up and play it easy and "safe" and went right back to fining my sweetheart my own "safe" way with my own plan **On My Own, once again now. One more time, by myself.** And then **I wonder why, I'm on my own.** Please forgive my intimidation over beauty.

Fears keep you down and depressed all day while it steals every bit of good God has for you. Have you noticed every time God points me in the right direction, Satan comes along right after that and tries to undo everything God just did? *"And as he was scattering the seed, some fell along the path, and the birds* (the enemy Satan) *came and ate it up."* Matthew 13:4. JKV.

Faith or Fear
Which One Dominates You?

It's impossible to please God without faith! Hebrews 11:6. Now if you want to buy something in America you must use U.S. dollars. Whether the item you want to buy is one dollar or one million dollars, you still need American money or you'll end up buying absolutely nothing. In Japan, their currency is the Yen. In Germany you must have Euros. But if you want to buy something from Heaven with your prayers, God requires His $currency$; "**faith!**" Faith is like discipline that most people don't want to do, (Proverbs 5:12) but you need discipline to get anything you want in life and in God's kingdom you need <u>faith</u> to buy anything from Him as well. Satan's dominating $currency$ is ☠**fear**☠ and if you want his curses haunting you for a lifetime, then you'll have to walk in <u>fear</u> or <u>feed</u> on <u>Satan's lies daily</u> to get <u>and keep</u> your fears alive and working in your life as you hide "<u>safe</u>" in his cage or in his **PRISON** of fear for a lifetime; not a wise move!

Now watch for God's method of freedom and make your choice. ²⁹ "*Then touched He their eyes, saying, __According to your faith__ be it unto you.*" Matthew 9:29. KJV. Again: ²⁸ "*For she said, If I may touch but His clothes, __I shall be__ made whole.*" Matthew 9:21. KJV. ³⁴ "*Jesus said unto her, Daughter, thy __faith__ hath made thee whole*" Mark 5:28, 34. KJV. ¹⁹ "*Then the disciples came to Jesus in private and asked, 'Why couldn't we drive the spirit out?'* ²⁰ *"He replied, "Because you have __so little faith__. Truly I tell you, if you have __faith__ as small as a mustard seed, you can say to this mountain, 'Move from here to there,' and it will move. __Nothing__ will be impossible for you."* Matthew 17:19, 20. NIV. ¹¹ "*If you, then, though you are evil, know how to give good gifts to your children, how much more will your Father in Heaven give good gifts to those who ask Him!"* Matthew 7:11. NIV. **⁶** *"But let him ask in __faith__, nothing wavering. For he that wavereth is like a wave of the sea driven with the wind and tossed. ⁷ "For let not that man think that he shall <u>receive anything</u> of the Lord.* James 1:6, 7. KJV. So, if you have no faith, you will get no response from your loving God! **<u>You must have</u>** and use Heaven's \$currency\$ to do anything with God.

Complaining about a problem without posing a **solution** is called **whining**!
Theodore Roosevelt

Now that you understand how to get things from Heaven, use the right \$currency\$ to please God and get what you want <u>within His will</u> using His established rules. But remember, God is not a cosmic bellhop that jumps every time you cry like a toddler for a new toy. But listen closely to God's words.

⁷ *"__If__ ye __abide__ in Me, and My words <u>abide in you</u>, ye shall ask what ye will, and <u>it shall be done</u> unto you."*
John 15:7 KJV.

But always remember God is sovereign; He makes the final decision predicated on His love for you and the **<u>level of faith</u>** He sees in you. As we grow in the Lord's faith daily, we learn new and deeper concepts and hopefully we start walking in stronger truths as we <u>hopefull</u>y learn from our past mistakes. And believe me I am preaching to myself more than anyone else. And always remember, **⁶** *"But without faith it is impossible to please Him: for he that cometh to God must believe that He is, and that He is a <u>rewarder</u> of them that __diligently__ seek Him."* Hebrews 11:6. KJV.

²³*"Jesus said to him, 'If you can **believe**? All things are possible for those who believe."* Mark 9:23. NKJV. Fear is the exact opposite of faith, and faith is the exact opposite of fear. You cannot have God's faith and Satan's fear at the same time; that is impossible! You must leave God's faith to gain Satan's fear; and you must leave Satan's fear to acquire God's faith in your life. Living in the middle between faith and fear will get you <u>nothing</u>! Solid trusting in God's faith will quench all of Satan's fears, while any amount of Satan's fear a little or a lot will destroy your faith as you gain nothing. Galatians 5:9. Now all we Christians have to do is decide which one we want and chase it whole-heartily with all our heart? *". . . Jews were broken off because they didn't believe God."* Romans 11:20.

Faith or Fear / How Can I Chose?

Two natures beat within my Breast
one is foul, the other is Blessed
The one I love, the other I Hate.
But the one <u>I feed</u>
will Dominate.

Isaiah 41:10

v16 Faith is the key that will unlock
every <u>spiritual door</u> in
God's kingdom.
v17 Now open the Door,
so you can get More.

Dad 1:16, 17

Never Let Your Friend Down

So now that God's plan was crippled by the doubt-casting enemy (2 Corinthians 4:8, 9) who provided all of these financial fears for me and monumental problems for God to solve, watch what my all powerful God does next to answer both Kay's prayers for a godly husband and my prayers for a godly wife despite me not looking or expecting the Lord's powerful provision.

So normally back in 2007 if I had work like a roofing job, or hanging new siding on a house or installing seamless gutters or whatever house repairs I might be doing to make a living, I'm out working at that job site making money to live and pay my bills in this world. But if I'm not working and while I'm waiting for business calls to come in from my website and advertising, or just word of mouth, I'm typing up my book so I can put out my novel and hopefully gain the attention of my future wife to be. Once it's out for sell I'm hoping she'll read my book of romance and then find the romantic author who wrote it and so we can finally meet and possibly have the Majestic Marriage I've always dreamed of having since the age of nine. So while I was busy typing up my book and having a great time doing so while waiting for the Lord to speak His wisdom as I love spending time with my Lord creating for endless hours all day, I get an interrupting business call from Chris Frank. Now Chris Frank, at that time, was a sell's representative from Liberty Roofing or I just called him my supply guy who gets me all my building materials like roofing shingles, vinyl siding, soffit, seamless gutters, drywall, et cetera for all of my building jobs. So I picked up the phone ☎ and said, "Hello." Chris said, "Hey Craig, Chris Frank here. How's it going?" "Oh I might survive this winter; you know how this rat race is, sometimes I think the rats are winning." Chris responded positive and excitedly stating, "Well then listen to this. There's a big new job up in your area. A doctor just bought the big building at the Clearview Mall right after the Ponderosa Restaurant and the triple AAA office building." [But the Arby's restaurant I believe was not there at that time 15 years ago.] Chris continued, "They need about 140 squares of shingles and a bunch of other stuff done; you could make a boatload of money on this job."

Now in the roofing world if you get a small house it's about 12 square. A square is 10 feet by 10 feet that equals 100 square feet or what we roofers call a "square". If you get a 15 square roof it's an average size house and 20 squares is a good size home with a nice profit; this was the norm in my neck of the woods and what I was used to receiving on a regular bases. At first I responded to Chris' announcement by stating, "Wow! That really sounds great." But then I remembered about the past frustrating bids and how I was disillusioned trying to get these big commercial jobs before and how many times I felt like I wasted many hours working all day on their bids just to find out someone else got the job and all I was left with was disappointment and regret for all my grueling time spent. Therefore I replied in discouragement, "You know Chris, I've tried bidding those really big jobs many times before and after six to eight hours of special order research and figuring out every intricate detail they want and then handing in that bid with great hope, you find out there are 12 to 20 other bids and half of them are all lower in price than yours are and then you don't even get the job after all that research, leg work and phone calls of bidding them." But Chris hearing my despairing opinion of these very large jobs countered my negative thoughts quickly. "No no, Craig you have a good chance of getting this job. They're up there right now; I was just there and saw them. If you go up there right now and put in a bid you will probably get this big job and make a boat load of money." I could hear the anxious pathos in Chris' voice and how desperate he was for me to get this big bid, which by the way would mean a great deal of commission for him as a sells representative. But he's also not the experienced contractor who put in countless hours in the past on many bids as I came up with zero dollars like I did many times bidding these big commercial jobs in the past which turned out to be a big waste of my time. But now you remember the big telephone company building in Cranberry at 2710 Rochester road that a master plumber, a painter and I the carpenter converted over to our new church building back in 1991 and 1992 after many months of ongoing work that I did get. Yes that's true, but all those ongoing months of endless work was all volunteer work as I never charged that pastor or the church I was going to a dime.

So hearing Chris' excitement I just patronized him and said, "Okay Chris, I'll check it out." But in my heart I had no intention of spending all my time on a bid that I figured had no chance of actually happening. So he reassured me once again it was worth all the time to bid this big job and with that last reassurance we ended the phone call. Naturally I went right back to enjoying my time with the Lord listening to His insight on spiritual matters and wanting to know more info about <u>how the spirit world works</u> and how we humans interact with those spiritual rules. Learning all the rules angels and demons had to abide by were exciting for me and so I was typing up the answers in my novel as fast as the Lord would reveal these truths so my future wife might read my book and seek out the author and hopefully we would live happily ever after. However, God had His own plan that I was completely oblivious too and so a few days went by and I was still sitting at my computer <u>making no money</u> to complete His plan when I business call came in. "Hello." "Hey Craig, its Chris Frank. So how did that big bid go? Did you get it?" Can you say, "Busted"? How about, "Egg on the face"? I never expected Chris Frank to call me back and checkup. I panicked and stuttered a bit, and then finally I regained my confidence and said, "Well Chris, I told you, those big bids never really do work out. They're typically just a big waste of time." But Chris Frank interrupted me, "No! I'm telling you, if you put in a bid you will most likely get it; really!" I didn't want my good friend to beg any more so I quickly agreed with him even though I still didn't believe I would ever get that big job. He continued to reassure me to put that bid in and so this time I said with <u>real conviction and positive confidence in my voice</u>, "Yes, Chris, okay, I will get right on that. Okay, alright; buy." This time <u>I was sincere</u> and had every intention of going up there to bid this job. But I was also right in the middle of a great thought in my book and all I wanted to do is finish typing that spiritual concept out so I wouldn't forget it and then I'll go up there and put in that big bid like I promised.

Now you might think I'm being irresponsible about work, but let me explain how the Lord speaks His words to a hungry heart excited to hear God Almighty reveal hidden truths to little old me. Several times at night <u>the Lord would speak His best ideas to me at three in the morning</u> or so while I was sleeping; but the first time He did that I decided to write that great idea out in the morning when it was <u>convenient for me</u> and not at a sleepy three AM. But when morning came and I was well rested I had forgotten His valuable input completely and so all of His grand wisdom and secret hidden insights and truths were lost forever. That's when I learned my lesson to get up even though it was three in the morning and write out everything He's saying at that time.

For those of you without experience, let me inform you how God often speaks in small steps for His children as this is all their limited mind can handle at the moment. Step one might be His opening word at three in the morning, but He may also follow that first word up with three to ten more steps till seven in the morning after that original thought He's longing to share with a hungry biblical heart that values His [1]Omniscient opinion. There's seems to be an unwritten rule with God about **paying the price** (1 Samuel 23:7-24:1-**19**-22 * Matthew 4:2 * Acts 21:23-28 * 2 Corinthians 11:23-28) and denying your own flesh to get these precious Omnipotent[2] powerful nuggets of truth and so I just get up gladly and write whatever He shares. *"Blessed are they who do hunger and thirst after righteousness; for they **shall** be filled."* Matthew 5:6. NIV. And then I always wait and listen for more juicy nuggets because God is an endless ocean of never ending knowledge and weighty wisdom He loves to lavish on His lovers of His soul that longs to hear His loving insight. Are you familiar with the **Kim Walker Smith's** song, Hurry? Listen to these powerful hungry lyrics.

♪ I give you permission to, interrupt my plans.
I know Yours are better than, all the ones I have.
I'm slowing down, tuning out, everything but You.
There's no rush, You're welcome,
to take up all the room.

---

[1] Omniscient: All-Knowing or Wise knowledge of everything.
[2] Omnipotent: Almighty, or All Powerful; able to do anything.

I don't wanna be in a hurry,

I don't want time to get in the way.

I just wanna give you the space,

to move in this place. I don't wanna be in a hurry ♪ .

I don't wanna miss, what You wanna say.

Extremely powerful worship song that will bring the power of God's Holy Spirit down on your hungry soul **if** you chase hard after the loving <u>Core of God's Heart</u>. If you like that one try <u>Make Room</u>, * <u>By Your Spirit God and * Throne Room</u>. So unless you want to lose all that God spoken wisdom or His precious insights on spiritual matters, you better get up at night and start writing as there could easily be a lot more He's willing to elaborate on to a hungry soul. So wanting to finish these highly valued thoughts from Heaven before I forgot them after a long bid, I chose God's wisdom over the money. It doesn't take long to replace one thought with another as I got wrapped up in this grand idea and then forgot all about my promise to Chris Frank to make that commercial bid.

So once again sitting at home <u>making no money</u> but happily typing up my novel I got another phone call. "Hello." "Hey Craig, Chris here. How did the big bid turn out?" It was Chris Frank, my supply guy; <u>my friend</u>! The one I promised I would certainly go up and put in a bid to that big job. And now he wants to know how that bid turned out and for the third time he is calling me! But I didn't put in that bid like a promised him I would do and so a look of pale white death crossed my face! I wanted to hide under a rock as I turned as white as a sheet and I felt as small as a grain of sand. "Oh Chris, I'm so sorry I forgot all about it." Chris Frank starts in again selling me on how if I just go up there and put in a bid I have a good shot of getting that big job.

What percentage of these multi amazing miracles does God have to do to answer Craig's Stubborn Love prayers of many years of pleading for a godly wife to show up in my life? God is definitely trying to do **His part** in this answer the prayer equation but someone is still **asleep at the wheel** and not catching on to God's best plan. And what does it take to get Craig out of his own plan and on board with God's plan? He not only has to provide the miracle job to pay for all my winter bills, year-end taxes and put all my financial fears to rest about this Bahama trip, but He also has to **beg me** to just stop doing my own plan **for a moment** so I can accept His plan that will actually work. This is why God's mercy needs to endure forever and why He had to say it 26 times; (Psalm 136:1-26) for people like Craig's determined **Stubborn Love** that just won't quit their own plan they believe in.

So I said in hast, "I'm shutting down the computer right now Chris. I'm walking out the door this very minute as we speak." And I really was walking out the door when I said that. I felt so bad I let my good friend Chris Frank down and even if I never get this job at all I will at least put in a solid quality bid and do my best to get it just for him alone if for no one else.

Well, just like I said, it took me all day just to figure up that very large bid and all of their special order details they wanted done but I handed it in at the end of that business day and then I said to myself, "Okay, I finally did it; the bid is in. Now when Chris Frank calls me for the fourth time I can say I did it and we'll have to see what they'll do with it. But I am absolutely not going to let down my dear friend again." I wonder how many times we Christians complain, "Why doesn't God ever answer my prayers when we rarely ever expect or wait for His answers? *"Wait for the Lord and keep His way, and He will exalt you to inherit the land."* Psalm 37:34.

Jehovah-Jireh Can Now Provide

Now the name Jehovah-Jireh means [19] *"My God shall supply **all** your needs according to His riches in glory by Christ Jesus."* Philippians 4:19 KJV. This is one of my favorite verses; however I have numerous favorite verses. But always remember, "God Can't Steer A Parked Car!" so you need to do **your part** so He can bless your efforts. Remember, Do nothing, get nothing. Do something, and God will bless what you do, **to the degree** that you do it; did you get that? So *according to the custom* of Craig (Luke 1:9 NIV) I was sitting at the computer typing out my book again when I got a business call. Ready to answer Chris Frank this time I said, "Hello". However, it was not Chris Frank at all, but the people with the big job I thought I was never going to get; they ask me a few questions and then wanted to know, "How soon could I start all this work?" I replied, "Well, sir, I'll have to check supplies on your choice of shingle color with Liberty Roofing but if it's in stock I could start this upcoming week if the weather is cooperative. He answered in the affirmative and so the big job to pay for everything was placed right in my lap as God once again was paving the road for me to, Go down and see Kay face to face.

So what have we learned here? If you're asking God for a miracle, be prepared to receive it; expect His Holy hand to provide the very thing you're asking Him for. Luke 11:9. Pretend God is a loving parent who longs to lavish good gifts on His children and you'll have the proper image of my loving God. Three months of work to finish that job may not sound like all that big of a deal to you, but I didn't have any debts, nor any bad habits like drinking, smoking, drugs, betting, or chew, nor did I run around with girls that do. But there was one problem I was not aware of but was about to find out. Now I'm the one calling up Chris Frank. "Hello." "Chris, Craig here. Hey you'll never guess." Chris interrupted and guessed, "Don't tell me; you got the big job?" Laughing a bit I said, "Yeah, I did." Chris responded, "I told you." We both had a big laugh over my poor opinion of never getting commercial jobs and then I said, "Hey, I went up there to get the half down check for the job but they said on big commercial jobs it's not done that way." Chris Frank said, "I know, they do it in incremental payments." But I responded, "Well how can I pay for all their materials they need if I don't have their money to get everything I need to do their job?" Chris explained, "I'll go to bat for you. I'll explain to Liberty Roofing that you are one of the few contractors that can be trusted with money. I'll tell them you don't drink or do drugs and that you're a real Christian and how you're always talking about the Lord to everyone and I will vouch for you personally and tell them you did plenty of smaller jobs before this and always paid every bill on time in the past. So you just let me work on them. I'm pretty sure you'll have your materials."

Now I know why Chris Frank was always calling me and wanted me to do work for him. It was for that very reason he just mentioned. A lot of contractors would drink all their money away and were never responsible to their customers. I used to go out on bids and the customers would say quite regularly, I called five contractors and you and some other guy were the only two who even showed up." My plumber friend John Ferguson who did all of my plumbing when I did bathrooms and kitchens told me he heard of a guy who only took the first half down from his customers and then never did the job at all but got in the habit of drinking all their money away. Contractors typically have bad reputation that made it hard on all good contractors who were trying to do business the honest and responsible way. But true to his word Chris Frank convinced the Liberty Roofing company this Craig Snyder contractor is a rock solid man who you can trust with money to pay his bills.

With Chris Frank vouching for me I can still see those materials that came up at the job site while I was still on this very large roof with a 40 foot truck and a 90 foot crane to boom all those pallets of shingles up on the roof the day I needed them and the rest of the building materials I had them leave on the ground where I could get to them when the time came for that part of the job. Along with those 140 squares of shingles which is 14,000 square feet, I had to construct and frame out a gable roof on one end of this building with tapering down walls to the 4/12 pitch roof and cover it with special order siding they wanted and a specialized rubberized roofing material to be installed on their partially rounded roof in front of this building. Then they also added to the bill the entire edge all around the building which then needed to be reframed with construction lumber and finished with aluminum metal bent on a break and installed over the frame work I just built. Then this building required long seamless continuous gutters installed all around the building as that finally finished up the largest job I ever had in my entire life; thank You Jesus.

After paying off the seamless gutter company and all the guys who helped me do this monolithic Job and keeping my promise to my friend Chris Frank to pay off his Liberty Roofing company I still had a nice profit to pay all my taxes, winter bills, and everything I needed to make this expensive trip down to see Kay in the Bahamas to meet my future wife as God's plan was starting to come together. God came through again in amazing ways to answer both our years of ongoing prayers for a soulmate.

God Carries His Children When They Need it

Now remembering back some 15 years ago I think the time line at this point was December 2007 and now my concerns of not being able to pay for everything were finally diminished as money was now <u>not the current problem</u>. So I went back to Kay's email, which I did not delete, and called up the cruise line she was dealing with and again keeping their privacy anonymous I'll just call them JES Cruises. The cruise ship prices were steep to have a cabin all to myself, so they had a half price cabin fee if you were willing to share your cabin with another Christian man. But I told them "I'm going by myself; I don't have anyone else to share the price of this cabin." They reiterated, "There are other single men you don't know going on these trips all by themselves as well and they don't have anyone they're traveling with either. However, most of them have already booked their reservations months ago and you're booking yours late. But there's still <u>a little time left</u> before we leave so someone <u>might call</u> in with the same need, therefore we'll keep you posted and <u>probably</u> call back with someone to help you with that cabin price."

The cruise line also informed me, "You'll need a Passport to go out of the United States and into the Bahamas." But I knew very little about personal documents as I was not much of a legal secretary doing paper work but more of a hands on guy who uses tools to create structures for my trade as a carpenter, roofer, builder, dry-waller, bathrooms, kitchens and anything else relating to building and repairing a house. So I started this unfamiliar paper hunt with just a photo driver's license I already had as I then <u>asked my Lord for His help</u> while hunting for this paperwork I knew so little about. As I understood the painful paperwork process, I needed to get a Social Security card first to help get the birth certificate second and both of them were required to secure this all important Passport or I would not be able to go on this trip at all in just over two short months' time. Now despite my parents getting Social Security cards for all of their six kids when we were all very young I must of lost it somewhere along the way. It was a race against time and a lot of leg work to see if I could get these necessary identification items to even qualify for going on this trip. Fortunately for me I found my original Social Security card and so I had my heavenly Dad the Lord to help me as I found out by calling if I waited on the snail 🖂 mail and this slow, we'll get to your paper work whenever we get to your paper work sad system, it would have been three long months to acquire my passport and that would be way too late. Therefore, I would have missed God's plan completely to see God's pick for my future wife He informed me about on TV in my dad's man cave. Now I started looking for my birth certificate first and I think it was ten days for the snail mail to return it; but my heavenly Dad informed me by asking educated people who knew more about paper work than I did, that if you just drive over west for a half hour to New Castle and fill out your application there and then handed it in, you could get this birth certificate in one hour if you didn't mind waiting. Fighting for precious time I decided that was the smart way as I needed those valuable ten days so I could then send in an over payment of I believe it was $170 to get my passport in record time sooner than the normal 90 days which would have been way too late. So all this paper work and driving over and paying extra is how the Lord had me out smart this slow sad snail mail system and assure me I'd have all my necessary paper work on time to qualify for this trip to see Kay and <u>without His input help</u>ing directing me I would have gone absolutely nowhere! So my heavenly Dad helped me through all of this unfamiliar legal paper work I wasn't very good at and <u>He carried me like the foot prints in the sand poem when I needed it most</u> and knew so little about this legal secretary work. As you can see so far, without God's help in everything I would have never made it at all down to the Bahamas to see Kay in person. So I was wondering in my quiet time, "Why would my heavenly Dad be doing all this help for me and countless miracles to boot <u>to constantly redirect my steps toward a curtain woman when I was never going in that direction at all if He didn't want us two praying Christians together for some godly heavenly purpose</u>? Therefore, I came to this obvious conclusion; <u>this must be God's will</u> for the both of us or He wouldn't have gone out of His way leading me and doing all those miracles if we weren't supposed to be together <u>some day in the future</u>. I figured, why would He point me in the wrong direction or why else would He go out of His way to help me every step of the way steering me in only one consistent direction if this wasn't His will. And even today in 2022 He must still want us both together or He would not have sparked my interest with that Patti LaBelle and Michael McDonald song **On My Own** when I was not planning to write any book at all plus the two other songs which I have not even told you about yet until we get to the end of this book. So I reasoned this must be His will.

v3 If you trust in Me, You'll always See
v4 I come through for You,
like I always Do
Dad 9:14, 15

Quenching the Enemy's Fire

When I hung up the phone with the cruise line and they made that unsettling comment, "Someone might call in with the same need, therefore we'll keep you posted and probably call back with someone to help with the cabin price." I was wondering and uncertain about this whole trip as I may have called in to late to even go what with this being my first time on a cruise ship and not knowing about all this time-required paper work to gather up all these necessary travel items. And now the cruise line was telling me I might not even go if another single man does not call them who needs to share a cabin as well. Waiting on my passport to arrive in the snail mail as precious few days were flying by quickly, I decide to focus on something positive like Kay's sweet face and so I was looking up her videos online and enjoying her music when I saw something that stopped me cold and threatened this whole trip to go and see her.

The dark kingdom saw God working with me and things coming together for us both praying Christians to go down and connect on a cruise liner ship and thus start our loving relationship in a Majestic Marriage. If are connection was completed, that would bring God great glory in Heaven and spread an abundance of love to lead others in God's powerful heart-changing love in this cold detached from love world our enemy has created almost everywhere. And so he and his dark fallen angels were looking for a way to Disrupt or Stop this godly man from God's connection to a praying Christian lady anyway they could.

Now I can't remember today the name of Kay's song video I saw but I do remember I like it a lot and played it over and over. The music video Kay had at that time in late 2007 I tried to look up some of those old videos I saw back 15 years ago in that era but she must have removed them. I don't know why, maybe she's all done with that dream of "hoping for a husband thing" and so maybe she got rid of those videos that reminded her of that old unfulfilled desire of getting married someday; but then again, what do I really know? Maybe she's just replacing the old videos to make room for the new ones.

Anyway, now in my memory alone I can only remember two things about that heart-stopping video today. I can still see in my mind's eye a broken mirror with her reflective heart-capturing face wearing red lipstick and that infectious dazzling white beaming smile every time she parts her sweet lips that lights up every drab room every time she enters one. But the part I can still see that stopped my hopes cold from going on this Bahama trip back then was a man in the video with his back to the camera and her slowly pulling back away from him as if she had just kissed him. When I saw this I thought to myself, "Father, if she already has a boyfriend then why am I going down there to see her?"

I pulled back that time line on the bottom of that video bar just a few seconds to see this heart-failing part again and again and with each time I watched, I came to the same heart-stopping jealous conclusion. I said to my Father, "I want a woman who is looking for a new man and ready for new love, not someone I have to draw away from some other man and persuade her to hopefully choose me to love over this other guy she obviously already likes. Father, I don't want to go down there just to get my <u>heart broke again</u>. But God seeing my plight sent my daughter to see me the very next day and as she entered the computer room the first thing she asked me was, "Hay dad, are you still going down to the Bahamas to see that woman, what's her name . . . ----- --------?"

I responded, "I don't know. Let me pull up this video and you look at it and then you tell me if I'm <u>too late</u> and if you think she <u>already has</u> a boyfriend?" Miranda, who had just turned 18 a month ago watched as I showed her the <u>heart stopping video</u> and when she saw the mysterious man or this so-called "boyfriend" I saw and Kay pulling away as if she had just kissed him, she said, "No dad, she's not kissing that man. That's why the camera was showing him from the back and her just pulling away. She's just trying to tell this video story using this man she probably hired for a prop so she could do that video; that's all." "Yeah, you think so?" "Yeah, dad, I don't think that guy is her boyfriend or she would have shown him off like she was proud of him." Smart girl; I would like to say she takes after her dad but then I'm the one falling for the devil's latest slick trick (2 Corinthians 11:3) and she was the one the Lord used to unravel the enemy's latest deception.

Now I wonder who would be trying to <u>Disrupt</u> or <u>Stop</u> our loving relationship before it even gets starts? Hmmm. And who would <u>exploit</u> the many abandonments I had as a young man and the many painful unfaithfulness' I suffered through growing up with in those past relationships as this dark prince is trying to tap back into those many past heartaches?

v2 When God is on the <u>Move</u>, Satan gets in his <u>Groove</u>.
Genesis 3:4 * Daniel 10:13 * Matthew 2:16 * 4:3, 6, 9 * 12:14 * Acts 14:19

v3 To foil God's <u>Plan</u>,
Daniel thrown into the lion's den. Daniel 6:16

and <u>Disrupt</u> or <u>Stop</u> God's <u>Man</u>.
Dad 2:2, 3

Kintsugi Pottery Repair

Have you ever heard of Kintsugi pottery repair? Dating back as early as the 15th century where these Japanese pottery master craftsmen would take tender care and great patients while repairing the customer's old broken pottery making golden seams while putting the fragile broken pieces back together like new? They did not see <u>worthless</u> junk <u>like the world treated me</u> after my heart was broke to just be thrown out as damaged goods or **worthless**, but they saw <u>valuable heirlooms</u> to be carefully <u>restored</u> and <u>treasured like new</u> as we value injured people in hospitals today. Once the Japanese pottery master craftsmen made all repairs and the golden seams cooled, these masters carefully boxed up those treasures safely with proper padding and then returned these priceless articles to their treasured owners like new. Down through the centuries, these repaired Kintsugi pottery items became so valuable to the buyers and collectors of that current day in the 1800s, that people began dropping and breaking their own pottery intentionally in order to have these patient gold working master craftsmen repair them in this special golden unique way to increase their value. Now watch for the second half of this parable.

This same tender, patient and caring way is how my loving Lord took time with me <u>to put me all back together</u> again using His finest gold ever after a life time of broken relationship<u>s</u> in school and my 18 year unequally yoked marriage broke my suicidal-soul in half. Yet My Lord didn't throw me away as **worthless**, but today my heavenly Dad tells me I'm <u>more valuable</u> because I went through **that deep level** of pain as I have become <u>a better person today</u> having gone through those terrible storms. Listen to how my heavenly Dad explained it to me. ³ *"Sorrow is better than laughter: for by the sadness of the countenance the heart is made better."* Ecclesiastes 7:3-5. KJV. Remember, *"The Lord is close to the brokenhearted and saves those who are crushed in spirit."* Psalm 34:18. NIV. So I say to you the brokenhearted, take time to sit in front of God's Holy throne in prayer with all your abandonments, pains, rejections and your broken tattered heart relationships and get to know my amazing God of Love and He'll repair you with tender loving care as He did with me like these *Kintsugi* Japanese golden pottery master craftsmen value pottery down through the centuries. Our Father is a loving tender caring God waiting for you. So if you spend time in daily worship and lay before God's throne and allow the Lord of Love to pour over your hurting soul as He did mine, He has great love that will wash over you cleansing your broken hurting soul and His mercy endures forever (Psalm 136:1-26) and His peace like a river will fix any hurt you may have. And here's the best part, you'll never have to say a single word to Him (Matthew 6:8) as He already knows how you're hurting before you even come to see Him; just <u>come in faith and be still</u>.

v18 If your latest love put you in <u>Pain</u>,
<u>lay before the Lord</u> as that hurt will <u>Drain</u>.
Matthew 14:23 * Mark 1:35 * 1 Thessalonians 5:16, 17 * Hebrews 7:25
v19 Before His throne you must <u>Stay</u>,
so your emotional pain He can take <u>Away</u>.
v20 He'll fix your heart like <u>New</u>,
2 Kings 20:5 * Psalm 34:18 * 43:1 * Song of Solomon 16:12

now loving another you can <u>Do</u>.
John 15:12 * Luke 6:31 * 1 Corinthians 16:14 * Proverbs 17:17
Dad 1:18-20

Like demons that can't stand to be in God's Holy presences (Mark 5:7 * Luke 8:28) so just being in God's throne room can fix a multitude of past pain and make you **completely whole again** and ready for loving another sweetheart. Stopping in at God's throne room is like wrecked cars on the highway coming to the finest auto body shop ever. Some come in scratched or dented fenders, or maybe wrecked front ends, and some are smashed up completely like I was both front and back ends mangled, and even totaled and considered to be **worthless**; but if you stay before God's throne long enough in prayer time, you, like the repaired car, will leave the auto body shop or God's throne room like brand new cars with a shiny new paint jobs and a clear-coat high-gloss finish ready **like new** for loving another soul. Give God a chance to love you.

But have you noticed every time the Lord points me in the right direction, the enemy tries to Disrupt and Stop that prompting with another crushing deception; like Kay already has a so-called "boyfriend"? Then My heavenly Father sends help to pick me up like Miranda the next day or God is like a parent who picks up a staggering toddler dusts them off, and then says, "Try it again." So with the Lord now quenching yet another fire-bomb from the doubt-casting, lie-loving demons, I decided to proceed with my heart totally renewed and in the open for love position once again.

As pepper is used very sparingly on food,
so a little truth is mixed in with
demon's lying words
to obscure the twisted facts
and give credibility to their blatant lies.
Dad 2:7

God Leads His Naïve Children In His Will

Now I still had a number of other items to purchase for this Bahama trip before traveling out of the country for the first time in my life and with each day I get closer to seeing Kay face to face, so my heavenly Father continues to ask me a very pertinent question, "What are you going to say to Kay when you see her?" or "Do you have a question for her when you finally see her for the very first time?" I heard those numerous promptings many times before but I didn't have an answer at that time and so I just replied in my mind, "I don't know" as I still haven't figure out what I'm going to say to this beautiful future wife God is sending me to see.

Now, I still needed to find some luggage to complete the next part of this traveling puzzle and so I thought back in time, "In all my travels in all my life to Walmart and the other food stores, I can't ever remember seeing any luggage anywhere." So avoiding the difficult "what am I going to say to Kay" question the Lord asked me, my question back to the Lord was, "Where do you buy luggage?" Again Lord Jesus who was well aware of my strengths and also very familiar with all of my weaknesses as well led me to a Big Lots store in my local small city because I remembered, or "someOne" put another thought in my head, that Big Lots had really low prices on some small tool items. For instance, Five dollar circular saw blades were only $2.99 and so forth at Big Lots. Since I was a carpenter and an A to Z man who did everything and anything regarding building and home repairs and whatever the customers wanted, tools were an essential part of my regular purchases. As I always used to say in my business, "You're only as good as the tool in your hand." So the purpose driven Lord was using my need and love for tools to guide me into His next piece to this travelling paradise puzzle to move His plan forward of this love seeking boy who is trying to meet his love seeking singing girl to answer our many years of ongoing prayers.

Now for you non-contractor people who don't live in small towns like I do and who don't need a wide variety of professional tools, this is not a problem for you. But for serious contractors, who live in small cities, finding good tools at great low prices is almost impossible unless you're willing to travel great distances to much bigger cities like Pittsburgh to get these must-have tools. So one day while in Big Lots purchasing smaller hand tools at low prices <u>I got the thought</u> to just walk around this store and see if they had any other tools at really low prices. Now while I was looking for whatever bargains I could find, I serendipitously[3] stumble across the very item I needed for this trip; black luggage. As soon as I saw it I thought, "Wow, <u>what's the chances</u> of finding luggage just when I need it for this last minute Bahama trip." Now keep in mind, I went my entire life and never saw luggage in any store at any time, and now like an amazing answer to prayer I <u>just happened</u> to find luggage at the last minute when I needed it the most? It pays to pray and have <u>God as your best friend</u> helping you through your life; never forget that. And it also pays to have a good relationship with that most powerful God in the universe as well. But remember when God is trying to lead you in His perfect will to answer someone's prayers and your own as well, you might just find an amazing long string of mini-miracles one right after the other because Lord Jesus is leading you to fine all the pieces to this multi-piece puzzle to paradise fulfilling His Holy will.

---

[3] Serendipitously: The accidental discovery of something pleasant.

Now pardon my naiveté over this next part, but I don't travel much at all. So I noticed one big handle on the top of this black luggage and so I got the thought to just grab on to it and surprisingly it moved up on sliding double metal poles revealing a long handle for pulling it behind you. Instead of the old luggage I remembered my parents carrying, I was now seeing for the first time this new much smarter design where the user could wheel this luggage behind them smoothly while walking in front like smart travelers do today walking long distances through the airport parking lots and down long airport corridors with ease. I said to myself having never seen this before, "Well isn't that handy? Boy I really stumbled across a great piece of modern luggage."

I know you're all giggling at my naiveté but living in a small town if you've never seen these things before, at some point you have to discover how the world has changed. Then I got another thought, "Will one large luggage be sufficient to fit all my stuff in?" I remember my parents carried two suitcases when they went anywhere." Then I got another idea to unzip it and look inside. But much to my chagrin there was another slightly smaller luggage in the larger one just like it. So then I thought, now I have two so I'll have enough room for everything. But then this second smaller size seemed heavy like the first one did and so I thought maybe I should unzipped it to look inside to see why it was so heavy. Sure enough there was another smaller piece inside that second one. By the time I unzipped every piece "I" discovered all five pieces and I'm sure Lord Jesus said, "Good work" to my guardian angel who was in charge of helping me find all these items I will need to go down on this Bahama trip and complete the prayers we both prayed for many years in the past requesting a soulmate each one of us could lavish all our stored up love on.

Time for Another Miracle

After I got home from purchasing this new luggage I got a call from JES Cruses who now tells me another single man is looking for a half off cabin price and would I accept him staying in my cabin for this week in the Bahama's. Having never met this man before, what could I say; so I said, "Yeah, I guess so." So now the cabin was secured and paid for and my all-important passport came in the mail and so I was already to go. But there remained **ONE** problem left; I still needed to secure an airline ticket. But again I was completely stymied as to where do you even get one? I actually started thinking to myself, "When you want food, you go to the grocery stores. If you want tools for my construction jobs, you go to Lowes or Home Depot. But an airline ticket; where in the world do you get one of those? I know today in our fast pace world I must seem like a little lost puppy who was born yesterday, but in 2007 having never booked an airline ticket in my life I truly did not know how to get that item.

But let me put it to you another way. If I removed you out of your familiar world you know very well and placed you into my construction world up on a two story roof where the wind is blowing and your standing on an easier 4/12 pitched roof at eight in the morning and said to you, the rain is coming tomorrow about three in the afternoon, so here is your roofing shovel. Now I need you to remove all these old shingles and I'll be back in one hour with a truck load of new bundles of shingles and then you can carry those bundles up this two story ladder on your shoulder and start shingling the roof. But remember, you must be done by early tomorrow before noon when the rain comes by three <u>if the weather man is right</u> and this roof better not leak in the customer's house!

Most people would say I can't shingle a roof or carry bundles up a two story ladder and I certainly can't do all of that by tomorrow. Even most men don't know how to change out a simple door knob if they had to because they never did that before. Most older woman know how to sew a button on a shirt, but when I tried it for the first time I spent over an hour trying to sew three buttons on my old worn-out winter work shirt and let's just say the workmanship was, "satisfactory at best." But I have to say I will never try that frustrating trying experience again. So you may know your business well, but you might also have no idea how someone else's business works at all simply because you've never done that business before.

So there I was stumped again trying to follow and obey what my heavenly <u>Father</u> was directing me to do to complete our prayers for a soulmate. Yet once again my heavenly <u>Dad</u> came to my rescue by <u>giving me a thought</u>, "Your sister Chris, flies out to see your mom, and she buys her tickets <u>on line</u>." That's when I got this <u>great new thought in my head</u>, "Hey Chris buys her airline tickets on line; yeah, that's where I need to go." So when we're stumped and can't figure out something important and then a moment later "<u>we</u>" figure it out. Do you think God is watching His highly limited but highly loved children? Do you think the God of Love (1 John 4:8) is willing to help His children when they're stomped and can't go any farther? If you had a child who needed help, would you help your own child if you saw them struggling to do what you told them to do? Sure you would, that's what parents do, help their children when they need it most. Now listen to the scriptures, [11]*"If you then, being evil, know how to give good gifts to your children, how much more will your Father who is in Heaven give good things to those who ask Him!"* Matthew 7:11. NIV.

And then the Bible also says, [2] *"You do not have, because you do not ask."* James 4:2. *"For everyone who asks, receives;"* Matt. 7:8. NIV. But remember God helps you when you're <u>doing His Holy will</u>." So if you and your weekend beer boys want to know where Billy Bob's Beer Barn is so you and the booze boys can get hammered tonight, don't expect the God of righteousness to help you sin.

Now after that God-given tip in the right direction came in my mind about my sister Chris buying her airline tickets on line, I proceeded to Google to get the last piece to this, "meet my wife puzzle", and get the Airline ticket I needed to complete this God directed task of, "Go down and see your future wife Kay". But after I punched in American Airlines and <u>back then</u> I saw all the many details, pages, side links and numerous ☠ad☠ options and choices to make mistakes with I thought, "Even if I think I might make all the right decisions now, on the day I'm actually at the airport and there's no time left to fix anything, I could easily find out I did something wrong. Then discover at the last minute I have no airline ticket secured at all. Then stranded at the airport with no ticket I might also discover the cruise line, the hotel room I booked and paid for in advanced are now nonrefundable as well. I could lose all my money and then discover I'm not going anywhere because I made a simple mistake in a profession I know nothing about like the people who can't shingle a simple roof in one day.

Therefore, realizing this part of the trip is very important and not feeling confident at all or willing to risk the money I already spent, I got my inexperience self off the internet that I <u>rarely ever used</u>. Now understand this: The only reason I even bought this computer was for writing my book of romance for finding my future soulmate and not for internet browsing and answering silly emails; so I ended up securing absolutely nothing.

But now I'm between **A Rock and a Hard Place**[4] having no clue how to purchase an airline ticket correctly and also having the confidence I need to actually know <u>for sure</u> I did it right. So once again I am stopped and laying dead in the water going nowhere. Now my heavenly Dad is watches His little naïve lamb trying to be obedient to His calling and His constant prodding will of chasing after a wife who almost lives in hotels half of her life and secures airline ticket regularly because that's her world she lives in. So once again Heaven helps out their children and so right after I got off line defeated on how to purchase an airline ticket <u>with confidence</u>, a few minutes later, probably when mother had a commercial break from watching her daytime TV, she opens the computer room door asking me for help. Knowing I knew how to get to the Pittsburgh International Airport and mom not wanting to make long trips anymore because she's getting old, she stated, "Chris and Louis are coming in from California <u>tomorrow</u> about 3:00 and I need you to drive me to the airport and we'll pick them up in my car because it has more room than yours." <u>Is God's timing not incredible</u>? I responded with a big grinning smile as <u>this was the answer to my prayers on how to get an airline ticket</u>.

So with a surprising happy sigh of relief I answered mom, "We should leave here about 1:45 tomorrow since it takes about an hour to get there?" Mom said, "That sounds about right." So I responded, "Okay, tomorrow at 1:45 we'll leave here for the airport and I'll go gas up your car so it's ready for the long trip." Now let's take a deeper look at this longshot miracle now unraveling in God's perfect heavenly timing. The only person in

---

[4] **A Rock and a Hard Place:** <u>Origin</u> of that saying: In ancient times the enemy would find a flat hard rocky area, then place a large 200 pound rock on their enemy's soft belly and as they struggled to breathe the rock would slowly crush and suffocate them so the victorious conquerors could get answers from them.

my birth family of six kids that actually knows how to secure an airline ticket is my younger sister Chris and her husband Louis and they are both coming tomorrow. Is this help from Heaven to complete the long list of repetitious miracles I need to bring a man from Pennsylvania who never even knew Kay at all just a few months ago to actually see her face to face on a ship in the Bahamas? Or maybe to the more cynical unbelieving (1 Corinthians 2:14) mind they might think it's all just simple luck and nothing more than a common coincidence the non-godly might say. But on the very day Craig is stomped about buying an airline ticket to see Kay and complete these many years of praying for a soulmate, Craig's only sibling who knows how to get an airline ticket shows up to answer those pressing prayers the very next day?

So I say, is God not our most amazing God? Does He not answer our many prayers when we pray? And how longshot amazing is it that Craig's sister Chris and Louis only shows up once every **TWO YEARS** from California to visit her mother where Craig just happens to be staying and the very next day she just happens to show up? Tell me what are the odds of just that one miracle alone? In two years it would be 730 days to one. But add that long shot miracle up with all the other astronomical chances of all the other involvements so far and the question of is there a God in Heaven who answers prayers is incredibly obvious. When you're in God's will, God instructs Craig's guardian angel to, "Help Craig as often as he needs it to get him down to that cruise line ship by February 25th 2008 so he can meet his future bride for the plans I have for them. Why? Because at that point in our lives the two praying Christians have filled up their golden bowl in Heaven and their **FAITH** is NOW sufficient to complete their same prayer request. So once those earthly prayers have been

$paid$ for by adequate $**FAITH**$ in Heaven, **THEN** God can go to work fulfilling their request for a spouse on Earth. God is well aware of our short comings. He has watched you grow up since birth and so He knows what you know and what you surely don't.

Like God knows Craig's abilities and how he's able to put on a roof as I have done this up to four stories high, or hang vinyl siding on a house, or install soffit and fascia or hang a one piece seamless gutter 72 feet long on a building or a house if needed without it bending and being destroyed. God knows Craig has built kitchens, hung cabinets correctly and constructed bathrooms and hung drywall properly so he can then tape and mud it and sand it smooth to finish with construction primer and custom colored paint for the customer. The Lord has seen Craig install ceramic tiles in a custom made shower or hang doors in new homes and do finished carpentry in any house new or old or even pour concrete sidewalks and steps if needed in his A to Z construction business. All these many custom learned skills most people can't do, God's servant Craig is able to accomplish simply because this path of learning is the road he went down in his life. 1 Corinthians 12:20-31. Other people might have gone down a lifetime road of singing worship songs and teaching Christians or whatever God has placed on their heart because God gave them a beautiful voice enabling them to sing and teach using the gift God gave them. All of God's children took different paths in their lives because He gave us all different gifts to complete this world around us, and make us dependent on each other for loving interaction relationships. And if we all **remain humble**, everyone can learn or receive help from each other (Ephesians 4:16-25) as we lavish our God given gifts and many skills God taught us if we share our past experiences with our brothers and sisters in the Lord. Ephesians 4:25.

Our Prayers in Golden Bowls

God sees all the many pieces we Christians need to these earthly miracles when He's answering our numerous prayers. Everything must fit like a highly complexed puzzle of precision planned and built by the King of the universe. How many people are involved and different places and numerous things all need to work synergistically and all at the exact times? Even split second timing had to be done by God when my dad was clicking the remote up or down to the TV and my mom grabbed it tossing it on the couch when he was at channel 40 the Cornerstone Christian channel. God chose that channel in a split second knowing the time when Kay would be singing and teaching the next day on my mom's old 1980 TV. God knew where I would be in front of that TV the next day after not watching TV for 6 years. Multiple miracles happening simultaneously sometimes must be done to answer even just one prayer despite the impossibility of Craig's stubborn love who won't watch TV to make just this one relationship start. But the deeper truth in Heaven is there are multiple hundreds of millions of people in the whole wide world all praying at the same time in hundreds of different languages and dialects. Therefore, Kay and my prayers are not the only prayers God receives on any one given day and yet He can harmonize millions of prayers all in perfect sequential order without making even one mistakes; and we humans think our super-computer on Earth are amazing. Having written biblical books before and so spending much time chasing after the Core Heart of God for His answers on spiritual matters, He revealed some of His hidden secrets on the subject of prayer. So let's look at some spiritual insight on what actually happens when we Christians pray to God.

Say I'm praying for a godly wife and the prayer sounds something like this. "Father, I come to your throne in the name of Jesus, holy is your name. Please Father forgive me for all my sins and cleanse me from all unrighteousness." 1 John 1:9. So while I'm praying, those light photons shoot through the vastness of interstellar space up to the planet of Heaven (Zachariah 6:1) to finally enter the throne room of God Almighty. Being Omniscient or All-Knowing, Lord Jesus knows who is praying and that Craig is one of His saved ones and one of His future brides to be (Revelation 19:6-9) when his death or most likely the Rapture occurs; Lord Jesus therefore steps in quickly and receives those praying photons first before they reach His Holy Father. Jesus now acts like our Holy lawyer in Heaven having paid for all sinful humans who choose to **Believe** and **Trust** and have **Faith** in our Savior's Holy selfless work on the cross ✝ paying for our transgressions or our wrongdoings so **OUR** sinful actions are cover in His precious blood and are no longer offensive to Holy God Almighty. The risen Lord Jesus beaming in all of His Shekinah glowing glory and spectacular spender acting as our intercessor or our go between (Romans 8:34) as He is now our heavenly lawyer to represent us sinners to His Holy untouchable for us sinners and unreachable Father. We sinners are unworthy to talk to Him directly or even be in God the Father's Holy presence (John 1:18) so our righteous Savior Lord Jesus justifies our sinful presence in His Father's Holy Heaven. 1 John 2:1-3. This is why Aaron the first high priest in the Old Testament had to make atonement for his own sinful self first (Leviticus 16: 11-14) and then for the godly Jews who also were sinners second (Leviticus 16:15, 16, 30 * Numbers 15:25, 26) *"for all have sinned and come short or the glory of God."* (Romans 3:23 KJV) as all humans are sinful and detestable to God's Holiness. ". . . *all our righteous acts are like filthy rags;*". Isaiah 64:6. So our Savoir Lord Jesus, who represents both us earthly <u>saved</u> sinful people to God Almighty the Father, and Lord Jesus the Son also represents God Almighty the Father to us <u>saved</u> sinful people, now speaks to His Holy untouchable unreachable Father on our behalf. 1 Timothy 2:5. Jesus justifies Craig's sinful presence in God's Holy throne room and interprets the pray I just made like this. "Most Holy Father, Craig Lyle Snyder, third child, second son of William Elmer Snyder and Marilyn Rose Wiles Snyder, is here to speak to You. He isn't coming to Your Holy presence on his own good merits or <u>his own level</u> of righteousness, but his sinful presence here <u>is based on</u> My Holy righteous actions on Calvary's cross 2,000 years ago as he is **Trusting** in My precious **blood** <u>to cover all his many sins</u> completely." Hebrews 9:22 * Romans 5:9. "*<u>Making peace</u>. . . to present you holy in His sight.*" Colossians 1:20, 22. NIV. Lord Jesus continues speaking on my behalf. "Now Craig comes to Your Holy presence, Father, to <u>beg forgiveness</u> for his many sins in My Hallowed name." 1 John 2:12. "*. . . the Righteous One . . .*" 1 John 2:1. "His prayer is that You might pardon Your <u>just</u> and <u>fair</u> judgment (Revelation 16:5, 7 * 19:2 * Psalm 9:7, 8 NIV) on his many sins. "*He rules the world in righteousness and judges the peoples with <u>fairness</u>.*" Psalm 9:8. NLT. "He is asking You most Holy Father to lead him to the right godly woman for the Majestic Marriage he seeks in your deep love of Oneness. Amen.". Do you see how Lord Jesus converts our simple words into something God the Father in all of His Holiness can accept and then can consider? Jesus intercedes for us <u>saved sinners</u> as He truly is our best friend.

So when we Christians pray <u>who worship's God</u> (John 9:31) in Spirit and truth (John 4:23, 24) by our actions, (Matthew 7:16-20) and try to do His will, (Isaiah 1:13 * Habakkuk 1:13) upon entering Heaven our prayers are answered **by** God the Father in His Son's name (John 16:23 * Proverbs 15:29) and placed in a Golden bowl. Revelation 5:8 * 8:3-5 * 15:7. Then that golden bowl with our incense (Exodus 30:34-38) or prayers that ". . . *is most holy to the Lord.*" (Exodus 30:10) is placed on hold **waiting to be filled up** by the key ingredient (Matthew 9:29 * Mark 5:28, 34 * Matthew 17:19, 20 * **7:7, 8** * James 1:6-8) by the one initiating these ongoing prayers. James 5:16. They must continue (Matthew **7:7, 8** * Luke 11:9) their heart felt prayers until these **8** ". . . *prayers of the saints* . . ." (Revelation 5:8 * 8:3 NIV) or their incense they pray daily fill up to the top or the very rim of that golden bowl in Heaven. Once the golden bowl is filled to the brim, God can **then** pour those prayers out on the recipient or in Kay's and my case on each other for we have been praying for each other not knowing back then who specifically we were praying for. But those who are petitioning these prayers, (1 Timothy 2:1 * 1 Timothy 5:5 * Philippians 4:6) must not have anxious impatient hearts as this would suggests to God a heart full of fear and panic, the opposite and the enemy of faith; which is the key ingredient and as you know it is impossible to please God without faith. Hebrews 11:6. A calm yet excited heart still depicts total trust in their Savoir and King and so this type of trusting peaceful heart pleases our loving Lord as we wait patiently for His perfect timing.

So now let's reveal this heavenly insight from Kay's perspective so she can see and understand God's seemingly complicated method simply and plainly. If Kay prays for a husband once, that one prayer or those few drips of incense that were converted are dribbled into a golden bowl in Heaven to start her answer and bring it to a climax someday **IF** she continues to pray and <u>fill</u> that <u>golden bowl up</u> with **FAITH** <u>believing</u> God will answer her prayers someday. But <u>if</u> she gets weary and stops at only one prayer, or not enough prayers <u>containing the faith</u> <u>needed</u> <u>to fill</u> the golden bowl up <u>to the top</u>, she will definitely not receive anything as typically our faith as Christians today is very weak and not like the strong faith of Jesus who only needed one prayer to raise the dead or move a mountain into the sea. Like the widow's son in the city of Nain: Luke 7:11–17 or Jairus' Daughter: Luke 8:49–56 or raising Lazarus from the dead: (John 11:1-44) et cetera.

Therefore Kay, like me, will have to continue our ongoing prayers for typically years on a large request of wanting a godly spouse before the required golden bowl in Heaven is finally <u>filled</u> <u>to the rim</u>. <u>Only when the golden bowl is filled</u> to the very top <u>with faith</u> for that desired idem, will she actually get the very thing she has been praying for and asked the Lord for over many years; <u>her</u> godly husband. But the same long process of chasing God with <u>ongoing faith</u> and asking year after year holds true for me. So I must also pray and fill up <u>the</u> **same** <u>golden bowl</u> she is filling with **FAITH** as both of us want God's choice for a soulmate and not just someone we find in the world <u>on our own</u> that we <u>settled</u> <u>for</u> because we <u>got weary in our well doing</u> of prayers. Galatians 6:9.

Now the size of the golden bowl is determined by the <u>size</u> of the praying Christian's <u>request</u>. If we <u>obedient</u> Christians (Romans 15:18) ask God for a good parking spot at the store when we go shopping, that thimble size golden bowl prayer might be answered in a relatively short time depending on how strong or weak our faith is and how often we pray for that prayer request. But if we ask our heavenly <u>Father</u> (John 16:23) for a godly spouse, each request we make is evaluated and weighed out like ". . . *tears in your bottle . . ." "You keep track of all my sorrows. You have collected all my tears in your bottle. You have recorded each one in your book."* Psalm 56:8. NLT. *". . . and the books were opened."* (Revelation 20:12) by the risen Lord Jesus who has all authority in Heaven and Earth. Matthew 28:18. It is Jesus who determines the value or the $price$ of that prayer request we want to buy from Him and so our corresponding size of golden bowl reflects that value or His price that we will need to pay or spend time filling up that golden bowl with our strong or weak faith to get that prayer request answered. Even though it is Lord Jesus who determines the size of that golden bowl which often determines the time we must pray, we determine how long it will take to fill up that golden bowl by how strong or weak our $faith$ is and how often we pray before we get our desired prayer request. Now as everything on Earth has a price you must pay to acquire that earthly item, so in Heaven you must also pay the price of your prayer request before receiving it. But you know US dollars are not the currency God requires in Heaven to gain your heavenly prayer request. You must use God-money or God's heavenly $currency$. Do you remember what that is? **$Faith$** is the currency of Heaven, and since we Christians typically have so little faith, (*Oh ye of little faith* Matthew 8:26 * 17:19-21 KJV) our weak faith in our prayers often take us weak Christians years to acquire enough incense (Revelation 5:8 * 8:3-5) to fill the golden bowl up and get our desired request down on His Earth (Psalm 24:1) we manage. Psalm 115:16. So before God will allow the angles to pour out (Revelation 15:5-16:12) these incense or prayers from the golden bowl on their desired recipient on Earth, their contents whether good or bad, must be filled. So we Christians must have sufficient $currency$ or enough $**FAITH**$

and this is why it often takes us Christians years to achieve our end goal in our daily prayers. Do you see the ongoing progress <u>needed to achieve an answer</u> from God Almighty? And do you understand the heavenly continuing process required and how only those with great faith in this Holy God and our willingness to be patient for years to get the prayers they want answered from this most Holy God we typically take for granted as we treat Him like one of us earthly sinners <u>on our low sinful level</u>? But learn a secret in speeding up your request and getting those desired prayers and your needs answered <u>much faster</u>. Always remember there is only one thing required for Christians to get our answers to prayers; <u>faith</u>! However, our desired prayers can be sped up considerably if we add one very powerful <u>soul intrinsic</u> ingredient; **fervency**! KJV: Colossians 4:12 * Romans 12:11 * James 5:16 * 1 Peter 4:8 * 1 Peter 1:22. The definition for <u>Fervency</u> means: enthusiasm, zeal, passion, <u>intensity</u>, fervidness. When you pray with fervency, the height of fervency is to pray with your <u>deepest longing</u> or your <u>most potent passion</u>. If this prayer is really important to you then let God know just how important it really is to you. So if you graduate up into ♦♦tears♦♦ pleading to God with your strongest heart-hoping crying aching soul, you will be at the highest height of <u>fervency</u>! ♦Tears♦ from God's love ones lets Him know **just how much they really want** and long for something very near and dear to your heart as <u>this moves God's Spirit</u> for His loving children like tears from our dear children moves the heart of us parents as well! Such as, "Father p<u>lease</u>! Send me a godly wife so I can <u>live a life of love-Oneness </u>with her and have someone to lavish all my stored up love on so we can bring You greater glory. Lord your Word say, [12] *"Though one person may be overpowered* *by another, two people can resist one opponent. And a triple-braided rope is not easily broken.*" Ecclesiastes 4:12. GWT. So Father I would like that triple-braided rope to be my godly wife, myself makes two cords and of course Your Holy Spirit in us both as this *triple-braided rope is not easily broken* by this sin-filled world. Together we three will live in great harmonizing love for You Father and will not be easily broken, not even by this evil world's ongoing lies." But now watch the power of fervency in this homemade parable. Mrs. Smith cleaning her son's bedroom discovers a porn magazine in his bottom dresser drawer and removes it and then she prays right there on the spot. "Lord, help my son to realize this is not appropriate viewing material; thanks Lord. Amen." But later when Mr. Smith comes home and his wife informs him of what their son has been doing, he confronts his son's evil habit with this satanic material, and tells him to tear it up right in front of him! Then the head of the house command's his son **he** must throw the ripped up pieces in the burn barrel out back and burn them right now! "*A number who had practiced sorcery brought their scrolls together and **burned them** publicly . . .*" Acts 19:19. Just like I burned all my Rock 'n' Roll albums in my parents' back yard fire pit after I was saved. This is also why God is going to burn the Earth soon in the Seven Year Tribulation (Revelation 8:7 * 11:5 * 14:9-11 * 16:8 * 17:16 * 18:8, 9, 18 * 19:3) as all sin must be completely and thoroughly destroyed and nothing destroys better than burning it. Hell. Then Mr. Smith commands his son to repent of this satanic sin in prayer out loud so our enemy and his father can record his son's every word and hear the sincerity of his voice as his son lets his father and the enemy know his most recent decision. After confessing his sin in prayer to the heavenly Father in the name of Lord Jesus (John 16:23) and asking the heavenly

Father to cleanse him from all unrighteousness (1 John 1:9) the earthly father knows through this process the enemy has just <u>lost their spiritual</u> **Legal Right** to influence his son any farther. Therefore, the enemy's hold over his son has been severed because of his new repenting decision to walk clean before the Lord and so any <u>Legal Rights</u> those spirits <u>had</u> to stay in their home are now gone **if** that is the only <u>ongoing sins</u> that whole family is doing at that time. Now it's the earthly father's responsibility as a godly Christian or the <u>Head of the House</u> in God's kingdom to set up his house in godly biblical spiritual order. He now prays in earnest sincerity using his **authority** <u>Jesus won back from Satan</u> on the cross who snockered that authority off Adam (Genesis 3:6) through his weak wife Eve (1 Peter 3:7) in the Garden of Eden as Adam got that **authority** or the title deed for the entire Earth originally from God our creator. Genesis 1:28 * Mark 6:7 * Mark 16:17 * Mark 6:13 * Mark 9:8 * Matthew 10:1 * Luke 9:1 * 1 Cor. 6:3 * Luke 10:9 * Luke 11:20 * Acts 1:8 * John 20:21. [12] *"Very truly I tell you, <u>whoever</u> believes in Me <u>will do</u> the works <u>I have been doing</u>, and they **will do** <u>even greater things</u> than these, because I am going to the Father."* John 14:12. NIV.

v4 A love for the truth,
gives a discernment for the false.
v5 To know truth,
you must first love Truth;
or our Lord Jesus the Christ!
Dad 5:4, 5 * John 14:6

Now speaking **out loud** or directly to Satan's kingdom the wise spiritually strong father speaks; "According to 2 Corinthians

10:3-5, by the weapons God has given me in His Word and the power of the Holy Spirit made available to me by the finished work of Jesus our Savior on the cross, He has determined that you **no longer** have the "Legal Right" or authority over this family or my son! You can no longer control him and keep him bound in sin and under your legal bondage anymore! So now, Satan, I speak a **Release** and a **Freedom** to my son as I know God's Holy Word! I also take authority over every **thought**, every **reason**, every **lie** and every **excuse** you're feeding him to deceive his mind. I command your mouth to be silent and **stop** feeding my son your deceptive lies from this day forth! Now, Satan according to the legal spiritual laws in scripture predicated on how **Jesus defeated you at the cross, I loose** my son from your **Deceptive Lies** as you now have no more power to blind his mind to the truth of God! 2Corinthians 4:4. I further tear down and demolish your Stronghold of **Pride** and cut it off! Psalm 118:10-12. I also cut off any and all curses from our ancestors' past sin through our generations (Psalm 79:8 * Exodus 20:5) and I cut off your future **Strategy and your Plans of Deception** over my son! I also speak complete destruction over your **control** over my son! Therefore, Satan, after being completely disarmed, (Colossians 2:15) I command you in Jesus' name to get out of his life, **NOW**! Acts 16:18. Release my son NOW; **let him go!** And now get out of my house! Out!"

Speak firm, authoritatively, with confidence and always in faith believing everything you said will happen. Remember Satan and his fallen angels and also his demons (they're not the same) do not respond to yelling, nor are they intimidated by you raising your voice; they're only responsive to the presence of Jesus and His Holy authority; this is why your strong faith is required. Now after you take authority over these thorny things, it is always wise to pray a **Hedge of Protection** over your entire family and your possessions as well. That prayer should sound something like this.

"Father, I (the Head of the House, or the reigning guardian of the house, or whoever is the designated authority) command a Hedge of Protection (Job 1:10) around me, my wife, my children, my house, and over all my worldly possessions! I thank You Father (John 16:23) for Your protection, (as you speak believing in *faith*) and that You are keeping me, my wife and my family, and all my worldly belongings safe. (Always speak and walk in faith in your life! Without faith you will receive absolutely nothing! James 1:6, 7.) *"For whatever is not from faith is sin."* Romans 14:23. KJV. *"When a strong man, **Fully Armed**, guards his own house, his possessions are safe!* Luke 11:21. NIV. But that verse is for a strong physical man; we are still talking about being wise in the Word of God and educating ourselves biblically and taking authority in the spiritual realm. [4,5] *"The weapons we fight with are not the weapons of this world. On the contrary, they have **divine power** to demolish strongholds. We demolish arguments and every pretension[5]"* 2.Corinthians 10:4-5. NIV. [11] *"Put on the full armor of God, so that you will be able to stand firm against the schemes of the devil."* Ephesians 6:11. ESV. When Paul says to ". . . *stand firm* . . ." he is referring to a military command as you are standing ready like a fighting soldier ready to defend your family spiritually against the enemy in war or ready to do spiritual battle against the evil dark army or our enemy; so, your family needs to all live spiritually clean before God on His Earth (Psalm 24:1) to bring God great glory. Matthew 5:16.

---

[5] Pretension: \pri-'ten(t)-shn\ The actions of speaking forward a claim; laying claim to something, or demanding their Legal Rights (demons') over something or someone is now destroyed!

The Cheetah or the Ox?

Watch this homemade parable for how to pray for results. The Cheetah was created by God with her sleek muscular light weight frame and designed purposely to run up to 90 miles per hour at a short burst of speed to catch her prey for her survival and to feed her young. But if the chase last more than a short sprint, the Cheetah's disproportional small heart ♥ which is much smaller than is needed to sustain this high pace fast chase, will cause her to tire rapidly resulting in her giving up the chase and forfeiting her desired **prey**. Likewise the first grade Christians are also a lot like the sprinting 90 mile per hour Cheetah chasing after God with our multiple ". . . *needs* . . ." (Philippians 4:19KJV) and our many ". . . *desires* . . ." (Mark 11:24 KJV) we want as we chase God with our short burst of speed while we're excited about our prayers at first. But if our *needs* and *desires* are not met in this short burst of time, like the Cheetah who quits, so we tire quickly and **Give up the short Chase** in our prayer time. Consequently, causing us like the Cheetah to also lose the **Prize** in our prayers we were chasing after what could have been ours. Are we as impatient Christians losing our desired prizes in our prayer time to quickly because our **hearts for Heaven** are just too small ♥ like the Cheetah who runs for a short burst and then quits? Maybe we just don't understand the rules to prayer yet? Are we conditioned by this fast paced microwave world we live in where everything needs to be done and conquered in five minutes or maybe we're just too **impatient** and **not willing to wait** (Psalm 46:10 * 37:7) for our Holy Father to move on our behalf in our daily prayers to get the good things we want and God longs to give us? Because the Cheetah has a small heart, she'll also chase easier slower prey like the lazy, (Proverbs 21:25) the undisciplined, (Proverbs 6:23) the weak, (1 Corinthians 1:27) the crippled, (2 Samuel 4:4) or even the helpless new born (Matthew 2:16) just like our enemy takes advantage of us. God designed the Cheetah's heart to be small on purpose to weed out the lazy, the undisciplined, thus automatically strengthening the heard that remains to be strong and healthy. God does the very same thing with the dark kingdom so only the dedicated or persistent Christians who endure are the ones who get God's grandest insights into His deeper heart as they are patient in prayer. The devil also with his limited power picks on the Christians who are undisciplined, or lazy in impatient prayer, or weak minded in lust filled flesh or crippled by **many foolish sins**, or Satan even preys upon the helpless new born saints who aren't educated on the spiritual rules very well or not grounded deeply in God's Word! Is this you? Did God set up the spiritual rules knowing the devil's craftiness that preys on the spiritually weak very much like the Cheetah who also picks on the physical weak to feed her voracious appetite for her and her young? Does this strengthening the heard method in the physical jungle teach us weaker Christians to dig in deeper to The Core Heart of God in our spiritual Church to live strong dedicated lives in God's holiness and leading them into His righteousness as they learn all about the spiritual rules and how to obey them for God's insight on spiritual knowledge?

Do these lessons on the Cheetah cause those who are truly hungry for God and His righteousness to chase harder and desire to grow in our knowledge of God like a Theopraxis[6] studies His ways

---

[6] Theopraxis: Comes from two Greek words: Theos = (God) and Praxis = (practice: or doing what pleases God) In our English Theopraxis is pronounced: Theologian or one who studies God's ways to know how to please Him better.

to know Him better and so please Him with a whole heart? By reading this powerful parable of *The Cheetah or the Ox* we now can understand God's spiritual rules on prayer and His strengthening the Church methods much better. Thus we bring <u>God greater glory</u> **if** we apply these rules in our prayer time what we have learned in our studying <u>God's Core Heart</u> by educating ourselves in His spiritual rules and so increasing our understanding of our Almighty loving God. So by this chasing of <u>God's Core Heart</u> method, He brings us <u>greater gifts on Earth and in Heaven at the Bema Seat Judgment</u> as <u>we will shine like the stars of Heaven</u>.

 *"Those who are spiritually wise will **<u>shine brightly</u>** like the brightness of the expanse of Heaven, and those who lead many to righteousness, will **<u>shine like the stars</u>** forever and ever."* Daniel 12:3. AMP. *"Then shall the righteous **<u>shine forth as the Sun</u>** in the kingdom of their Father."* Matthew 13:43. KJV. *". . . we shall be like **<u>Him</u>**; . . ."* 1 John 3:2. KJV. *"Who shall <u>change our lowly body</u>, that it may be fashioned **<u>like His glorious body</u>** . . ."* Philippians 3:21. KJV. *"God wraps Himself up in **<u>Light</u>**."* Psalm 104:2. NIV. *". . . **dazzling white** . . ."* Mark 9:3. NIV. *"And when Moses came out and told the Israelites what he had been commanded, they saw his face was **<u>radiant</u>**."* Exodus 34:35 * Mark 9:3. NIV. Acts 6:15 * Exodus 34:30-33 * Ezekiel 1:1-4 * Mark 12:25 * Matthew 22:30 * Hebrews 1:7 * Luke 24:4 * Luke 1:19 * Matthew 18.11 * Revelation 1:16. *"those that are led by the Spirit of God are sons of God."* Romans 8:14. NIV. Those who are truly hungry for more truth and knowledge from God produce more good fruit for Him to educate and help others to greater eternal blessings for ourselves in Heaven? <u>Is this anything you want</u>? Then you will be rewarded for this deeper devotion on Earth and in Heaven forever. I believe this is God's mature method He wants for all of us.

Now, on the other side of our homemade parable; the *Ox*,

has a large ♥ heart <u>designed</u> by God the Father and <u>created</u> by God the Son and <u>brought to life</u> by God the Holy Spirit working synergistically <u>as one</u> to get us closer to the God Head. Yet though the Ox must drag a heavy plow behind him anchored deep into the hard stubborn sod uprooting rocks, stiff clay and ripping out roots all day long, still the Ox bucks up under the hard difficult load pulling the plow all day long <u>Without Complaining</u>. Philippians 2:14. This harder work than the quick Cheetah is done until the field is prepared for helping us humans as the harder clay sod is broken up for the planning of our good seeds from God to grow our food and strengthen our survival is all made posable by the power of the *Ox*.

And in the same way our longer harder prayers dig deeper into <u>God's Core Heart</u> as <u>those who burrow inward get better seed from God</u> to grow the Christians with better spiritual food thus strengthening ourselves, our family and all others who have a hungry heart to hear God. These kind of deep dedicated Christians continue to pray for their deepest desires until **the spiritual job is finished** very much like the strong Ox plowed up the entire field until the job was done for planting our food to get our physical needs and all our essentials met. So the more <u>mature Christian</u>, like the <u>Ox</u>, may pray much longer, listening to the Holy Spirit's <u>eternal</u> insight more than the novice first grade Christians speaking their earthly <u>temporary</u> desires and worldly wants to God, as if God needed to learn something from our sinful souls! Matthew 6:8. This humble patience we Christians use while waiting on God and His wisdom to speak His intrinsic insight in prayer brings a godly spiritual Harvest to those that are truly hungry for more truth in the Church like an earthly farmer who can reap in the harvest and then share all his crops with the hungry physical world around him. So what the mature Christian has learned through his patience in prayer from his wise all-knowing God by taking more time before the throne of God can now benefit other weaker Christians like the Ox benefited the community with crops the farmer harvested. The more mature Christian prays deeper and listens longer for God's still small voice like the Ox plows longer than the Cheetah runs and the Ox digs up rocks, roots and stubborn stiff clay just as we Christians also dig up strongholds, bind demons, and prays for stubborn sinners' worldly hearts to receive their salvation before time runs out and the Rapture is here. This is why the mature Christians are slower in prayer but does much better in results while gaining the more abundant harvest because they are patient and willing to wait on their Holy God to speak knowing the grand gifts God can grant them if they are willing to pray with a ♦♦fervent heart♦♦ for His hallowed holiness. With a compassionate and loving soul, displaying perseverance praying long prayers in privacy (Matthew 6:6) until the job is done. As the stubborn stronghold defiant stony hearts (Ezekiel 11:19) are broken, the demons are bound, and the unsaved come home with a humble heart like the prodigal son did as his godly Father prayed for his wayward worldly son. The Ox may take a lot more time in prayer than the sprinting quick Cheetah, but at the end of the slow moving Ox's prayer as they listen to God and gain on His insights, the Ox stays in heavenly prayer longer getting greater and deeper answers from God till the heavenly job is done (1 Thessalonians 5:17) and the earthly people are closer to God. So Christian, the next time you enter your hidden prayer closet chasing after your multiple earthly

". . . *needs* . . ." and your many worldly ". . . *desires* . . ." whose heart will you choose to take with you, and whose heart will you most likely emulate this time after our lesson of the Cheetah or the Ox? Will it be the small Cheetah-size ♥ heart who quickly quits after a short five minute prayer because you didn't want to miss another "important" episode of Gilligan's Island that you've already seen 57 times? Will you learn to have the new <u>stamina</u> and <u>endurance</u> like the mature Ox who digs in deeper for your precious ". . . *needs*. . ." or your highly desired ". . . *desires* . . ."

you desire like the large ♥ heart of the *Ox*? Will you graduate

to plowing up strongholds or praying with 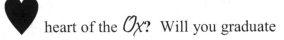fervency♦♦♦♦ over lost love ones and walk in patience and passion until the heavenly power from God comes down from the throne to change earthly sinner like mature Christian that get results for their families? The Rapture is coming soon. Now listen to God's Holy Word.

[7] "***If*** *you remain in Me and My words remain in you,* <u>*ask* **whatever** *you wish*</u>*, and it will be given you.*"
John 15:7. NIV.

Also keep in mind, [15] ". . . *the battle is not yours, but God's.*" 2.Chronicles 20:15. NIV. Our Lord is similar to the Marines, as He is looking for "<u>A few good men</u>" when it comes to prayer to do godly work for Him; <u>is that you</u>? But when you pray you only have to do <u>your part</u>, live clean and <u>pray in faith</u> trusting the Word of God and your Holy heavenly Host. But always understand, let God do <u>His</u> part and your faith will increase thus your prayers will be answered sooner and you will be an affective prayer warrior getting all God has set aside for you. Others who pray quick short throw-up prayers hoping something will stick in Heaven like cooks throw spaghetti on the wall to see if it's done as they are impatient and don't take the time with God. Your job is only to pray and **Believe** in His power and in His Word you have hidden in your heart. Psalm 119:11. God's job is to work the miracle, **not yours**; understand the difference? Don't ever feel like you have to do the healing or the miracle by yourself; that's Satan's stinking thinking and you'll crush your own Faith trying to do God's Holy job!

Though we pray for an Hour, still only God has the Power. If we try hard to be He, Our prayers we'll never See.
Dad 2:3

Just remember, Almighty God will be Almighty God; and you, the simple humble trusting servant, will continue to be the simple humble trusting servant! Always remember you are just a simple tool like a modest pencil in God's hand believing in your all powerful God and His power. This is why a humble heart should always be your best friend and humble is always your most beautiful garment you wear and wrap around yourself to be, attractive. This is also why the spirit of pride is always ugly and only demons and fools wear this dreadful spiritual arrogant garment! Ezekiel 28:17. So remember, Lord Jesus delivers the demonized! You simply pray **Believing** in Him and His power to do the job. We Christian rest in His power. Matthew 11:28-30. That is why **He** gets ALL the Glory! But those we pray for get all the healing and all the heavenly help we believe for; or the deliverance for them we have chased hard after believing total victory for!

Creative Craig Creates

"The Lord will fulfill His purpose for me." Psalm 138:8

v1 Looking for <u>Romance</u>, cause you Love that <u>Dance</u>.

v2 You hope for true <u>Love</u>, that comes from <u>Above</u>.

"An excellent wife is the crown of her husband . . ." Proverbs 12:4.

v3 Yet Satan has picked out his <u>Fuel</u>,

by making this trashy tramp his new <u>Tool</u>.

v4 So God will judge you, cause you broke His <u>Rule</u>.

"Anyone who does wrong will be repaid for their wrongs." Colossians 3:25.

v5 Now she comes on <u>Strong</u>, while singing her <u>Song</u>.

v6 Her morals are <u>Wrong</u>, but you still ♩ sing <u>Along</u>.

". . . they have closed their eyes so their eyes cannot see . . ." Isaiah 6:9, 10.

v7 She says you're her favorite <u>Jewel</u>,

while claiming she's <u>Cool</u>,

yet she still dresses like a <u>Ghoul</u>.

"The woman approached him, <u>seductively dressed</u> and sly of heart." Prov. 7:10

v8 Now she calls, "Come into the <u>Pool</u>,

and gaze daily at my <u>Dual</u>."

v9 Where you can always <u>Drool</u>,

and forever be my <u>Fool</u>.

"Do not be deceived: Bad company corrupts good morals." 1 Corinthians 15:33

v10 But be careful where you <u>Look</u>,

cause you know Satan's a <u>Crook</u>.

"From the roof David saw Bathsheba bathing." 2 Samuel 11:2

v11 <u>Avoiding God</u>, you look for a <u>Sign</u>

then Satan, points to his sin of looking on <u>Line</u>.

"... *The <u>boundary lines</u> have fallen for me in pleasant places;* .." Psalm 16:6

v12 Just sit back and <u>Stare</u>, as you notice she's <u>Bare</u>."

"... *anyone who looks at a woman lustfully has already committed adultery with her in his heart*." Matthew 5:28

v13 But God says, "If you <u>Lust</u>, your soul will <u>Rust</u>."

David says: "*my bones wasted away through my groaning all day long.*"
Psalm 32:3

v14 He says, "You must walk <u>Wise</u>, to get the <u>Prize</u>."

"*Do you not know that in a race all the runners run, but only one gets the prize? Run in such a way as to get the prize.*" 1 Corinthians 9:24 (Run with God).

v15 "If she lowers her <u>Shirt</u>, while she's on the <u>Flirt</u>,

don't drop your <u>Gaze</u>, or your eyes will <u>Glaze</u>."

"<u>*Put to death*</u>, *therefore, whatever belongs to your earthly nature: Sexual immorality, impurity, <u>lust</u>, evil desires* ..." Colossians 3:5

v16 Still you look to <u>See</u>, as she says it's all <u>Free</u>.

v17 While Satan speaks to <u>Thee</u>, "Be all you can <u>Be</u>."

"*The thief comes only to steal, kill and destroy* ..." John 10:10

v18 So God says again listen to <u>Me</u>, "Before you <u>See</u>."

"*Do not follow the crowd in doing wrong.*" Genesis 23:2

v19 If sin you are <u>Glancing</u>, and dream of <u>Romancing</u>,

v20 Your demons are <u>Dancing</u> 1 Kings 18:19-28

while Hell is <u>Advancing</u> Isaiah 5:14

Dad 6:1-20

A wise man makes learning joyful.
Dad 1:1

v1 Careful as you <u>Look</u>, cause in Hell you'll <u>Cook</u>.

v2 God speaks to you <u>Sir</u>, as you still look at <u>Her</u>.

v3 With just one <u>Glance</u>, you're in a <u>Trance</u>.

v4 With just one <u>Sin</u>, your demons are <u>In</u>.

v5 Now you hear voices and wonder who they <u>Are</u>,
but she says, "Never mind that, lets hit another <u>Bar</u>."

v6 All sin sounds <u>Great</u>, until it's way too <u>Late</u>.

v7 With just one lustful <u>Date</u>, you've taken her <u>Bait</u>.

v8 Now you must <u>Pay</u>, for that one quick <u>Lay</u>.

v9 So you work all <u>Day</u>, for Satan's one night of <u>Play</u>.

v10 You've played the <u>Fool</u>, while gazing at her <u>Dual</u>.

v11 Now look My <u>Way</u>, as I have something to <u>Say</u>.

v12 You peeked to <u>See</u>, what Satan had for <u>Thee</u>.

". . . we have done wrong and acted wickedly." Psalm 106:6

v13 She looked so <u>Fine</u>, now Satan says, you're <u>Mine</u>!

v14 You went down the dark <u>Trail</u>, but now you <u>Wail</u>.

v15 So now your soul will <u>Yell</u>, while you rot in <u>Hell</u>.

v16 The deeper into sin you <u>Fall</u>,
the more you'll scream and <u>Bawl</u>.

v17 Though it seemed <u>Odd</u>, you had no time for <u>God</u>!

v18 You did not <u>Repent</u>, so now you're in <u>Torment</u>.

"And in Hell he lifted up his eyes being in torment<u>s</u> . . ." Luke 16:23

v19 With her one grand <u>Grin</u>, she has suckered you <u>In</u>.

v20 Satan's demons are <u>In</u>, as you're living in <u>Sin</u>.

Dad 7:1-20

v1 You should have gone <u>Home</u>, to stop this <u>Roam</u>.

v2 But she looked to <u>Good</u>, and said, "You <u>Should</u>."

v3 She says, "Let's get a <u>Room</u>; so love can <u>Bloom</u>."

"*. . . no one who touches her will go unpunished.*" Proverbs 6:29b

v4 With sweet <u>Perfume</u>, she now opens up your <u>Tomb</u>.

v5 But think for a <u>While</u>, as she's giving you a <u>Smile</u>.

v6 Your morals will always <u>Fail</u>, when sin's on <u>Sale</u>.

v7 Now falling <u>Headlong</u>, as you're not that <u>Strong</u>.

v8 She's stringing you <u>Along</u>, still you sing her <u>Song</u>.

v9 And you know it's <u>Wrong</u>, to look that <u>Long</u>.

v10 Now you wonder, "Is this really where I <u>Belong</u>?"

v11 So beware of the <u>Stare</u>, that takes you <u>There</u>.

v12 You took this <u>Path</u>, but not to get God's <u>Wrath</u>?

v13 You hoped for her <u>Fun</u>, but ended up with <u>None</u>.

v14 Satan binds your <u>Soul</u>, with his deceptive <u>Control</u>.

v15 These evil voices will <u>Call</u>, and you will <u>Fall</u>.

v16 But is this really the <u>Love</u>, you were dreaming <u>Of</u>?

v17 Where's your <u>Grin</u>, since she snookered you <u>In</u>?

v18 But remember, God knows where you've <u>Been</u>,

while you're living in <u>Sin</u>.

v19 You wanted <u>Romance</u>, and you took your <u>Chance</u>.

v20 Now she gained <u>Control</u>, over your foolish <u>Soul</u>.

Dad 8:1-20 / <u>**1 Corinthians 6:9, 10**</u>

Forgive that little interruption, sometimes I get on a creative roll.
That message is for the uneducated that have wondering eyes.

God Sends Help From Faraway

Now it's back to *My 20 Miracle Prayers For A Wife.*

So yesterday came and I drove my mother down to the Pittsburgh International Airport as we picked up my sister Chris and her husband Louis. The ambient air in the car was joyous as everyone in the vehicle was celebrating this long awaited reunion and so the following happy morning came and they were out in the kitchen cheerfully visiting with my mother they have not seen in two long years. Now on my hopeful side of this ongoing proceeding puzzle to compete this Bahama trip, all that was left for me to do to get these elusive airline tickets is to simply ask my own sister Chris if she would come back to my computer room and secure my ticket with the proper procedure that I was not sure of and she already knew how to do. So it sounds all too simple at this point doesn't it? But it wasn't simple at all. I sat there in the morning in my computer room hesitating to ask my own sister for help because she was a staunch devoted Democrat. She and I have had our hard conversations on political differences before and after all those past hard words of disagreements I assumed she might reject my request for a favor and then I'd not get any help at all. And the absolute last men I wanted to ask help from was my brother in-law Louis. Not because he wasn't a kind and friendly man, because he certainly was. In fact that's why Chris married him because of his infectious lovable personality that absolutely everyone including my own daughter Miranda loves. But the last time they were here at mom's house two years ago our two political sides clashed with me on the right, and their opposite democratic views on the left. That conversation shall we say was not exactly a warm and fussy sweet moment and now I'm supposed to just go out there and ask them for help and would you do me this big favor? Remembering these thoughts I was therefore very hesitant to approach either one with confidence and so I thought my best chance at success was to try my own sister. So, nervous and feeling trepidation the enemy was slowly filling my mind up with a foreboding gloom as I <u>finally left my computer room</u> and started down the long hallway toward the kitchen where they were visiting with mother. "<i><u>Do not fear, for I am with you</u>; do not be dismayed, for I am your God. I will strengthen you with My righteous right hand.</i>" Isaiah 41:10. NIV.

V19 Demons will never <u>relent</u>, while looking for a weak <u>moment</u>.
"However, this kind does not go out except by prayer and fasting." Matt. 17:21

V20 They'll **exploit** anything at <u>All</u>, just to make you <u>Fall</u>!
Dad 4:19, 20

Now remember our enemy <u>can't create</u> **anything**, but he can **<u>exploit</u>** any <u>weakness you might have</u> as he tries to make our **naturel flaws** we already have <u>worse</u> for their easy to control will and I remembered all too well our last heated conversation just two years ago was not very friendly. But I desperately needed help to complete this trip I already put money down on and so if I didn't get it, I'll not go on this trip at all. So coming down the hallway toward the kitchen I could hear them both talking with mother and so I turned the corner into the kitchen and right off the bat there was Louis with his back to the sliding glass door and facing right in front of me as he turned to see me entering the kitchen.

I wasn't sure what to say or what sort of greeting I might get but much to my chagrin Louis pipes up first and says with a great big welcoming smile, "Craig, how are you?" I was slightly stunned, but I thought, "This is your lead in so tell him how you're doing." Well he seemed in a good mood and so I said with a troubled pathos in my voice, "Well I'd be a lot better if I could figure out how to secure an airline ticket." Chris was at the kitchen counter facing mom as this was the reason she came but Louis' dominating "life of the party" personality spoke up again with a pleasant tone of voice asking, "Are you going on a trip?" Hearing the positive atmosphere continue I answered feeling a little more at ease, "Well, I am if I can figure out how to book this airline ticket." Louis, with his positive infectious dominate tone, inquired, "Where are you going?" I answered happily as this conversation was definitely headed in the right direction, "Fort Lauderdale to catch a cruise liner ship for a week in the Bahamas." Louis, who used to live in Fort Lauderdale for years, and still having an optimistic attitude responded by standing up and heading for the long hallway replied, "Well if you need an airline ticket I can help you with that."

So my heavenly Father seeing my unease nervousness and troubled hesitation steered that conversation rather well I thought. Now walking down the hallway Louis said, "You're back in your computer room right?" Following my brother in-law back down the long hallway I said, "Yeah, I'm just not sure how this is done and I can't have any mistakes." Louis marching right into the computer room in full confidence as booking airline tickets is just like breathing for him and so this was his big chance to help out his naïve little lamb brother in-law who rarely ever leaves the deep dark cave I live in almost continuously, so he was my hero that day.

So Louis sitting in my big black Lazy Boy chair as I took the side black executive business chair looking on as he hit Google and said, "What airlines are you traveling on?" I replied, "American". As he was punching in the name he was speaking out loud to me, "And you're going to Fort Lauderdale. And it stands to reason you'll be leaving out of Pittsburgh. So what day are you leaving?" "Well the cruise starts on February the 25th but I already have a hotel room booked the night before so I can be ready first thing in the morning." Louis is thinking out loud again so I could hear his decisions, "So you want to leave the day before on the 24th, right?" "Yeah." Then Louis ask, "They have an 8:00 AM or an 11:00 AM which one will work better for you." "Well, we better make it the 11:00 one as I need time to get ready and get down there; plus I want an extra hour just to play it safe just in case anything should go wrong." "Having booked airline tickets many times before, Louis was well familiar with all the details and so he said, "Would you like an aisle seat or a window seat?" Since flying wasn't my common thing and with me being a visual person I thought it might be nice to look out the window and see the sights of takeoff and landing since I'm such a novice. So I replied, "Window seat". Louis checked the box ☑ and then asked, "And what day and time are you coming back?" "Well the last day of this cruise is the second of March but I'm not sure what time of day it's over, so maybe we should make that flight later in the day so I have plenty of time to get to the airport." Louis is scanning through and then says, "They have one flight here for 11:00 AM or another one at 3:00 PM. Which one do you think will give you enough time?" "Well let's just choose the later one since I'm not real sure." "Okay, what credit card are you using?" Handing him my VISA card I said, "Right here." Louis typed in the numbers and said, "Okay, it went through; now turn on your printer." Louis hit print and sure enough all my instructions for travelling on this week trip to the Bahamas were printed out for me to look at and carry with me and show the American airlines."

Then Louis farther instructed me, "Now when you get to the Airport you'll be looking for the American Airline's desk. They will already have your information in their computer and all you'll have to do is show them your papers on your flight that we just printed. These papers already have your flight number, your gate number, you're leaving from, your time of departure and your return information as well. You have nothing to worry about; it's all done." Talk about putting your trouble heart at ease. I would not have been able to do any of that on my own and would have messed it all up and would have surly missed the whole trip if Louis did not help me secure that airline ticket. Plus I had full confidence he knew what he was doing and so my heart was at complete ease; as my Lord wanted it. God's helps His children when they need it most. *"Do not fear, I will help you."* Isaiah 41:13.

And for those who think you can install a roof on day one all by yourself with no help or guiding instruction from someone who has done this many times before, who do you think you're kidding? That roof you tried to install on your own will leak like a spaghetti colander under a running faucet.

By the way Craig, Louis was not angry, or uncooperative, or unwilling to help at all. He was just his normal happy-go-lucky willing to help self like always. So maybe we political people should not think so ill of the other apposing political side. Once again our enemy makes trouble through fears where there really are no reasons to dread at all. Psalm 53:4-5. NIV.

The Fish Out of Water and The Genius Within

Now on February the 24th 2008 one day before I see Kay and difficult as it was for God to get Craig ready in everything he needed for this trip to Fort Lauderdale Florida and then out of the country on a cruise liner ship to the Bahama's I was finally ready to travel outside my cave. I had my all-important passport so I could travel legally out of the country and my American airline flight papers to present to the airlines and all the JES Cruises necessary paper work they wanted and my hotel reservation paper work for one night as well and then of course I had all my Kay entertainment advertisements and all necessary papers for her itinerary that week. I tell you I felt like a legal secretary on wheels. And for all my family members who know me well and wonder how I got all that paper work accomplished, I tell you if it wasn't for my heavenly Dad, it would have never been possible. Have I ever told you now much I hate paper work? I'm more of a hands on guy with ⚒tools; give me something to fix or build and I'm happy all day long or happily at home in my comfort zone.

So I drove down to the Pittsburgh International Airport and parked in their extended parking. That's when I saw the incredible need for the new luggage with wheels and extended slide handles God set me up with in Big Lots as the travelers must journey for what seems to be "miles" of walking. I found the American airline desk and dropped off my big luggage first as I asked them where do I go from here. They instructed me where to fine airport security and so God reminded me this adventure I'm on is a step by step faith journey. Everyone had to pass through Airport security as security was upgraded considerably after the 911 incident in New York and so we all placed our carryon luggage on these conveyer belts, along with your laptop if you had one and even your shoes had to be taken off and examined internally.

Then they had metal detector wands they would wave over you closely while your luggage and shoes went through the X-ray imagery machines. After my stuff passed through and they took out my <u>liquid mineral bottle</u> and said, "You can't bring any liquids on the plane." That's when I made a foolish comment as I jokingly said, "Yeah, you never know, I might be a bomber." When I said that unwise comment, the airline inspector took one look at me and determined I must be a new traveler like some <u>fish out of water</u> and so I got **GRACE** from God as he said quite sternly and seriously, "<u>Don't say that</u>!" I found out later if they suspect anyone they think might be a bomber or even have a knife concealed on them they will pull you aside and do an in-depth search including a cavity search. Ouch! So I put on my shoes gathered up my stuff and <u>quietly moved on</u> but this time a little wiser. Now the travelers are all back to scurrying in this hurried rat race with luggage trailing on wheels chasing us all rushing in this continuing gallop. I kept looking up where they had all the signs to multiple gate numbers to go in this direction or that way as I simply followed these overhead indications. After going down very long different corridors with moving walkways that move even quicker, I finally did find my gate number at that time which today as I'm writing on December 28, 2022 I can't remember what that number was. Once there I checked with the desk clerk making sure I was at the right gate and that this gate had my flight number with the up to date time of departure. I just remembered <u>today</u> while I was waiting for the departure time <u>back then</u> to elapse I was reading a book that Kay and someone else wrote as I was learning more about God's pick for my future wife to <u>someday</u> be.

The time came and we all boarded ✈ as I found my seat number by the window that Louis checked the box on my home computer. Then I saw everyone else placing there carryon luggage up in these overhead bins and so I followed their lead and did the same. Then reading about Kay's personal life, I learned all the more as she revealed further inside information about herself in her book. Therefore, I got more excited to see her and start our relationship of sweet love. Now if you've ever flown <u>coach</u> in an airplane before, you know that if you gain five pounds, you might have to hold your breath the entire trip or it's possible you'll not fit in their "size-<u>two</u>" seat. I think a highly trained group of anorexics must have designed the layout on these planes and I'm not even a chubby guy. So with a little bit of Vaseline I was able to crowbar myself into this window seat. Plus the curved ceiling above me crowding me even farther and my laptop positioned between my feet leaving me no room to move my legs and just enough room to relax and breathe gently; don't you just "<u>love</u>" flying <u>coach</u>.

Next I discovered on the plane it's the battle for who occupies the one armrest between the two passengers. And if you reach to scratch your nose you just lost ownership of that armrest; oh the comforts of home make flying a pure joy. Sorry for the humor, the situation just seemed to call for it. So I just looked out the oval window during takeoff and saw us all slowly gaining speed on the runway and then suddenly rising up swiftly 100, 500, a thousand feet up through the clouds as <u>God was in the process of answering Kay's and my prayers</u> while He made this fish out of water having **<u>zero</u>** chance of coming to see her actually happen.

I know I must seem like a new born fish flying in a jet to those that travel regularly but God showed me something one day that gave me a new prospective. I was watching a documentary on the South Pole and how hard life is on these Penguins at -102 degrees below zero in the winter with the wind howling at them. I also saw how slow they walk with that reciprocating waddle they do and then thought to myself, "What a slow moving animal, not one of God's best creations." But then I saw their genius that God had created inside these slow moving creatures once they entered the frigid icy sea water. They moved with lightning speed through the water and even faster than the Sea Lions who were trying to eat them. So it is with this hidden genius phenomenon with ordinary people as <u>we discover their hidden genius inside them</u> as well. Like my youngest brother Kirk who has been an electrician for almost 40 years now will sometimes ask me for inside knowledge about finishing drywall at his house or the proper way to install laminate wood flooring I've helped him with before at his home. These construction things I consider to be basics and no big deal in my world of building knowledge as he might seem like those slow moving Penguins to me not knowing my basics. But years ago on the day he asked me for help in my area of expertise on one of his big jobs, I saw he installed this main power electrical panel grid you might have seen in the laboratory on an old 1931 Frankenstein movie in this old Hospital building that seemed like it could light up half the city of Butler. It was then very obvious to me you could now see Kirk's genius as his gift God trained him in was making me seem like I was the slow moving Penguin this time. So if I seem to you like a fish out of water while traveling, just remember, you haven't seen all the amazing things I can do, that would reveal my genius to you.

The Hunt for a Loving Heart

After I woke up in the hotel and caught a taxi to the dock I exited the taxi looked up and saw just 30 feet away this mammoth ship that stood a hundred feet high from the first deck and virtually up to the sky, or so it seemed. It also when on down the dock for a thousand feet long and then I found out later this ship was also a hundred feet wide. So adding up the square footage on this enormous ship there was one million square feet to get lost in a sea of 5,200 people I don't know <u>and the only reason I even came down here</u> was to meet and speak to one person; <u>Kay</u>. So with all these people and all this square footage, how is God going to put the two of us in one tight spot for our own privet conversation? Therefore, if there is to be a privet moment for us to meet and talk, only God will be able to arrange that magic moment as I found out Kay normally travels about the ship with her group of friends and love ones who regularly go with her on these annual trips. God had finally gotten His will across to me after many attempts of me missing His whole plan that Kay was my soulmate He had chosen for me and the future wife I had prayed about for many years.

Now there was more paper work to be done before boarding this ship and so I remember them pointing to a set of tables where you had to check in and answer a few more questions. Today I could not tell you what those questions were but one particular question caught my eye that I still remember them asking? "Are you married or single?", and the paper had a small box to check for each choice. Now at first I wonder, "What does that have to do with boarding a ship. I thought, why would the ship staff care one-way or the other whether the passengers were married or not?" That's when I got a new thought, "Kay is still praying for a husband and she must be very careful not to get to friendly with a married man as this would not look good to her Christian image and could also get her in a lot of trouble with their wives as well. Not to mention what the enemy might try to do to her untarnished reputation as walking holy before the Lord she observes." And with the Lord cluing me in on that question I proceeded to my destination to find my proper cabin number I'll be staying at for the next week on this "<u>wife</u>" connection.

The staff people gave us passengers who were fans of Kay's a schedule to all her events and their starting times and a schematic of the ship's layout as well showing all ten usable decks for the passengers as other lower "staff only" decks were off limits to the public. Now this enormous ship was the size of a floating city or the Empire State building laying down that I was never in before, but being a typical man of <u>logic</u> and <u>reason</u> I systematically determined what deck I needed first and then started looking at cabin numbers to find mine. Surprisingly, having never been on a cruise ship before I found my cabin in record time. Now this was it! This was <u>D</u>-day. The day I <u>D</u>iscover after all these months of preparation who God picked out for me. For all the Lord's miracles up to this point He did in preparing me to be ready to meet my future bride to be (Esther 2:12) was riding on what I <u>did</u> and what I <u>said</u> in these next few days <u>if I got the chance to speak</u>.

I arrived and saw the small efficiency cabin but then I got an "**<u>exciting</u>**" new idea to, "**Just go see kay NOW!**" as I was motivated to see her after reading her book and so I left my carryon luggage and laptop at my cabin. Now I had no idea where she would be on such an enormous ship so I put my male logical mechanically inclined mind to work for me as I looked at this ship's schematic and skimmed through these many diagrams.

Looking for the auditorium where possibly Kay might be signing, the schedule informed us fans she was preforming that first day at 5:00 to welcome us all here. I was hoping she might be practicing on stage and warming up on the microphone for her first show tonight. I believe the second floor had an auditorium on the schematic and then so did the third floor as well with the fourth deck X-ed off as unavailable for occupancy to complete the height of the auditorium ceiling. Since I'm a builder and used to reading blueprints, I instantly understood this visual mystery as most auditoriums have high ceilings for sound quality effects and so this ship required two and a half floors to accommodate this one large professional sound stage. I calculated this would be the highest probability to possibly see Kay and so that's where I boldly headed.

But the ship schematic used ship terminology like Port, Starboard, Bow and Stern for points of reference. Having never been on a ship before they might as well been talking Greek as I had no idea what any of these terms meant. So standing in the ship's very thin and very long hallway on deck two, I think, it was impossible for me to tell if I was going toward the front of the ship or the back. Seeing a crew member in a hurry carrying our big luggage to each cabin, I stopped to ask him which way was the back of the ship? He said pointing at my schematic, "The **Stern** is the back of a ship. The **Bow** is the front. The **Port** is the left side when you are facing the front and the **Starboard** is the right side. Since he kindly indicated I was already heading in the right direction I started to walk faster and this time with zeal to see Kay.

But the Lord questioned me with the same thought again as He did numerous times before while preparing me for months in my mind, "What are you going to say when you do meet Kay?" I was not sure about that but I also was not in front of her yet, so I just put off that thought for the moment. The way I envisioned our encounter, she would be on stage holding a microphone saying things like, "Testing, one two three; testing." Or, "Okay, let's take that one from the top and do it one more time." After all it was still hours before the first show at 5:00. Anyway I proceeded on the second deck to locate the ship's auditorium doorway. Looking at the ship's schematic I was sure this was the right doorway to the auditorium but it turned out to be a long curved hallway that led to the front of the stage and later I found out there was a side door off that curved hallway to enter a set of steps up to the actual stage. That's where the performers would be singing and this was <u>not at all</u> the lime light <u>nor the attention</u> I was looking for and certainly not what I wanted for me. I didn't want to interrupt Kay's singing nor did I want to be at the stage where <u>she might see me</u> looking in where I <u>might not be allowed to be</u>. I had hoped rather to just walk in quietly through the back upper baloney and maybe sit in silence in the back row and simply admire her beaming beauty and listen to the beautiful gift God had given her while she was singing.

So now realizing I'm at the wrong door on the second floor, I knew I wanted to be on the third floor at the balcony level and so I proceeded up one level to the third deck. Now I'm looking at building grade thick and heavy double doors. Each door was three foot wide as the building code would require them by the Fire Marshal's rules. I knew these double doors were the right doors to view Kay <u>hiding myself in the back baloney</u>. But there was a paper sign taped to the right door stating something like, "Staff members only!" So I understood I was not allowed to go in.

My dad raised all of his six children up <u>strict</u> and we were taught to obey all authority with responses like, "Yes, sir. And, no ma'am." I also knew famous people like their privacy and don't prefer a lot of clamoring fans <u>all the time</u> demanding autographs and, "Can we just get a quick picture with you?" Some fans impose their domineering will on the famous that are <u>somewhat of a slave</u> to their own stardom as they are highly recognizable and get noticed everywhere they go, so privet moments can be very difficult to achieve and possibly demanding to them all the time. And sad to say, there are even impatient fans that boldface asks interrupting while the star is already talking to other kind and polite fans that patiently waited their proper turn to converse with the famous. So, these impatient fans that can't wait their proper polite moment just boldly interrupt placing undue pressure, "Can we just get a quick photo with you?" That interruption places an awkward pressure on the star who now must decide <u>discreetl</u>y to keep everyone calm, who to address first and who to put on hold and how the star should now handle these p<u>ush</u>y embarrassing "<u>me now</u>" people. These persistence impolite people ruin the peaceful nicer moments for the patient and kinder fans as the star who now must deal with these demanding impatient p<u>ush</u>y personalities.

Well I didn't want to be an interrupter but then I also did not come all this way for a simple autograph or some picture for my scrap book which I don't even have as those things just will not do for me. No I was on a <u>M</u>ission of Lov<u>e</u> for <u>a soulmate</u>, someone I can share all the love God has given me <u>with a special heart</u> built by God, custom designed and made by Lord Jesus or a sweet lady with the Holy Spirit inside waiting just for someone like me. I was always taught to respect authority and obey all rules like well posted signs Kay had taped on the door. But this was my <u>once in a life time moment</u> and so I thought, probably no one will even see me walk in anyway as I will just slip in quietly and sit discreetly in the back row and silently listen to Kay's singing.

The Moment

So very much out of my character I decided to <u>disobey the rules written clearly</u> on the paper taped to the right side of the door as I was <u>rolling the dice</u> and <u>taking my chances</u> with love and fate. Therefore, very <u>sheepishly</u> and <u>quietly</u> I slowly opened the big ship door with <u>great caution</u> resembling the Cowardly Lion who was going down the long corridor to meet <u>The Great and Powerful Wizard of Oz</u> while <u>violating this rule</u> as I gently walked in with my heart-hoping plan where Kay would be on stage singing, but that was not the case. I had only gotten in the door about four feet when I stopped and saw two ladies talking about 18 feet away while I was looking at their side profile and so they did not see me <u>yet</u> <u>where I was not allowed to be</u> as they were facing each other and so <u>I was safe</u> for the moment. <u>I thought</u> the Lord had set me up perfectly to start out this opening conversation between our two heart-hungry-for-love souls with the advantage to this first meeting given to me the new comer.

Relating this to a football analogy, she obviously had the home field advantage as she has done this cruise ship thing before ten different times already; yet I was definitely the novice rookie visiting team increasing my nervousness as I was still in awe over this monumental floating city so different from my little computer room at home. Having been on this unfamiliar ship for less than one hour I still haven't gotten used to the immense size or the awe inspiring granger of this ship yet and now I'm looking closer at the two ladies I saw at first and noticing <u>Kay</u> is one of the two talking to the other one <u>right in front of me</u>. This is not the ideal scenario

I had envisioned at all where all I had to do is just hide quietly in the back row and watch Kay on stage from a distance and avoid my shyness of talking to females; especially famous beautiful ones who sing on stage. But the Lord saw me boldly entering this auditorium as **I created** this open window to meet Kay **forcing** our moment to happen **NOW** and not later and so seeing the short time left slipping away the Lord then spoke to my mind, "What are you going to say to her?" Being a visual person I was becoming all the more mesmerized as I was gazing at her beaming beauty and so my soul was slowly filling up with awe-struck spellbound panic and so I replied while staring and soaking this heart happy moment all in, "I don't know, I didn't foresee all this happening right now." I could hardly focus my thoughts being so close to the famous star as my eyes were starting to glaze over with elation.

Seconds later and seeing the time running out the Lord spoke again stating the near future as I heard the prompting, "Well you better think up something quick she'll be coming this way and will be walking right through the same door you just came in a moment ago." I saw Kay talking to a lady who I assumed was associated with JES Cruises and as I absorbed her beauty I felt twitterpated.[7] But if I was not prepared to talk to her before with my mind starting to freeze up with panic when the Lord questioned me, the pressure was then dialed up tenfold when her conversation was finished with JES Cruises and then she turned toward the door I just came in. Now just like the Lord warned me here she comes walking toward the same door that I just came through only a few feet behind me. Now D-day was finally here and so she sees me

---

[7] Twitterpated: In a state of nervous excitement or smitten, love struck, romantically infatuated. Twitterpated was first used in 1942 in the Walt Disney movie Bambi.

standing there <u>inside the door</u> <u>in direct violation of her sign she taped to the door</u>. Like sneaking into the Holy of Holies when you know you're not supposed to be there and then I made direct mesmerizing eye contact like I was staring at an angel. While my eyes were riveted and locked on her <u>I saw her as the authorit</u>y who posted that sign to the door and I know <u>I'm not supposed to be in here</u> breaking the rules in an area <u>I was clearly told to</u>, "**<u>Stay out!</u>**"

But she was kind and did not point my violation out, but only put out her hand in a warm and friendly greeting, and then she parted her sweet lips as that dazzling white smile beamed straight through me like a laser beam. At that moment I was <u>completely petrified</u>! Like meeting President JFK back in the early 1960s or the Queen of England for the first time if that helps you understand how I was feeling. But petrified or not I did manage to reach out my hand to accept hers as we held hands for the very first time and then she said, "Hi, I'm ----- --------." It was obvious in those next few seconds it was now my turn to respond back to her kind and friendly greeting. But I was so overwhelmed having never spoken to a lady that stunningly lovely before, ". . . *like the face of an angel* . . ." (Acts 6:15) and as <u>close up</u> as she was beaming in all of her glorious beautiful. Luke 2:9 * Acts 12:7. Just like many others who got a visit by angels <u>they were overwhelmed</u> (Luke 1:11-13 * 29, 30) but those ancient people in the Bible didn't shake the angel's hand or get a one on one eyeball to eyeball face to face meeting at <u>close range</u> like I did either. Eyes completely glazed over with glee and in this solidified state of shock I could not even remember my own name as my mind was paralyzed with wonder and amazement as my thoughts went completely blank. I was not even able to speak to save my own life if I needed to. So give it a name, star-struck, overwhelmed, nervousness, did you ever look directly into the Sun and quickly realize <u>it's just too much</u>? *"Turn your eyes from me; they overwhelm me."* Song of Solomon 6:5a. Living in my small backwards home town and freshly out of my <u>familiar quiet cave</u> where I study quietly all day, I couldn't handle that level of sudden beaming beauty being **<u>so close</u>** as well as she was looking directly at me and was expecting a <u>casual light-hearted warm and friendly response</u> while I stared back mesmerized and totally petrified.

Between the fact that I <u>broke the rule</u> she taped to the door I just entered and the fact that there I was seeing my future wife God told me was mine right in front of my eyes for the very first time as we touched and held hands, <u>it was just too much for me all at once</u>. Drinking in her incredible beauty <u>that close up</u> she melted my heart with that electrifying brilliant smile piercing right through me like cupid's arrow. But there I was, just like the Tin-man <u>standing stiff</u> in the red poppy field sent by the Wicked Witch of the West causing me to sleep <u>like a statue</u> in the falling snow while gazing at the Emerald City glittering in all of its glory and splendor without his oil can <u>I was rusted solid</u>. At this awkward pin-drop quiet moment with me not responding at all and standing there stiff like some <u>Wooden Indian</u> outside a cigar store, and Kay hearing nothing from this <u>mute</u>, she withdrew her hand and walked around the rusted stiff Tin-man and out the same door I came in.

The moment I had waited for all my life since nine years old <u>was now gone in a flash</u>. Then the enemy <u>who planned all this</u> started right in as they had set this whole <u>forced meeting</u> up **NOW** to <u>Disrupt</u> and <u>Stop</u> our hearts from merging together in happiness that the enemy hates, "You blew it completely", as they continued with their condemnation telling me how **worthless** I was. The enemy had me seeing myself as a complete failure; crushed and defeated, already to go home; <u>where they told me</u>, "<u>I belong</u>.

The Raw Simple Truth

In one of the five trips I took to see Kay I remember walking through a skinny hallway on the ship right before the jewelry store **by myself** as usual where they were selling those new big bulky wrist watches when I saw a small six by nine picture on the wall to my left of Russian Miss World 2006. She had brunette hair just like Kay did and I stopped to look and said to myself, this Miss World is very pretty, but even she still can't hold a candle to Kay's incredible DNA as God made her special for someone? Either that or what a colossal waste of incredible beauty He made; like a brand new Lamborghini Revuelto sitting in the garage for 50 years that nobody ever drives. Another time I was in the front of the dining gallery with a very large crowd just where you enter to the right and everyone talking and then Kay walked in and she just barely caught my peripheral vision as my head turned automatically in a split second to pin point her iconic incredible heart-stopping face. Within a minute, one of her fans asked her if they could get a photo with her as she is incredibly photogenic and then she flashed that brilliant dazzling smile for someone's camera as that side of the room just lit up with happy.

When Kay enters a room she's a head turner and if people stop and suddenly listen when E. F. Hutton speaks, then when Kay enters a room all the male heads suddenly turn and stop what they're doing to pause and reflect on her incredible DNA. And, [40] "... *if I should hold My peace, the stones would immediately cry out the truth.*" Luke 19:40. NIV. You cannot hold back illuminating brilliant looks like that as they pierce right through the fog of mediocrity that surrounds us regular folks like the Sun piercing through the storm clouds of this drab and dreary world of grays and browns. I was like a wondering ship lost at sea in the blinding dark that suddenly spotted the beaming piercing light of a powerful lighthouse on a starless night cutting through the murkiness of this average world till her radiant beauty grabbed my attention and locked up my gaze in her lovely looks. Have you ever seen a brilliant hot pink flower standing out alone in a field of common brown weeds? Song of Solomon 2:2. Others may not see things as I do, but this is just my raw and simple honest opinion. One time I went looking for Kay's videos on line and saw an older bald man dressed in black and sitting in a red chair named Tony Campolo who had a talk show and Kay was his guess or his co-hostess on that show I saw. At the end of their conversation while looking at her all this time he stopped and made a comment about Kay's looks stating, "My wife and I were talking about you before I came here today and she said to me what I agree with that here you are a single woman and you are, and this is not to flatter you this is an objective statement, one of the most beautiful women I know, really quite beautiful." And when he said that very complimentary statement Kay's only response was a very meek and soft, "Thank you." Someone might say you're just infatuated with her, that's all. But no, I'm really not; I will not fall in love with someone I really don't know yet and her and I have never really had even one heart to heart conversation as I just could not face her and have a relaxed conversation up close. There must be a lot of discussion and positive time for me to spend before bonding can occur for true love to germinate and connect our hearts together in real love.

Have you ever heard of "Imprinting"? Imprinting in nature is like a new born Zebra when they are just starting to focus their eyes seconds after they're born. This is when the new born's mother will stand broadside to the new born Zebra about ten feet away as the colt will start to focus their eyes and begin looking at their mother's pattern of black and white stripes as these stripes are like snowflakes and no two zebras' stripes are identical. This gazing upon the mother's pattern on the new born Zebra's subconscious mind is what causes this visual bonding process of imprinting the correct image on the offspring's mind. This way the mother is accurately identified among a staggering sea of other seemingly identical Zebras in a very large heard so the new born knows where to get its first meal of nourishing milk before their sense of smell is developed and takes over identifying each family member. But this very same imprinting or visual bonding also occurs with humans, Kay, as the more you look on a curtain unique face like a one of a kind snowflake and slowly study and memorize her each exclusive feature, **the more you will bond** to that distinctive face you've been focusing on. That's why wise business men have a picture of their wives on their desk at the office to see all day. That wise move strengthens their bond to each other and also reminds them their secretary who they do see eight to ten hours a day if there's over time, is still only a secretary and not a back-up wife as other good men have fallen into these imprinting pitfalls. Kay and I have only spoken a few very short times, but some day if fate permits or God arranges it, I would love to give that imprinting with her a try, only with the bonding door wide open. There's a unique feature in me I haven't told you yet Kay. I am what I call a vision-person. A term I made up to describe people like myself who learn deeper understanding as I normally receive greater insight from vision as the Lord explained it to me than audio as most people are normally limited to. I see in my mind's eye what the Lord shows me and visualize things in a way most people never do as this is how I try to teach as well using physical <u>visual</u> props, as I believe the Lord did while on the Earth teaching His disciples. If He was talking about God providing for His children like in Matthew 6:25-34 <small>KJV</small> He said, ²⁸ "... *Consider the lilies of the field, how they grow; they toil not, neither do they spin:*". I believe Jesus would point to the lilies of the field right in front of Him and His listeners would have a <u>visual reference</u> for <u>greater clarity</u> while His disciples had a <u>greater understanding</u> through this visual viewing prop. Or if He was talking about our godly walk like in Matthew 13:3, ³ "*A farmer went out to sow his seed.*" Jesus would again point to a sower on the path in the distance right in front of them so His disciples could <u>see</u> the illustration <u>for greater and deeper perception</u> which also makes memorization easier because you can <u>see</u> and <u>hear</u> it. When there is two different ways into the mind like hearing and seeing, the listeners and viewers receive and understand to a much deeper level of comprehension which is why Jesus did this teaching method when He taught. I see a lot in my mind in <u>this visual way</u> and teach others like the Lord did with this sower on the path using physical visual props people can see. I originally had well over 20 pictures in this book you're reading now but I had to remove them as I didn't know how to incorporate them <u>legally</u>, therefore much to my disappointment they were discarded. But with this gift He gave me, maybe that's why God selected someone with your beaming beauty for a visual person like me. All of the reasons that Lord Jesus is still trying to put us together and all the plans He has instore for us to do after we meet I still don't know; but He has shared a few amazing things so far that I believe will certainly happen and I would love to share them with you if we ever get a moment of intimate time together.

The Aftermath

Now like a good Father watching His little children slip and fall down, it's now time for the good heavenly Father to pick up the broken hearted troubled troglodyte[8] like a toddler who tumbled and tripped over his quark of shyness, dust him off stating, "Try it again", while the Father reassembles all the tattered pieces back together again. God told me that mistake was caused by a zealous heart longing for love but <u>didn't wait</u> for his Father's leading and so I jumped in head first because I just wanted to meet my new bride <u>now</u> instead of waiting on the Lord's perfect timing. So walking out of the auditorium where I stumbled and failed with my future Heart, I was now depressed and broken-hearted while I got a new thought in my mind as the Lord saw me disappointed and shattered in many pieces with the enemy grinding me into the ground like so many old used worthless cigarette butts.

My Father said, "When you enter a **<u>hot tub</u>** that is very hot, you don't just dive in head first like a swimming pool with a normal regular cool temperature. You test the water cautiously first with the tip of your toes to see how hot it is. Then you slowly enter a hot tub <u>little at a time</u> as you go in the hot water up to your ankle and then slowly get used to that. Then you advance to your other foot <u>slowly</u> getting used to that. Proceeding patiently you then continue up to your knees, and after 15 minutes of <u>slowly</u> getting used to the very hot water you can finally sit down in this extreme hot water as you have carefully and <u>slowly adjusted your normal temperature to match this hot tub</u>. <u>This is what you should have done</u> with meeting Kay, <u>slowly gotten used to her hot beauty</u>

---

[8] Troglodyte: A person who lives in a cave and doesn't get out of the house very often as I don't. A stay at home hermit or someone who is very old-fashioned.

over the course of a relaxing week on the cruise ship in the warm Bahama Sun like I had planned your meeting. All her beauty that overwhelmed you in the auditorium was a gift for her to display especially for you two to enjoy as I know how I created you as a visual person who appreciates the world visually as I have displayed My creative work on Earth and in the clouds of sunlight.

But living in your small bubble of Butler plus your hibernating habit of not getting out that often to mingle with this depraved world, you're not used to that high and lofty beauty level she has. You needed to see her extraordinary level of looks over the course of a week **slowly** getting closer to her a little bit at a time like the hot tub parable I just showed you in your mind. Eventually at the end of the week you would have been able to enjoy a casual relaxing conversation with Kay face to face discovering all the hidden gifts I placed inside you both. Then communicating after more intimate talk you two would have started to gradually notice how well you both bond together like two perfectly fitting puzzle pieces that's been separated for far too many years waiting to connect your gifts as two souls in one heart. Even seeing her close up only inches away by then you would be used to looking at her face that intoxicated and overwhelmed you in the auditorium as you would have adjusted slowly to her unusual outstanding looks like sitting in that hot tub you took time to adjust to while then laughing and having fun together. You simply needed to **take your time** and slowly get accustom to her striking looks over a week of fun in the Sun like I wanted.

This arrangement I've made between you two is not something that happens every day and you need to test every spirit (1 John 4:1-5) that you hear and are unwisely quick to follow out of your excited zeal. That quick thought told you to run ahead and find Kay **NOW! Don't wait!** The enemy had you rushing in to meet her <u>knowing you were ill prepared</u> in your mind to see her <u>up close</u>, nor were you prepared as to what you were even going to say to her as an opening statement. I asked you dozens of times in all of those many months I was preparing you for this <u>once in a life time</u> single meeting. Esther 2:12. "What are you going to say, or do you have some statement ready to ask ----- when you meet her?" And each time you replied, "I don't know." "

After the Lord spoke that educating thought but rebuking statement to my mind and I was <u>still</u> greatly disappointed, I replied <u>in hurt</u> to the Lord as I'm casually accustom to doing, "Why didn't You give me something to say?" As I am always seeking His input? "You know I have trouble talking to girls. Especially ones as stunning as her?" "Craig, I can't live your life in your place and make all your choices for you! I will move Heaven and Earth to put My praying children together if that is what it takes. But I will not <u>make</u> or <u>force</u> someone to fall in love with anyone else. That is a violation of a person's <u>freewill</u>; and I have given all people saved or unsaved a **<u>freewill to choose</u>** their own path and their own spouse and to decide for themselves who is right for them. My decision to put you two together is still My perfect will, but as you know I don't always get everything I want <u>on this wicked Earth</u> as I have given this Earth <u>like a gift</u> or <u>**a test**</u> to mankind."

The <u>M</u>essage Bibl<u>e</u> says that verse this way.

¹⁶ *"The Heaven of Heavens is God's, but He has* **put <u>us</u> in charge** *on the Earth."*
Psalm 115:16

The NIV Bible says that very same verse like this.

16 *"The highest Heaven belongs to the Lord,*

*but He had **given** the Earth to mankind."*

Psalms 115:16. NIV.

In this verse, the word "*. . . **given** . . .*" in the Hebrew manuscript is, "*. . . natan . . .*" #5414 KJV; or 5989 NIV and it means: **Entrusted to, Give Over, or To give an Assignment to,** or **to have someone MANAGE something for someOne.** In the same way a store manager manages the store for the owner, so we humans, created in God's image, are to manage the Earth by His rule of righteousness (Psalm 96:13) tainted by our freewill to choose.

Watch as I explain. We humans are to "*. . . Rule over . . .*" and "*. . . fill the Earth and subdue it; . .*" (Genesis 1:26, 28) everything on the whole Earth as an extension of God who created us or as an ambassador of Him for God in all of His righteousness. So God gave the Earth over to **all humans** to manage the Earth as we see fit, but we were supposed to understand His righteous rules in the Bible that we read as He commanded us to follow. Deuteronomy 28:1. Yet after we earthly sinners make our freewill of choosing, listening to the prince of darkness our enemy Satan and all his fallen angels plus hearing and falling victim to the voices of so many demons we yield to by our sinful actions, we tend to follow God's enemy more like our parents Adam and Eve rather than God and His Holiness. So we may be free to choose right or wrong, but God is also free to judge us for all our choices we made whether good or bad, obey or rebel, accept God or reject His Holy will.

Spiritual Law

How the Spiritual Law <u>Actually Works,</u>

Listen closely as I explain the scriptures: *"Then God said, 'Let <u>Us</u>* (the <u>Trinity</u>) *make man* (all humans saved and unsaved) *in <u>Our</u> image in <u>Our</u> likeness and let them **rule over** . . . <u>all the Earth</u> . . ."*. Genesis 1:26 * Hebrews 2:7, 8 * 1 Corinthians 15:27. Then Genesis 1:28 says, *". . . God blessed them . . ."* (Gave authority to) and commanded them to *". . . fill. . . subdue . . .* and *. . . <u>Rule over</u> . . . every living creature . . ."* However, we humans do not have complete ownership of the Earth (Psalm 24:1 * 50:12b * 89:11) to do as we see fit <u>without God also having His ability to **judge** our actions right or wrong we humans do daily</u>. But we are instructed only to <u>manage</u> this planet (Psalm 8:4-8) for God by His laws of <u>righteousness</u> as He has <u>given the Earth to us to set up</u> or run it but not in flagrant blatant sins rebelling against His clear written rules in the Bible. We often redefine God's well established laws to follow Satan that God gave us to live by and rule this world and all humans with His love. Lots of uneducated people, even weak Christians who don't understand the Bible very well, judge God far too harshly as they stand confused wondering why this All Powerful Holy God let's all this evil happen in the world today. But because most humans don't study God's Holy Word they foolishly misunderstand and credit God for all the wickedness on the Earth when it's really mankind and our daily rebellious ways fighting our loving living God who first placed man-kind <u>in Paradise</u> because He loves us.

*"You **made him** (humans) **ruler** over the works of Your hands; You put everything under <u>his</u> feet."* (Authority given)
Psalm 8:6

The Lord knew I was well familiar with Psalm 115:16 and so He did not tell me that verse as I have explained it. The Lord now continues. "So at the end of their lives they cannot put their decisions back on Me and so they stand in judgment good or bad for their own wise or foolish choices. Therefore, I will not make you two fall in love <u>with My words</u> so you can court her, Craig. What you say to each other and how you both respond to each one's reactions is all up to you two. I will not interfere with human <u>freewill</u> or <u>matters of the heart</u>. I still have a beautiful atmosphere in the Bahamas as Kay chose My suggestion well, then I leave the romance up to your souls and what you two <u>want to do</u>, obey or disobey My spiritual laws. <u>I have prepped you now for several years writing with you in your many books</u>; but once you two are together, that's as far as I go, My hands are off and you two are left to choose your own soulmate, whether you get it right or miss it completely I'll not interfere with your choices."

Again readers, I must remind you non-Christians, God does not speak every word as I have written them out but only <u>a concept</u> in my thoughts at the speed His children can understand them. Then when I convey in a book those same thoughts He spoke, it's up to me to write out His thoughts longhand the way I understood them so you can be a part of that intrinsic interaction conversation between God and what He says to His praying children.

v3 In love, God will point the <u>Way</u>, but never tell you what to <u>Say</u>.
v4 God can take your Test, and turn it into your Testimony.

Dad 3:3, 4

Does Fear Hold You in its Grip?

Do you know what's the #1 fear in humans? For the vast majority of us, people rank fear of **public speaking** as their number one fear they never want to face. Or not knowing what to say in a pressured moment like I just had while meeting with Kay in the auditorium. Did **Moses** fear Pharaoh at any time? Yes; in Exodus 2:11–15. NIV. Moses did flee from Pharaoh out of fear. "*Then Moses was afraid and thought, "What I did* (accidently kill an Egyptian) *must have become known*" and so Moses was afraid and fled from Pharaoh. Where in the Bible 📖 does it say Moses had stage fright? Moses battled with public speaking phobia, pleading with God to spare him a leadership role because of his lack of eloquent or stuttering when he spoke. Exodus 4:10 * 6:12.

How many times did God tell **Joshua**, Do not be afraid? Joshua is told to "*be strong and courageous*" NIV **four different times**, three times by God, (Joshua 1:6, 7, 9) and once by God's people. Joshua 10:25. And, three more times, Joshua is told that <u>God is with him</u>. Joshua 1:5 twice and Joshua 1:9.   Why all this repetition you ask? Simple, <u>Joshua needed the encouragement</u>; <u>just as I needed encouragement</u> from my heavenly Father.

Was the great **Elijah** who was taken up in a whirlwind and who was involved with God doing many miracles afraid also in the Bible? ³ "*<u>Elijah was afraid</u> and <u>ran for his life</u>.*" Look at verse ⁴ ". . . *Elijah requested for himself that **he might die**; and said, 'It is enough; now, O LORD, **take away my life**;*" 1 Kings 19:3, 4. NIV.

What were Jesus' fears? **Jesus** knew that all the <u>sin</u> and <u>sickness</u> of the entire world would come on His body while being nailed to a Roman rouged cross <u>full of splinters</u> and left in agony to suffer and slowly die a horrible suffocating death while demon bulls and dogs or like vicious lions ripping at His flesh swirled around Him. Psalm 22:12-21. He also knew the Father would turn away from Him because of our sin as He would feel abandoned (Matthew 27:46) for the first time in His eternity for the world's sins from our past, present and future would be poured upon Him having never sinned (2 Corinthians 5:21) or deserve this terrible treatment at all. Jesus knew every detail of what was about to happen to Him as He spent endless hours with His Father in prayer up on the mountains many times in His three years of ministry. Luke 5:16 * 6:12 * Matthew 14:23 * Mark 6:46 * John 6:15. And while He was in the garden of Gethsemane, He was afraid again asking His Father, [39] *"And He went a little further, and fell on His face, and prayed, saying, O My Father, if it be possible, let this cup pass from Me: nevertheless not as I will, but as Thou wilt."* Matthew 26:39. KJV. Do you know fear and faith are two sides of the same coin as we all experience both fear and faith in our lives many times over as this phenomenon of fear is a part of our normal lives.

V1 "A teacher is like a candle.
They consume themselves
to light the way for others.
V2 As Jesus poured Himself
out on the cross,
His words lit the way for
you and me"
Dad 5:1, 2

Jesus, the Greatest Candle or Teacher this world has ever seen!

So whether we fear **pain, poverty, heights,** 🕷 **spiders, snakes, the IRS, intimidation** like I did with Kay's beauty, or just someone bigger like a perpetrator, trying to murderer us, Jesus can understand our fears. God knows all things, He has addressed fear or its derivatives 524 times in the Bible as He knows <u>fear</u> is the **chief weapon** of our enemy and <u>**everyone**</u> must deal with a certain level of fear many times in their life before it is over.

The road to strong Faith,
is paved with many Fears.
Fears you must get <u>Past</u>,
if you expect your faith to <u>Last</u>.
Dad 10:15

Even at the moment when we are born we are plagued with two innate fears: The fear of <u>falling</u> and the fear of <u>loud</u> or <u>sudden</u> sounds. So as you can see, God is very aware that fear is quite common in all humans as He is the One who created us all. But we Christians have an advantage over the unsaved as we have found peace and comfort in the Holy Spirit to calm our fears knowing He is with us <u>and where we are headed brings us peace.</u>

Man is forever restless,
until he learns
to rest in
God!
Dad 9:12

The **King** or the **Fool;** Choose?

Do you remember me saying back in 1991 and 1992 I was selling carpet at Prezant's Carpet and a new sales lady with better than average looks came in who wanted to just meet the other salespeople she would be working with? And I said I struggled just to look her in the face and carry on a simple conversation as she spoke to me <u>way to close</u> as my self-image at that time was still fairly weak. But don't misunderstand me; I was also the top sales person at the Butler Prezant Carpet store who spoke to the public some days 12 hours at a time and dominated every conversation with them. I also once sang a B. J. Thomas song on stage called, "<u>What A Difference You've Made In My Life</u> in front of a crowd of over a hundred people during a very small talent show at a Christian coffee house called the Lamb's Resting Place that I was the President of in 1982 after only two year of my salvation. We also invited in the local public and put on a Christian theatrical play at this coffee house to help save the lost and I played one of the main unsaved actors who later got saved or Born Again. I've also boldly and spontaneously witnessed to well over a hundred unsaved people or my own A to Z business customers countless times or anyone else that would listen to me as I mimicked the boldness of John the Baptist in my 25 years as a carpenter contractor while I felt quite at home talking about my favorite subject; <u>God</u> and the Bible.

As long as the subject is something I'm familiar with and there's not a pretty face staring just <u>inches away</u>, I can even dominate the conversation when talking to a lady without hesitation and even take the lead steering the conversation in any direction I choose for it to go. But when it comes to jumping in quickly and being a "smooth operator" who has a new loose woman every night or one of those slick talking guys who uses those silly Hook Lines to "hook" or start up a relationship for their one night stand that ends in the morning after the thrill is over to hook their next victim, that's just not me. So I just can't do those quick Hook Lines or those fast relationships. Like the Lord said about the hot tub, I have to take the relationship slow and get to know her over time and take each advancing level little by little till we're both ready and able to progress to the next tier. So now that I think about it, I'm sure the enemy did wreck our God planned meeting after years of preparation as he knew I could not handle the quick connection very well while diving into the hot tub relationship with Kay's extraordinary looks head first and all at once like it did. Like my Lord said, I should have waited on His "Slow to Know" method and His Gradual School Rule technique rather than Satan's famous "Plow Now!" and his Don't Wait for Fate that he likes to do as the enemy was afraid this whole love connection relationship might actually work and then where would his dark kingdom plan be for stopping Love from Above.

I remember back when I was 18 or so and my friends and I were out in Herman just a few miles from my home town in Butler and my two friends who were always chasing girls at that age struck up a conversation with this group of young women and while they were talking I thought I knew one of them. So I waited for an opening in the conversation and then quite innocently I made eye contact and asked this one girl, "Don't I know you from somewhere?" She responded, "Really? That old line?" I was confused with her response. I had no idea what this "line" thing was that she was talking about. Hearing her offended rejection response to my curious question I didn't continue the conversation with her any farther as I could tell somehow I offended her as I misunderstood her comment. Later on I asked my best friend Mark, "What did she mean when she said, "That old line?" Do you know what that is?" My secular friend <u>at that time</u> explained it to me and that's when I understood what these Hook Lines were that people use to hook their next victim for a one night stand. But I can tell you I've never used a Hook Line to meet anyone as that whole approach sounds like such a lying scam and I'm only interested in honest transparent relationships with no lines, no head games, just be yourself and always be truthful as that makes the <u>best</u> and <u>deepest</u> relationships.

Once I hired two men to help me bend sheet metal on my 10 foot brake for one of my jobs and the one man was telling me he used these Hook Lines to start relationships that night and then that fast relationship was quickly ended the following morning. I must have sounded pretty naïve to these young bucks who were living their life in the fast lane with Satan as I knew so little about that life when I asked that young man out of curiosity, "How many women have you had?" He thought a few seconds and then calmly responded <u>with no shame on his face</u>, "Oh, about 150." I snapped back in sheer shock, "<u>150!</u> You're only 23 years old and you've already had 150 girls!" Seeing my utter surprise he defended himself by questioning me back as he responded, "Well how many women did you have by the time you were 23?", as he thought this behavior was common ground for every guy. I replied, "I didn't even get saved or Born Again till I was 23; and I didn't have any! Psalm 112:1. You obviously don't get to know them well before you dive right in, do you?" I guess I just grew up differently as I walked <u>A</u> Different Roa<u>d</u> than most males my age. I heard of a lady on line kind and talented quoting <u>CS Louis</u> once, who said . . .

"I find in myself a desire that nothing in this world can satisfy and the most probable explanation is that I was made for another world."

Zechariah 6:1 * 1 Peter 2:11 * Hebrews 11:13.

When I was 18 my 17 year old best friend would rather pick up his younger 16 year old friend Mike to go cruising around looking for girls while I did not show these same aggressive loose desires like he and my best friend did. Then after I got saved my two good friends saw me destroy my entire rock 'n' roll album collection and they thought I was foolish as I switched from the god of rock 'n' roll over to my Savoir Jesus my new best friend forever. That's what stopped all my unsaved relationships as I then went down to the local Christian coffee house called the Lamb's Resting Place (Jeremiah 50:6) and by two years the Lord had me running the place as President. We had worship every Saturday evening with local small time Christian artist and supported four missionaries. We also had Bible study every Thursdays night as my mentor John Dollar, who was saved many years before me like the Apostle Paul taught the class. John also started the Open Door Bible Club and made me his Timothy the vice President of that Bible study.

My secretary came along watching me cold call knocking on doors asking strangers for donations for Bibles for Africa. We ended up sending over 100 Bibles to Reverent Enius D. Didimu in Malawi. But **the reason** I was so shy all my growing up years and lacking confidence was explained to me by my Lord as He spoke to my mind one day a principle in the Kingdom of God.

Then one time when my only daughter Miranda got her first real boyfriend and there was a bit of trouble in their relationship I told her then what the Lord explained to me that day to give her some fatherly guiding advice and steer her in the right direction. So I said to her while visiting with her in her apartment.

In the heart of every man there's a **King** and a **Fool**. And oddly enough it's the woman in the man's life that determines who he will be and who she will surly get. If this uneducated woman speaks ill of her man, tearing him down in front of other people or saying things like, "If anyone will get it wrong, you sure will! You can't do anything right!" Then she will surely get this low level of man <u>she has spoken into him</u>; and he will behave like the **Fool** <u>she has breathed into existence</u>, treating her badly like fools do and everyone else around him displaying this bad worthless ingredient <u>she spoke into him</u> daily. But if the same uneducated woman changes her <u>destructive tongue</u> and <u>criticizing strateg</u>y and then starts to build up that same man, <u>encouraging him</u> with positive words and building up his confidence, saying things like, "If anyone will do the right thing, I know you will. You're a good man; I know you'll get it right." Now this wise woman who took time to <u>build up her new man</u> daily transformed the old **Fool** <u>she</u> <u>made</u> into a very special new **King** she has always wanted and is now <u>speaking into existence</u>. This new **King** <u>she has spoken into</u> <u>reality</u> will then treat her like a special Queen and everyone else in his life likewise: did you get that tip of the **King** and the **Fool**?

So Kay, you might ask yourself, "Where has my future husband been all these many praying lonely years?" <u>Sadly</u> <u>receiving and believing the enemies ongoing endless lies</u>. Being told I was **worthless** (Luke 17:1) by those who were willing to let the enemy use their <u>sharp tongues</u> for Satan's wicked work tearing me down and avoiding the **King** God surly placed inside waiting to be let loose by a "<u>wise</u>" and "<u>godly</u>" woman. The Lord said the king in me was always available all along like it was in any man's life, but the dark kingdom using <u>unsaved tongues</u> wanted to make **Fools** rather than **Kings**; so the condemnation just continued daily hammering me for <u>endless decades</u> <u>to keep this good biblical man down</u>. Miranda understood my words I spoke to her that day that the Lord explained years ago. So before our relationship starts up Kay with the Lord's plans to follow, who would you rather have loving you; a **<u>King</u>** or the **<u>Fool</u>**? <u>My</u> Life is in Your Hand<u>s</u>.

v5 It's not who you are
that holds you back,
but who you <u>think</u> you are!
v6 You're the King's kid,
<u>so act like one!</u>

Dad 3:5, 6

Kind words live in our memories
Proverbs 16:24 * 15:23 * 15:26 * 25:11 * 13:2 * 18:20 * 10:20, 21

for years watering our hearts
"*. . . comfort one another with these words.*" 1 Thessalonians 4:18

like love does to a
1 Corinthians 13:4, 7 * "*Love never fails . . .*" 13:8

love-starved souls
Proverbs 17:22 * 12:18 * 15:4 * 12:35 * Romans 14:19

or as rain to a thirsty garden.
Dad 3:7

But harsh words poison
Proverbs 18:21 * 15:1 * Colossians 3:12 * Galatians 5:22

the heart and destroy our Hope.
Ephesians 4:29 * Proverbs 15:1, 2 * 29:11 * James 1:19, 20

Like a fowl sewer
"Reckless words pierce like a sword . . ." Proverbs 12:18a

taints a clean stream
Ephesians 4:31 * Proverbs 15:18 * Psalm 37:8 * James 1:20 * Colossians 3:8

as I then considered a Rope.
Dad 3:8 *". . . there is a future for the man of peace."* Psalm 37:37 ESV.

At the end of my unequally yoked marriage I just wanted to Die.
As the enemy spoke death to me through yet another Lie.

v 9 Build your spouse's Soul,
". . . but the tongue of the wise brings healing." Proverbs 12:18b

help them out of that Hole.
v10 Positive words are your Role,
"Pleasant words are a honeycomb, sweet to the soul and healing to the bones."

as a new sweet man will be your Goal.
v 11 Let love take its Toll,
"While we were still sinners, Christ died for us." Romans 5:8

then his heart will be Whole.
"The man told the Jews that it was Jesus which made him whole." John 5:15

v12 If you feed his soul with God's Love
"Rather speak the truth in love . . ." Ephesians 4:15

then you'll finally get
"Now may the God of hope fill you with all joy and peace . . ." Romans 15:13

what you've been dreaming Of.
Dad 3:9-12

Just One Bed

So after the rusty <u>Tin Man</u> failed at *The Moment* with Kay just inside the auditorium, I thought my love life was truly over and it was back to my same old four walls at home again when I came back to my cabin like a whipped pup dragging his tail to unpack my suitcase. The enemy convinced me I was now caged up like a prisoner and locked on a ship called, "Depression" for a week of daily disappointment as I thought I was going to be all alone for the rest of my lonely life. Then things got worse, I no sooner got to the ship's cabin when my roommate showed up who I never saw before and he came in and saw the very same problem I did; **only one big bed** for the both of us right in the middle of this one very small room and so there we both were, two men staring at that one big bed and wondering, "Who thought up this?"

Suddenly I had a vision of that old movie back in 1987 <u>Planes, Trains and Automobiles</u> where John Candy who played Dale Griffith and Steve Martin as Neal Page was stuck in the business world trying desperately to get home to his love ones for Thanksgiving. So from the New York's business world headed for Chicago the snowy weather canceled all airline flights into O'Hare and then they ended up in Wichita. They could only get the last room available in a hotel with only one queen size bed. When they both entered the hotel room and were looking at that one bed for the two of them with shocked panicky faces, I saw myself as Neal Page staring at that one bed. And so now this new guy I never met before, who I found out <u>snored like a rusty chainsaw all night</u>, and I were also looking at this awkward "**one bed**" situation like Dale Griffith and Neal Page did with their eyes wide open and a stunned look on our faces wondering, "What is this? And I wondered which one of us was going to sleep out in the hallway."

But like a knight in shining armor this staff ship worker stopped in a few minutes later as we were hanging up our clothes and eyeing this unusual haunting problem while putting our belongings away and then the ship staff worker said, "I'll have this changed around in just a few minutes." So while putting away our things we stood and watched this ship worker divide the one big bed in half into two regular size beds that he separated with a three foot wide aisle in the center to enter each bed <u>separate</u>ly.

Now that our hearts started working again I slowly got prepared for the first show but in my heart I wasn't even sure if I was even going to go after all those many months of preparation and then that first blatant blunder in the auditorium before Kay. <u>Yielding to</u> these depressing thoughts this gave the enemy room to continue speaking his endless words of <u>condemnation</u> over me as I did in fact freeze up like a Popsicle and wrecked *The Moment.*

Now remember, Satan can't create anything but he does **<u>exploit</u> <u>weaknesses</u>** like my shyness to speak to a beautiful lady. So he spoke defeating words of failure and said you should just hide your face somewhere till it's time to go home to avoid having that embarrassment happen again. Walking in <u>fear</u> is a sin, as "*the just shall live by <u>faith</u>*". Hebrews 10:38. NKJV. <u>Any sin</u> gives our enemy the <u>Legal Right</u> to enter our lives and start speaking negativity to our souls. So the enemy stayed on me constantly stating over and over, "Months of preparation and all you did was <u>flounder</u>; you're **worthless**, absolutely and completely **worthless**!" But remember, <u>Step One</u>, demons try to Disrupt or Stop whatever God is doing in a Christian's life. Let's learn more spiritual rules.

Understanding Spiritual Rules

Understanding spiritual rules is crucial if you want to be an effective spiritual warrior and truly comprehend the **real truth** in this current *Twisted* Satan-obsessed system the uneducated humans call, <u>normal life</u>. So let's take a <u>small</u> in-depth look at our enemy's ability to cripple the unsaved humans and even us Christians who our enemy always tries to <u>Disrupt</u> or <u>Stop</u> God's will working in our lives as this battle between halos and horns was a very big part of my faltering with Kay and losing 15 years of bliss. <u>Step Two</u>: Demons try to bring <u>hurt</u> that last a lifetime so they can continue using this <u>hurt</u> <u>they just created</u> against us like the shame of <u>embarrassment</u> I had at *The Moment* Kay and I met for the first time in the auditorium. They do this to feed their ongoing condemnation for past mistakes the dark army tries to **exploit**; like <u>being afraid</u> or in my case intimidated or highly overwhelmed by a pretty face I was not used to as they **exploited** the shy weakness in me causing me to freeze up while trying to simply talk to a nice kind and talented beautiful woman. However, God has placed rule-restrictions on the dark kingdom so these <u>fallen angels</u> or <u>demons</u> (they're <u>not the same entities</u>) cannot just run rampant as <u>they have limitations</u> and cannot go totally unchecked with their own evil desires of destruction in our lives. There are God created <u>real</u> and **spiritual** ". . . *rules and regulations* . . ." (<u>Numbers 9:3, 14</u> * **Job 38:33**. "*Reflect on what I am saying, for the Lord will give you insight into all this*." 2 Timothy 2:7. (spiritual eyes to see and understand with) that He made before mankind's time on His newly created Earth that even most Christians aren't aware of.

God laid down restricting rules for the angels and especially the dark army like He did for us humans in the Ten Commandments and the hard Old Testament Laws no one could keep followed by the new laws in Paul's writings based on faith in Jesus the Christ who paid for all us sinners **IF** we believe in His Holy work on the cross. Let's learn some of these restrictive rules: Demons cannot enter human homes or even our lives unless these thorny things are invited in by us humans purposely requesting their evil presence. But you might ask the obvious question, "Why would anyone invite an evil fallen angel or a demon spirit into their life? Yet surprisingly people do this very foolish and terrible thing all the time even Christians do, every time they **sin repetitiously**, that falls under God's rule of, "All humans have a Freedom of Choice". So it's our **ongoing sins** we humans **do** and **choose** that does the asking of evil fallen angels or demon spirits (not the same thing) into our lives. Our actions are much more truthful to God and accurate as they carry more weight or greater truth revealing to everyone in the spirit realm like God and the dark kingdom as well about our true intentions or our inner heart motives. Our repeated actions reveal what each person truly wants in their life more so than our cheap words do we humans often don't follow through with. Look at the scriptures. [31] "*And the Lord said, Simon, Simon, behold, Satan hath **desired** to have you, that he may sift you as wheat.*" Luke 22:31 KJV. The NIV Bible say, "*Satan has **asked** to sift you as wheat.*" The ESV translation say, "*Satan has **demanded permission** to sift you like wheat.*" The NAS1995 translation says that "*Satan has **demanded permission** to sift you like wheat.*" So these demons cannot just do any evil they want without permission from God Almighty abiding by His established rules (Job 1:6-12, 2:1-8) they **must** abide by and so **if we ask these thorny things into our lives**, they are then allowed in but not until we ask. But now you ask the obvious question, "Why would God Almighty, ". . . *Holy and true* . . .", (Revelation 6:10) **grant permission** to evil fallen angels or demons of all evil things into our lives to hinder the humans or worse His beloved Born Again children and tempt us all the more into sin?" Good question, you're now starting to learn the spiritual rules of how the spirit world actually works you know so little about. So here's the answer: God gave us all a ". . . *freewill* . . ." (Lev. 22:18 * 22:21 * 22:23 * 23:38 * Num. 15:3 * 29:39 * Dt. 12:6 * 12:17 * 16:10 * 23:23 * 2 Ch. 31:14 * Ezr. 1:4 * 3:5 * 7:13 * 7:16 * 8:28 * Ps. 119:108 * Prov. 1:25 * Isaiah 63:19 * Luke 7:30 * Acts 7:51 *2 Thess. 2:10-12) **to choose** right or wrong, obey God and His rules or rebel against God and His Holy Bible and do as you please or as your fleshly desires lead you into more naturel fleshly "fun", or "sins" you rebelliously want to enjoy. (Sexual perversions, drugs, alcohol, stealing . . .) Thus we tell God or reveal to Him every day who we truly want for our eternal master to follow or live with eternally; Satan or God. Every decision we make 20 or 30 decisions a day we are constantly telling God Almighty or revealing to Him daily whose kingdom we truly love and want for our eternality. But we are also alerting Satan's kingdom with evil fallen angels and demon spirits (both are not the same) as well that we want them in our lives!!! Do you understand these first few spiritual rules and how they work so far as I have explained them?

If we choose to do sin **regularly**, Satan has the Legal Right by God's eternal rules and our Free Will to choose to lead us in the way of wickedness because we have just asked Satan by our ongoing disobeying sinful actions that we keep doing with our willingness to **choose** sin regularly. As we continue choosing sin continually, Satan and his kingdom of darkness will continue gaining greater control over us with every sin **we choose** to do as these evil fallen angels or demon spirits lead us deeper into more sin for more of their control over us and our daily choosing sin-loving soul. However, if we earthly sinners choose our Savior's Holy work on the cross and **Believe** and **Trust** and have **Faith** that His Holy works now transfers over to us sinners, then His Holy works are applied to us sinners and then become our Holy works as if we had done them ourselves, as we are then just as good and righteous as Lord Jesus or God. If we do this believing process, then our sins are cleansed and then nothing stands between us cleansed sinners and our Holy God, therefore, we will make Heaven our eternal Holy home when we die or get Raptured. Since **believing** in Jesus as our Savior and **trusting** in His Holy works on the cross to cover our many sins is all we have to do, this seems pretty simple. But let me explain the word "**Believe**" in this homemade parable so you thoroughly understand all that it means.

A prophet comes to Andy and Billy's house stating an asteroid from space will hit their house tomorrow at 3:00 PM. Both Andy and Billy say they "**Believe**" what the prophet said will happen. Andy immediately packs up everything he owns in his car and then drives a mile away to a new safe location and unpacks. The following day at 2:59 PM Andy looks through his binoculars back at his old house through the picture window and sees Billy still lying on the couch and watching old reruns of Gilligan's Island. One minute later the old house is completely obliterated by the asteroid. Since they both **said** they "**Believed**" the prophet's word, why weren't both saved? Because Andy put his **Believing** or his **Trust** or his **Faith** into **action**, where Billy just said the words but never Did the **action** at all stating, "Yes I believe" but he never acted on what he said he believed. So what's the moral or the lesson in this homemade parable? Saying you believe but not acting on what you say is absolutely worthless and you'll end up in eternal Hell for saying words you don't really believe in and following through with real actions that tells God you truly believe. Therefore, "*Examine yourself to see whether you are in the faith; test yourselves. Do you not realize that Christ Jesus is in you; unless, of course, you fail the test?*" So how can you ". . . *fail the test . . .*"? By talking about your faith but not walking in it, or acting on your beliefs, so you have no good works from Jesus following your easy to say words because your **Believing** was talk only or your **Trust** in Jesus and His Holy works on the cross was not real for you. Neither was your **Faith** activated as you said you have faith but you never placed that faith in Jesus with real actions as you simply talked about it and never **acted on** what you said just like Billy never acted on what he said either. So **talk is cheap** and is easy to say, but actions like dying to your flesh is never easy and requires long suffering which you will not really do unless you truly **Believe** what you have been saying is really true. So if you really **Believe** Jesus is your Savior and you're truly **Trusting** in His Holy works on the cross to save your sinful soul, you will walk ". . . *with **gratitude*** (actions) *in your hearts.*" Colossians 3:16. When you truly "belief", you will truly **try** to walk obedient and be respectable like a real Christian with good works that follows your true believing heart. Not that your good works that followed your believing did anything to save your soul because **your good works** CAN'T save your soul at all. But rather those good works followed your believing because you were truly grateful for the good works that Jesus did **for you** on the cross for all those sinners like you and me who call on His hallowed name for salvation. Therefore, when you observe in the Bible and it says, [30] ". . . *what must I do to be saved?*" and they answer is, [31] "***Believe*** *in the Lord Jesus, and you will be saved.*" Acts 16:30, 31. We now understand what is required in that word "**Believe**". Good works and godly actions will always <u>follow</u> a heart that truly **Believes** like Andy did who packed up his stuff immediately and left <u>truly</u> **Trusting** the prophet's words with <u>active working</u> **Faith**.

So, since we are truly saved <u>and</u> if we don't ask for demons to come in our house by our sinful actions, we can take authority over them and demand they leave <u>our lives</u> as they must get out of our homes <u>now</u>! [3] "*For though we walk in the flesh, we are not* ***waging war*** *according to the flesh.* [4] *For the <u>weapons of our warfare</u> are not of the flesh but have divine power to <u>destroy strongholds</u>.* [5] *We destroy arguments and every lofty opinion raised against the knowledge of God, and <u>take every thought captive</u> to **obey** Christ.*". It's very important to read and understand God's Holy Word or His Bible. If you don't read or understand the Bible yourself, then at least find someone who does read and then listen to what they say like a good godly pastor; but it's best to get your spiritual information <u>directly from God</u>.

So remember what we do by our actions informs both God's kingdoms and Satan's dark kingdom of our eternal desires and spells out quite clearly whose kingdom we truly want to live in for our eternity; God's happy Heaven or Satan's hateful Hell where those who go <u>burn in fire pits forever</u>. Now if you want the demons to leave your house, than <u>stop sinning</u> or stop asking them **by your foolish actions** to come into your home. But if we continue choosing sin regularly, the evil fallen angels <u>or</u> demon spirits (they're not the same) gain a <u>greater grip over us</u> because we <u>keep asking for them</u> **to come into our lives** <u>by our sinful actions</u>.

Our regular efforts of dying to our flesh <u>shows God by our daily actions</u> (Matthew 7:16-20) who we are trying to please and by those action whose kingdom we truly want running our lives on Earth; God's or Satan's kingdom of darkness that <u>will blind our eyes to the truth</u> and eventually keep us from seeing any of God's truth. Jesus sees our many decisions and records our daily choices (Revelation 20:12) in His books and then knows our true intent toward Him and His righteous kingdom. So, all your choices will be recorded and written down in Heaven that our <u>HARD</u> to do actions are truly trying to line up with His kingdom of righteousness more so than our <u>EASY to say</u> words. But now you ask, "Why does <u>Jesus</u> tell us to <u>do good works</u> in Matthew 3:8-10 * 7:19 and other verses while <u>Paul</u> tells us we are saved by <u>grace alone</u> and not by works?" <u>Ephesians</u> 2:8, 9. Some Bible doctrines are <u>complexed like college courses</u> that take hundreds of pages to explain as God's ways and methods are deep. We can't take time for that <u>deep answer</u> now but remember we Christians have a <u>Relationship</u> with our Savior Jesus <u>who died in our place</u> and so we are <u>Grateful</u> to our sweet future Husband and <u>long to please Him</u>. So when we get weak and caught up in our sinful fleshly actions, we then "<u>should</u>" want to apologize with a sorrowful heart informing our future Husband who sacrificed His life on a Roman cross for us sinners and so we inform our spiritual Husband we will certainly <u>try harder</u> not to sin again this time. Now do you see the <u>Relationship</u> we Christians are "<u>supposed to have</u>" and not a set of religious rules the religious people **do to be "<u>good enough</u>"** to get into Heaven which cannot work as, ". . . *all our righteous acts are like filthy rags*." Isaiah 64:6. This is why you can't do good works and use them to get into Heaven as we Christians don't have a <u>religion</u> like the misguided religious world <u>praying to statues</u> and mother Mary as they think their prayer will be answered faster as if Lord Jesus was too busy and supposedly overwhelmed with other prayers. Matthew 6:7. This line of thinking is earthly and comes from uneducated religious people and their own limited reasoning. This is why Jesus wants real Christians to have a <u>Relationship</u> with our future Husband <u>to be</u> in Heaven; <u>do you see the difference</u>? So thinking this way <u>we Christians walk with our Lord daily discussing everything we do with Him</u> as if He were walking right beside us all the time. Therefore, it's pretty hard to sin if your spiritual Husband you're going to merry in Heaven is right beside you; isn't it? So we Christians walk in <u>Gratitude</u>, <u>Gratefulness</u>, <u>Thankfulness</u>, and <u>Appreciation</u> as we feel <u>Beholden to our Savior</u> at all times and this proper attitude keeps us on a closer and godlier walk. These are the <u>words</u> that describe our saved indebted hearts to Jesus that Christians walk in; not hoping God can't see our true intent that can't wait to sin on every weekend. We show Lord Jesus daily we want to <u>honor</u> and <u>respect</u> Him as we <u>will soon be with Him</u> in Heaven. We treat Him the same way He treated us when He pulled us condemned sinners out of the flames of Hell (Jude 23) where we sinners were surly headed before He came down from Holy Heaven to <u>pay for our salvation in full</u>. Our sins are supposed to be honest mistakes we <u>accidentally make</u> because our flesh is weak and Satan is tempting us into those sins. Not regular sins <u>we look forward to</u> guzzling down with our favorite booze-sin to get tipsy on every weekend for our fleshly sinful pleasures. Do you see and understand the different bond in our close loving **relationship** to Lord Jesus and how we are to treat our <u>forgiving fiancé</u> we're about to get married to forever in Heaven very <u>**soon**</u>?

Are you understanding this sincere level of **<u>TRUTH?</u>**

But what happens to people who choose to reject God's truth? Let's look at this subject of truth through God's eyes and find out what God's rules are about **TRUTH** and **Lies**. Now the more we humans love truth, the more truth and insight into His kingdom and His Core Heart God reveals to us and gives us to treasure up in our own souls. If we continue chasing God for days or even years as I do for even more truth, He will inform those that love His truth with even more abundant truth and then we'll end up with greater insight on God's deeper laws few know from Him on the subject of truth because we love truth which turns out to be God Himself. John 14:6. However, just the opposite is also true; the more we humans turn our backs on truth, the more **BLINDERS** Satan is "allowed" to place over our eyes to see and recognize truth when it comes to us by God's rules of our **Free Will to Choose** truth or **Choose** lies or choose right or wrong or obey or rebel. If we choose wrong or rebel, Satan will then blind us from the very truth **we turned our backs on** and didn't really want because we wanted to do the sins we want and love to do without feeling God's conviction or feeling guilty for our sinful actions so we simply rejected God's truth to avoid the conviction we didn't want. Acts 28:26-27 * Matthew 13:4. *birds*. Now listen closely to this blinding part: the more you reject the Bible or someone speaking truth to you like I'm speaking now, the more **blinders** Satan's kingdom is "allowed" by God's rules of our "freedom to choose" to cover your spiritual eyes with his *Twisted* darkness so you can't see the very truth you really didn't want. Whether you understand the Bible or God's rules, you are making choices for your eternity and digging yourself a deeper hole or fire-pit to burn in forever.

So when you hear anyone speak truth or the Bible, God's Holy angels are watching you closely recording your response you just heard. Then your guardian angel, (Hebrews 1:14 * Exodus 23:20 * Psalm 91:11 * 97:10b * Acts 12:14, 15 * Matthew 18:10:11) enter your reply to that person who told you the truth as the guardian angel record your responding actions to that godly word you just heard in books stored in Heaven. Revelation 20:12. If you're unsaved and have rejected the truth you were told many times on Earth, you ". . . *will have to give an account on the Day of Judgment for every careless word you have spoken. For by your words you will be acquitted,* (freed from judgment or pardoned from your sins) *and by your words you will be condemned.*" (sentenced to a fire pit in Hell for rejecting God's truth many times. Psalm 28:1) Matthew 12:36, 37. NIV.

If you're saved, since you're **Trusting** in Jesus to cover all your sins by **Believing** in Him and having **Faith** in His blood on the cross, then **ALL** your sins are paid for, your good works you did on Earth are all that remains. So, you'll be rewarded for all the good works you've done for God's Kingdom, unless your motives were selfish or greedy, then of course you'll *suffer loss of rewards* (1 Corinthians 3:15) for your impure selfish greedy motives. So while we're still on the surface of Earth (Deuteronomy 32:22 * Job 11:8 * Psalm 9:17 * 55:15 * 86:13 * 116:3 * Prov. 9:18 * 15:24 * Isaiah 5:14 * 14:9 * Ezekiel 31:14, * 16-18 * 32:27 * Matt. 12:40 * Luke 12:5 * 16:23 * Rom. 10:6, 7 * Eph. 4:9) as there's no such thing as "☠soul sleeping☠", we can still choose to hear truth. But if you resist truth and turn your back on it, your ability to recognize truth comprehending with God's understanding will then start to diminish in your mind. Satan will have the Legal Right by God's rules of **freedom to choose** to blind you as you'll start to disregard truth and see it as wrong. Then spiritual darkness will continue clouding your spiritual eyes as your normal wise judgment will become slowly darkened to God's real truth while you continue rejecting the real truth you really don't want. So seeing truth will start to seem foreign to you as Satan's lies will continue replacing God's truths that you're now ready to dismiss all together. If you continue to reject truth over time, before long all truth will seem upside down to your new darkened way of thinking as your opinion of right turns to wrong or truth is now switched over to the world's lies and now you're willing to **Believe** wrong is now right and start **Trusting** in this wicked world and having **Faith** in the devil's worldly system. You have foolishly switched yourself over to the fleshly sinful flow of this wicked worldly system as breaking godly rules seems good to your new lifestyle in y<u>our now</u> dark sin-loving *Twisted* opinion.

This detailed explanation I've just showed you explains how some political people got to their incredible twisted darkened position over many years of turning away from God's truth and then in their current warped mind, after all that time rejecting truth, murdering babies seems to be justifiable to their thinking as they must have their sex without consequences. After many years of exchanging God's truth for Satan's lies, even something as twisted and off the wall as homosexuality (Genesis 19:1-11 * Leviticus 18:**22** * Leviticus 20:**13** * Judges 19:16-24 * 1 Kings 14:24 * 15:12 * 2 Kings 23:7 * Romans 1:18-32 * 1 Corinthians 6:9-11 * 1 Timothy 1:8-10 * Jude 7) in their now blinded depraved darkened minds is somehow today okay as they say, "<u>It's</u> just another life style". Despite God's Holy Bible stating, [26] ". . . *you must not do any of these detestable things.*" Leviticus 18:26. ". . .*detestable*. . .", or ". . . *these <u>abominations</u>* . . ." means, **very** <u>wrong</u> or **BIG** <u>sin</u> in God's eyes. ". . . *because they <u>exchanged the</u> **truth** about God <u>for a</u> **lie** . . . Because of this, <u>God</u>*

gave them over to shameful lusts. Even their women exchanged natural sexual relations for unnatural ones. **²⁷** *In the same way the men also abandoned natural sexual relations with women and were inflamed with lust for one another. Men committing shameful acts with other men, and received in themselves the **due penalty** for their error.* **²⁸** *Furthermore, just as they did not think it worthwhile to retain the knowledge of God,* (**Bible**) *so God gave them over to a depraved mind,* (Satan is allowed to blind them with spiritual **darkness** because they didn't want **truth**) *so that they do what ought not to be done.* **²⁹** *They have become filled with every kind of wickedness, evil, greed and depravity.* (when you reject God or truth you only have Satan's lies left). *They are full of envy, murder, strife, deceit and malice. They are gossips,* **³⁰** *slanderers, **God-haters**, insolent, arrogant and boastful; they invent ways of doing evil; they disobey their parents;* **³¹** *they have no understanding,* (Satan is allowed to **blind their eyes** by God's rules of letting us humans **choose** right or **wrong**, truth or **lies**, so they **cannot see truth** or hear God's righteous ways any longer. Psalm 38:13) *no fidelity,* (no loyalty) *no love,* (heartless, calloused souls, cold in kindness; killing innocent babies with no shame or no concern as if God's precious babies were worthless having no value at all) *no mercy.* (those that give no mercy to others, will in return get no mercy come their own day of judgment. Matthew 5:7) **³²** *Although they know God's righteous decree* (**Bible**) *that those who do such things deserve death,* (reaping what they have sown on Earth to be sentenced to eternal death in Hell for their **love of lies** and turning their backs on **TRUTH** as Satan did. Isaiah 14:12-14) *they not only continue to do these very things but also approve of those who practice them."* **Romans 1:25-32**. **¹⁶** *"Have I become your enemy by telling you the truth?"* Galaltians 4:16. ɴɪᴠ. The Bible says, **²⁰** *"Woe to those who call evil good and good evil, who put darkness for light and light for darkness . ."* Isaiah 5:20.

NIV. Today's twisted world advocates evil as good and condemns good as evil. **8** "*. . . but for those who are **selfish** and <u>do not obey the truth</u>, but obey <u>unrighteousness</u>, there will be **wrath** and fury.* **9** *There will be **tribulation** and <u>distress for every human being who does **evil**</u> . . . but <u>glory</u>, <u>honor</u> and <u>peace</u> for everyone who does good . . .*" Romans 2:8-10. ESV. Do you see the difference? Watch for the future of these kinds of people. "*Now the Spirit expressly says that <u>in later times</u>* (<u>end times.</u> Like now <u>at the end</u> right before the **Rapture** of the <u>Church</u> or those <u>truly saved</u>) *some will <u>depart from the faith</u> by devoting themselves to deceitful spirits and teachings of demons, through the insincerity of <u>liars</u> whose consciences <u>are seared</u> . . .*" How do you get a ". . . <u>*seared consciences*</u> . . ." by <u>choosing</u> to <u>ignore the truth over much time</u> or <u>turning your back on truth</u> you truly don't want! There'll be a day when you're in Hell burning and screaming in terrible pain and you will be asking yourself, "How did I get here?"; and the answer will come to your mind, "You chose to turn your back on God's truth <u>repeatedly</u> because up on the surface of Earth when you were alive, "*There was no fear of God before your eyes.*" Romans 3:18. NIV. By this foolish decision you then received spiritual blinders placed on your eyes by the dark <u>kingdom</u> that <u>you yielded to</u> and so from that day forward you were <u>not able to see the truth</u> any longer.

So if you have been caught up in the dark actions of the malevolent political world (<u>Ezekiel 12:2</u>) and followed their twisted Satan-loving God-hating actions and now don't want God's truth either, Satan will then continue darkening your fading failing understanding of real truth as your opinion will continue trending toward dark sinful actions like Satan's dark kingdom. If you persist in <u>blinding your own mind</u> even farther to all of God's truth as well so that all you do see is Satan's lies, your own crippled understanding of truth will then be darkened and so you will think the same way Satan's dark heart thinks. Acts 28:26-27. Wise up!

_{V1} Satan whispers to You,
you don't have to be True.
_{V2} Just accept my Lie,
so you'll be a sly Guy.
_{V3} As now you're not Shy,
about living his twisted Lie.
_{V4} Satan will always let you Sin,
as you sit now in your sinful Grin.
_{V5} It's easy to Do, just never be True.
_{V6} But God says learn to love My Truth,
you have lost from your Youth.
_{V7} Then you will See,
Satan's been lying to Thee.
_{V8} Just turn from your Sin,
cause your demons got In!
_{V9} Satan will tell you all is Well,
as he opens up the gates to Hell.
_{V10} You'll get your own fire Pit,
and the flames will never Quit.
_{V11} You have exchanged truth for a Lie,
so now who's the wise Guy?

Dad 9:1-11 ". . and *all liars* shall have their place in the Lake of fire." Rev. 21:8

¹⁴ *"So justice is driven back, and righteousness stands at a distance; truth has stumbled in the streets, honesty cannot enter.* **¹⁵** *Truth is nowhere to be found, and <u>whoever shuns evil becomes a prey</u>.* of Satan. *The L*ORD *looked and was displeased that <u>there was no justice</u>.* Isaiah 59:14, 15. NIV. Does that not sound like today's upside-down world?

But you might ask why would God allow that darkening, blinding process to happen to the people He loves on Earth? John 3:16. Because God gave us humans a **free will to choose** right or wrong, God or Satan, Truth or lies and you simply didn't want God's truth like some in the political world who hate all godly truth and have been <u>steering the spiritually uneducated astray for years</u> trying to establish Satan's <u>New World Order</u> with the anti-christ in charge of the whole Earth. Revelation 6:1, 2 * 20:10. Satan's satanic system can then rule over all the deceived people like God's Word says <u>he will do</u> by this eye-darkening (2 Thessalonians 2:7-12) process just like Satan tried to do through Hitler conquering Europe years ago trying to rule the whole world back in the 1940s.

Eventually if you continue to reject the Bible or God's truth like the sin-loving political people has already done down through the years of moving even <u>farther every election to the twisted left</u>, or closer toward Satan's darkened heart, your ability to understand real truth and make wise decisions as you once did when you were younger will diminish daily <u>as</u> their lying hearts have. So if you avoid truth or God's Bible, your good common sense and wise opinion <u>you once had</u> will fade out slowly like a dying lightbulb in a flashlight with low batteries draining all wisdom into <u>dead light</u> or <u>no truth</u> at all. If you continue rejecting truth your ears will become dull of hearing any of God's truth as Satan is "<u>allowed</u>" to continue making you <u>spiritually deaf to all truth</u> simply because you don't want to hear the real truth that convicts you of your daily sins the Bible told you not to do. Jeremiah 6:10 * 2 Timothy 4:4, 5. Your eyes now cannot see God's Holy ways very well either because of your constant denying the truth you still don't like as it doesn't fit into your now new sinful carefree, sin any way you please, lifestyle. The Greek version to Isaiah 6:9, 10 reads, "*And the Lord said, "Go and say to this* (stiff-necked stubborn) *people, 'When you hear what I say, you will not understand.* Satan has blinded the minds of those who do not want the truth. *When you see what I do, you will not comprehend.* Your understanding is clouded by Satan. *For the hearts of these people are* **hardened**, (calloused hearts made of stone hardened by ongoing sin; Ezekiel 36:26, 27) *and their ears cannot hear*, (deaf ears to understanding God's truth because they did not want truth revealing their sinful ways) *and they have closed their eyes so their eyes cannot see*, (they cannot see what they do not want! They don't want truth anymore as sin Is now what they want to do and they just don't want the conviction that the truth brings?) *and their ears cannot hear*, (hearing truth grows more dull) *and their hearts cannot understand*, (Satan has blinded their minds by way of **their freedom to Choose Sin** and love darkness) *they cannot turn* (repent) *to Me* (God) *and let Me heal them.*" Isaiah 6:9, 10. "*The wrath of God is being revealed from Heaven against all the godlessness and wickedness of men who suppress the truth by their wickedness.*" Romans 1:18. NIV. These people who don't like truth have drifted so far away from God's Holy Bible, their ability to see and hear God's truth has diminished into almost nothing or spiritual blindness and deaf ears that cannot understand real truth any more. Satan' kingdom will eventually have you believing his ungodly ways are actually good as you have slowly switched over to his dark kingdom one rejection of truth at a time. Listen to the scriptures, "*Jesus said, 'The knowledge of the secrets of the* *kingdom of Heaven* (truth) *has been given to you,* (those who are hungry to hear the truth as I do daily) *but not to them.* (those who reject the truth and don't really want it because the truth points to all their sins <u>they don't want to give up</u> **John 3:19-21**) *Whoever has* (God's <u>truth</u>) *will be given more,* (God wants us to *hunger and thirst after righteousness as they* <u>*shall be* filled.</u>" Matthew 5:6 or chase hard after Him <u>for more truth</u> and His knowledge, deeper insights and those that <u>love His wisdom</u> as I do chasing the Core of God's loving and eternally wise Heart daily) *and he will have an abundance.* (like me who chase after <u>God's Core Heart</u> are totally **addicted** to God's truth when He speaks because we love His Holy heart and can't wait to hear even more). *Whoever does not have,* (God's truth and doesn't really want it) *even what he has will be **taken** from him.*" Matthew 13:12. (Satan is **Allowed** to **take** God's truth from those that don't want it as he darkens their understanding and blinds you from the truth you don't really want; **did you get that?** [4] *"In their case <u>the god</u>* (<u>Satan</u>) *of this <u>world system</u> has blinded the minds of the **un**believers, to <u>keep them from seeing the light of the gospel</u> of the glory of Christ, who is the image of God.*" Corinthians 4:4. ESV. This is what I'm talking about as this principle of being blinded from the truth as it comes out of the Bible you should read daily. [19] *"And this is the judgment: the <u>light</u>* (<u>truth</u>) *has come into the world, and people <u>loved the darkness</u> rather than the light <u>because their works were evil</u>.* [20] *For everyone who does wicked things hates the light* (light exposes their sins and so they don't want that <u>light</u> or <u>truth</u>) *and does not come to the light, lest his works* (sins) *should be exposed.* (people try to hide their sins in darkness because deep down they know the Bible is right and sin is wrong) [21] *But whoever does what is true comes to the light, so that it may be clearly seen that his works* (his actions) *have been carried out in God.*" John 3:19-21. So if you love truth, as I do, and have fun chasing the very <u>Core of God's Heart</u> all day long, like I enjoy, God will continue feeding you (James 4:8) more insight and more knowledge and revealing greater hidden heavenly secret truths that most Christian don't take the time to know such deep <u>enlightening wonderful insights</u>. Bottom line, if you reject God's truth, all that is left for you are Satan's lies that darken your understanding of real truth and blinds your understanding thus it takes you to Hell all the quicker; so I have to ask you, <u>is this really what you want</u>?

Now are we gaining on our biblical mind and increasing on our understanding of God's spiritual rules and how the deeper insights of God's spiritual laws really work? So if the "<u>c</u>hristians" <u>never show Jesus</u> by their **actions** they're making an <u>effort to walk in truth</u> before Heaven, (Hebrews 4:11 * 2 Peter 1:3-**5**-11 * Matthew 7:16-20) all of Heaven will know those professing "<u>c</u>hristians" talking righteousness like the hypocritical Pharisees did, those people will end up in Hell as their **ACTIONS** told Lord Jesus the real truth in their life. Now that we've learned about truth, we return to the spiritual rules about <u>evil fallen angel</u> **and** <u>demon spirits</u> longing to gain greater control to cripple our witness as they <u>watch our sinful actions closely</u>. The more we sin, the more control or <u>spiritual power</u> they gain over the <u>uneducated sinners</u> who does not know the rules and <u>their control over us</u> is what the Bible calls, <u>strongholds</u>. (2 Corinthians 10:4) as Paul was writing to us Christians [1] "... *unto the* ***Church of God*** *which is at* <u>*Corinth,*</u> *with* <u>*all the saints*</u> *who are in all Achaia.*" 2 Corinthians 1:1. KJV. The stronghold the enemy had over me was the big lie that I was **worthless** like a [7] "... *thorn in the flesh, the massager of Satan to buffet me,*" (2 Corinthians 12:7 KJV) as Paul was also buffeted by these destructive God-hating <u>fallen angels</u> <u>**or**</u> <u>demon spirits</u> or this "... *thorn in the flesh* ...". Then as long as <u>I believed</u> I was truly <u>worthless</u> like they convinced me I was, and <u>not good enough for Kay</u>, their stronghold over me was secure. But after 10 more years of Bible study when I **stopped believing** in their endless lies of **worthlessness**, they lost their Legal Right over me and so the stronghold was broken. As I was [5] ". . . *bringing into captivity every thought to the obedience of Christ.*" (2 Corinthians 10:5) the spiritual door for Kay and I to move forward with our relationship was available once again which is why I am writing this book today in 2023. Now watch closely in the Strongest Strong's Exhaustive Concordance of the Bible, James Strong has the definition for the word "*strong*" in the verse 2 Corinthians 10:4. And that word "*strong*" is #3794 **ochyroma**: in the Greek. Translated into our English, that parenthetical definition is (**Stronghold, fortress**; or even **PRISON**). Romans **7**:**23**. This is where I was being held as a Prisoner in the spirit realm in their **PRISON** by the demons' stronghold that I yielded to by being afraid of Kay's beauty and the long standing lie that I was **worthless** all those many years as I accepted that lie as the truth. Therefore, this endless luring us into sin is their constant strategy for more spiritual power over all of us Christians, especially if God is using us for His Holy will to answer our years of prayers.

[16] "*Don't you know that when you offer yourselves* (walking in sin) *to someone* (God or Satan) *as obedient slaves, you are slaves of the one* (God or Satan) *you obey—whether you are slaves to sin,* (slaves to Satan) *which leads to death,* (Hell) *or to obedience,* (God) *which leads to righteousness?*" (Heaven). Romans 6:16. NIV. Consider also, "*Jesus replied, 'I tell you the truth, everyone who sins is a slave to sin.* (slave to Satan) *Now a slave* (unsaved) *has no permanent place in the family,* (God's family; Heaven) *but a son* (saved) *belongs to it* (Heaven) *forever.*" John 8:34, 35 * Ephesians 4:17-25. Jesus also said, "*You will know them by their fruits.*" (or your actions) Matthew 7:16-20.

Demonic Power Levels 1-10. Let's start with level **1**: Most uneducated Christians believe fallen angels **or** demon possession is thought to be restricted to only the unsaved; but this religious myth is just not true. Those that remove demonic spirits from individuals regularly will tell you they get as many Christians as non-christians in their spiritual practice that need the unwanted thorny things thrown out of their lives. Demons or fallen angels have the "Legal Right" by God's rules to enter Christians as well because **regular sin** or our **freewill to choose** wrong over right, or disobey over obey is God's rule for demons entering us humans saved or unsaved as we make our daily choices and get tempted into sins just like the unsaved sinners do. So either you the Christian are going to master Satan **by** obeying God regularly, **or** Satan is going to master you **by** you bowing down to him through his rebellious rules of ongoing sin he wants you to keep on doing even after you're saved so he can **continue** controlling you as his slave; **understand**? *"Jesus replied, I tell you the truth, **everyone** who sins is a slave to sin."* John 8:34. Paul writing to Christians **also** informs us, ". . . *you are slaves to the one whom **you obey**."* Romans 6:16. Watch the scriptures closely to understand how we Christians are slaves to our ongoing sins; [14] *"We know that the law is spiritual; but I* (Paul, a sinner, as we all are) *am unspiritual, **sold as a slave to sin**."* Romans 7:14. NIV. All humans like Paul are, ". . . **sold as a slave to sin**." So when were we ". . . **sold as a slave to sin**"?

In the Garden of Eden when Adam was commanded by God, *"But of the tree of the knowledge of good and evil, thou shalt not eat of it; for in the day that thou eateth thereof thou shalt surely die."* Genesis 2:17. KJV. Then Adam listening to his wife Eve, ate of the tree God told him not to eat from. So by this disobedient method, Adam, the first man, rebelled against God and at the same time **obeyed Satan** by eating from the tree God commanded Adam not to eat from. This is what Paul is talking about to the new Christian Gentiles back in his day who never read the Old Testament or understood the law as Paul is educating the new Gentile Christian convers when he says, ". . . ***sold as a slave to sin***" in Romans 7:14. This is why Satan is ". . . *the god of this world system* . . ." 2.Corinthians 4:4. ESV. Or Satan <u>and</u> all us sinners who continue sinning are the ones responsible for all of the evil in this wicked world today.) Remember, *"The Earth is the Lord's, and everything in it, the world, and all who live in it."* (Psalm 24:1. NIV) yet Satan rules over humans because of our original sin of obeying Satan through Adam's sin rather than God who told our first father Adam not to eat of ". . . *the tree of the knowledge of good and evil* . . ." in the Garden of Eden. So God the Father not wanting us humans to live in this sin-state forever and so be separated from Him forever burning in Hell, sent His only beloved Son, Lord Jesus down to live a life on Earth as a man and so Lord Jesus ". . . *became flesh . . .*". John 1:14. Jesus could then live the perfect life that Adam did not and then being perfect with no sin, He could then die on a cross for all mankind to redeem all humans **IF** we choose Lord Jesus as our Savior to cover our sins with His precious blood. But all humans wanting to be saved from Hell's fire and go to Heaven, **MUST** choose to **Believe** in our Savior Lord Jesus that God the Father provided for us. We must **Believe** Jesus is God and we're sinners destine for Hell who needs His righteousness applied to us for our salvation **Believing** in His <u>Death</u>, <u>Burial</u>, and <u>Resurrection</u> to save our own lost souls headed for Hell's eternal fire.

Now watch closely what the apostle Paul says for <u>the **clue**</u>, [15] *"I do not understand what I do.* (What is Paul talking about?) *For what I want to do* (obey God) *I do not do,* (Paul wants to obey God and all

His rules, but **he can't**) *but what I hate I do.* (Paul hates the sin he is doing)
16 *And if I do what I do not want to do,* (If Paul sins but really doesn't
want to) *I agree that the law is good.* (Paul is saying the fault is not on
God's laws, but on him the sinful Christian as he wants to obey God **but can't**).
17 *As it is,* **it is *no longer_I* myself who do it,** (do what? Sin! Paul is
saying <u>I'm not the **one**</u> sinning) *but it is sin* (**?**) *living in me.* (So if Paul is
not the one sinning, than <u>who</u> is**?** Paul is saying it is <u>sin</u> living <u>in me</u> that is
sinning; **not me**) **18** *I know that <u>nothing good lives **in me**,* that is, **in**
my sinful nature. (Paul continually uses the words ". . . **in** *me* . . . or ". . . **in**
my sinful nature." *For I have the desire to do what is good,* (than why
doesn't Paul do the good he wants to do?) *but <u>I cannot carry it out</u>.*
(So Paul ". . . *desires to do what is good, but he **cannot carry it out**.*" **19** *For
what I do* (sin) *is not the good I want to do;* (like obeying God) *no, the
evil I do not want to do,* (sin) *this **I keep on doing**.* (what is <u>driving Paul</u>
to sin <u>against his will</u> as he longs to do good?) **20** *Now if I do* (sin) *what I
do not want to do,* (disobey God's rules) *it is <u>no longer I who do it</u>,*
(Paul's says it's not him that sins, so <u>what</u> or **who** is <u>driving him</u> to sin when he
doesn't want to sin**?**) *but it is <u>sin</u>* (<u>demons</u>) *living **in** me that does it.* (as
I said before, <u>sin</u> <u>driving Paul</u> to disobey God is an <u>action</u> like lying, stealing or
murder and <u>actions</u> do not have the **will** to work against you the Christian nor
do <u>actions</u> have the ability to **choose** sin or **desire** wrong doing, nor do
<u>actions</u> have an **entity** to <u>choose</u> or <u>desire</u> or <u>work</u> anything against you as
<u>actions</u> are not alive to **decide** to do anything) **21** *So I find this law* (of sin
or these fallen angels or demons spirits) *<u>at **work</u>:** When I want to do
good, evil* (or fallen angels or a demon spirit) *is right there with me.* (so if
these fallen angels or demon spirits are **in** <u>Paul</u>, the best Christian this sinful
world has ever produced, is it not clear to you that it is not Paul who is sinning
but these fallen angels or the demon spirits **driving** Paul to sin as they do us
Christians as well**?** **22** *For in my inner being I delight in God's law;* (is
this not our desire as sincere Christians to walk godly before our loving God?)

²³ *but I see **another** law at work* (these <u>fallen angels</u> or the <u>demon spirits</u> <u>working against my will</u> to do good and obey my God) ***in** the members of my body, <u>waging war</u> against the law of my mind* (can <u>actions</u> **wage war** against us Christians? Or do demons attached to sin **wage war** against us regularly**?**) *and <u>making me</u>* (Paul) *<u>a **prisoner** of the law of sin</u> <u>at work</u> within my members.* (can <u>actions</u> "<u>*make you*</u>" do anything? **No**, actions don't have a **<u>will</u>** to **<u>war</u>** against you.) ²⁴ *What a wretched man I am!* (Paul is saying he is wretched because of these fallen angels or the demon spirits **working against** his **will** to do good and obey God) *Who will rescue me from this body of death?* (Paul is saying, how can I obey God with these evil things constantly **working against** me) ²⁵ *Thanks be to God, through Jesus Christ our Lord!* " **Romans 7:14-25**. NIV. (the blood of Jesus covers our sins <u>we struggle</u> to not do. But remember Lord Jesus needs to see you **struggling to do good** and **trying to obey** His rules with **<u>active faith</u>** like <u>Andy did</u> by packing up his stuff and not like <u>Billy who only talked about it</u>).

God's opinion of the human heart. "*The heart is **deceitful** **above all things**, and **desperately wicked**.*" Jeremiah 17:9. KJV. Do you see the demons inside of us? The American S. Bible says, "***exceedingly corrupt***". The Berean Study Bible says man's heart is, "***beyond cure*.**" "*Jesus did not need man's testimony about man, for He knew ?what? was **in** a man.*" John 2:25. NIV. So if Paul one of the greatest Christians ever, if not thee greatest, <u>cannot do the good he wanted to do</u> and Paul does do the sins he hates, is this struggling Paul not like us Christians today as we face this **struggle** as well? And if Paul still struggling to do good <u>but cannot</u> says, ". . . *it is **no longer I** myself who do it,* (sins) and *the evil I do not want to do, this **I keep on doing**. . .*", as the demons are ". . . ***in*** . . ." Paul, ". . . ***waging war*** *against the law of* (his) *mind . . . <u>making me</u>* (Paul) *<u>a</u> **prisoner** <u>of the law of sin</u> at work within my members . . .*" then Christians today can certainly have demons **<u>in</u>** them as well.

Paul says, ". . . *For I have the desire to do what is good,* (than why doesn't Paul do the good he wants to do?) Then Paul says, ". . . *but I cannot carry it out.*" as he is losing this spiritual battle in this unholy war with the demons that are **in** him and so the question today is, "Who of us does not have demons today? Now you might start to believe, "Well then maybe everyone has demons today." But not so fast with that idea as we always go to the Bible for God's insight and His holy answers as Jesus speaks, [43] *"When an evil spirit comes out of a man, it goes through arid places seeking rest and does not find it.* [44] *Then it says, I will return to the house I left.* (or the possessed person he was just **in** before he got cast out) *When it arrives, it finds the house* (or the spirit's old host he was possessing) *unoccupied, swept clean and put in order.* (this means **not possessed** any more but **free from demon spirits** or fallen angels whispering evil in their minds. So by this lesson we have learned at least **some people** are not demon possessed) [45] *Then it goes and takes with it seven other spirits more wicked than itself,* (as this original weaker evil spirit that got cast out is now counting on the strength of his new stronger spirits he recruited to secure his old home **in** his original host he was once in) *and they* (the now eight spirits) *go in and live there. And the final condition of that man is worse than the first. That is how it will be with this wicked generation.*" Matthew 12:43-45. So now we stop and ask you, "Are your <u>Pet Sins</u> you still love to do and these evil spirits guiding you in evil daily to their wicked future in Hell really the demons you truly want in your life steering you toward more sin so they can get a better hold on you? And what about these verses, [14] ". . . *a man approached Jesus and knelt before him.* [15] *'Lord, have mercy on my son,' he said. 'He has seizures and is suffering greatly. He often falls in the fire or into the water.'* This demon was trying to kill the boy. [16] *I brought him to your disciples, but they could* *not heal him.'* If you do not have **sufficient faith**, nothing will happen. [17] *'O <u>unbelieving</u> and perverse generation,' Jesus replied, 'how long shall I stay with you? How long shall I put up with you? Bring the boy here to Me.'* [18] *Jesus rebuked the demon, and it came out of the boy, and he was healed from that moment."* Matthew 17:14-18. NIV. When the demon came out of the boy, that boy had no demons. So again it is possible for humans to not have demons. But can Christians really cast demons out of possessed people? Look at the scriptures, *"Jesus called His **twelve** disciples to Him and <u>gave them **authority** to drive out evil spirits</u>."* Matthew 10:1. After Jesus sent out the 72 they returned saying, *"Lord, <u>even the demons submit to us</u> in your name."* Luke 10:17. Watch again, [16] *"Once when we were going to the place of prayer, we were met by a slave girl who <u>had a spirit</u> by which she predicted the future. She earned a great deal of money for her owners by fortune-telling.* [17] *This girl followed Paul and the rest of <u>us</u>,* (<u>Timothy</u>, <u>Paul</u> and <u>Silas</u>) *shouting, 'These men are servants of the Most High God, who are telling you the way to be saved.'* Demons always try to <u>Disrupt</u> or <u>Stop</u> what God is doing. [18] *She kept this up for <u>days</u>. Finally Paul became so troubles that he turned around and <u>said to the spirit</u>, 'In the name of Jesus Christ I command you to come out of her!' At that moment the spirit left her."* So Christians have the authority to cast evil spirits out and set the sinners free from them.

So do you dominate Satan with your righteous efforts of **continuous trying** to walk a godly walk so <u>God can see your true intent</u> and <u>regular striving heart</u> <u>toward righteousness</u>? Or does the dark kingdom dominate you with your continual <u>Pet Sins</u> you still want and love and <u>continually keep doing</u> as you <u>still live your life</u> **in the flesh**? (Masturbation, drugs, alcohol, enjoying <u>violent</u> movies, or <u>soft porn</u> movies, or movies focused on <u>fear</u>, (Satan's <u>chief weapon</u>), or movies of satanic power being displayed as you enjoy them watching wizards fly on broomsticks and casting spells). Sin is not "cool", it's just binds you to Satan's control and not to be enjoyed or taken lightly! All of these foolish choices informs the spirit realm like God or Satan whose kingdom you really like and truly want in your life. Remember this short **life** here on Earth is just a short **test** to see what you truly desire for your eternity ever after. So who is your master you are submitting to and unwittingly placing over you so he can work his control over you for the remainder of your earthly life? And who is the foolish underucated blind slave not knowing the spiritual rules as you go through life thinking all is well? Do you know which kingdom rules over ☠Hollywood☠? We are all very near the end where Lord Jesus is ready to call us real Christians home to live with Him in Heaven forever as He has prepared a special dwelling place for each of His pure brides. So will you be ready when He calls, "*Come up Hear*."? Revelation 4:1. Learning the spiritual rules of truth can be a scary place, something for you to ponder today before it's too late. Watch as God is educating Cain the murderer on His spiritual rules in Genesis 4:7. [7] "*You will be accepted if you **do** what is right.* (**Actions** tell the real truth in a person's soul as to whom that person, saved or unsaved, truly wants) *But if you refuse to **do*** (**actions**) *what is right,* (or choose to stop sinning and obey God. ". . . *sold as a slave to sin.*" Romans 7:14, 15.) *then watch out! Sin is crouching at the door, eager to **control you**. But you **must** subdue it* (master sin, or obey God rather than obey the dark kingdom) *and be its master.*" Genesis 4:7. NLT. Now since sin is an action like, stealing, lying or murder and actions can't *crouch at a door* (Genesis 4:7. NLT) nor can actions **desire** to control you, but demons spirits or Fallen angels who are attached to these sinful actions can ***crouch at a door*** or ***desire to have you*** (Luke 22:31 KJV) or demon spirits or Fallen angels can be [7] "*__eager to control you__*" (Genesis 4:7 NLT) who then do you think is **tempting** you or **steering** you into more sin for their control; the actions that cannot do anything; or these evil entities leading you to Hell? Understand that all sins come with evil entities attached to them as these sins you continue to do gives the dark kingdom their much needed "Legal Right" through God's rules as you're allowed to **choose** right or wrong, obey God or rebel against Him with your freedom to choose. So God is saying it's the demon spirits or fallen angels that can *__crouch at a door__* who are always, [7] "*__eager to control you__*", not the actions like stealing, lying or murder that cannot do anything as they are simply an action with no **driving will** or **desiring** evil **entity**. Therefore, **regular sin** is all that is required to inform God and these evil fallen angels **or** demon spirits of humans' true intent, and your deepest desires. So our **daily sins** are all that is needed for these thorny things to gain the Legal Right set up by God's eternal rules eons ago to enter any human saved or unsaved. Do you see what the Lord has been teaching me all these years since 2005 and why I put His teachings ahead of everything including my own work, money, even my highly desired romance?

Now after your **ongoing sins** have let these evil entities into your home first, they look all around your home at every one of your personal possessions knowing these possessions have been **your regular constant choices** you have personally **chosen**. So these personal sinful items you have chosen to be in your home, gives them all the stronger Legal Rights to be in your house and in you as well, so be very careful what items you choose to place in your home. Therefore, head of the house, if these wicked weird wolfs get control over you through your sinful choices, by God's laws, they will have control over all that is yours; like your children, because your children are yours. ". . . *visiting the iniquity of the fathers upon the children unto the third and fourth generation . . .*" Exodus 20:5. Your sins dad and mom, are corrupting your children to the third or fourth generation; so it's time to learn the real truth and be aware of the spiritual rules and how they really work so you and your family don't lose the spiritual war you're not even aware you're in daily in Satan's ever expanding sinful world for his control over **YOU**!

Let's try another education: Do you have video games in your home? Are these the kind of video games where you seek out people and then learn to shoot and kill them? Does the video "game" have you being the shooter who learns how to kill and murder? Do you not understand Satan is training you how to learn to **devalue life** as the dark kingdom advances your mind one step closer to the real act of murder? But you argue, "I'm not going to murder anyone!" People making campfires in the woods don't plan on burning down the forest either, but it does happen. Satan wants you to shoot without hesitation or thinking as he teaches you to disregard your morals? But you reason again, "It's just a game; it's not real!" But learn Satan's inside secret; the dark kingdom doesn't really care how you are desensitized as your once kind-hearted mind and spirit is now growing colder as it's being hardened every time you play this so-called "harmless" game. You keep chasing murder for "fun" and learn how to harden your spirit while you learn to kill without any remorse at all; just pull the trigger and be happy, how simple as you have now learned, "killing can be fun". What if you watch a romantic movie and learn how to love; as **you pick up on** being kind like the loving actors you're watching and by doing so you learn how to love others? Those kind of love-growing movies are available today on

Hallmark; and if you seek love, you'll find love; but if you seek sin, you'll find sin. Why not choose <u>Love</u> over <u>Murder</u> and get closer to God building up your rewards in Heaven and being a godly light to others? You've learned to <u>shoot with a cold heart,</u> <u>without hesitation</u>, and <u>shoot with no remorse</u>. But you argue, "No one is dying, it's just "harmless" entertainment! It means nothing"

Really? It's hard to see spiritual matters with the pure eyes of God when your mind is still <u>clouded with daily sin</u> you're used to as you have been chasing wickedness for so long. So let's try a different approach to get you to see the light through the pure eyes of God. What about "R" rated movies that show naked woman? Is this lusting also just "harmless" entertainment? But you argue, "I'm not lusting!" Let me understand what you're saying. So you are a male, and God Almighty has geared all male minds to like and prefer the looks of naked females for His marriage institution and His procreation purposes and repopulating the Earth in a Holy matrimony but you now tell me you're somehow not effected by God's programing and His design He put into your head of looking at naked females and getting physically excited; is that right? Stop lying to yourself; or worse, stop <u>desensitizing</u> your mind to God's pure ways. It's time to wise up and <u>stop playing with Satan</u>; he wants you to play his <u>desensitizing</u> sin games with him so he can lead you astray into more sins you don't even recognize and take you to his ultimate goal for you; <u>Hell</u>. What happens if you go to a godly church with real worship music and solid doctrinal teaching? Eventually the Christians who frequent these churches will lead you into your salvation as the Holy Spirit fills your soul then you will end up getting saved, Born Again and filled with God ready to go up to Heaven when Lord Jesus calls, *"Come up hear."*. We need to choose our environment wisely to start down the right road so we end up in Heaven like God wants us to be with Him. But Satan wants you to start off on the wrong road so you'll end up in Hell where you'll spend eternity burning. Listen to the scriptures. "... **_raging fire_** ..." Hebrews 11:34 * "... **_unquenchable fire_** ..." Matthew 3:12 * "... **_thrown into the lake of fire._**" Revelation 20:15 * "*the punishment of **eternal fire.**" Jude 7 * "... *into Hell, where the **fire never goes out.**" Mark 9:43. Your environment you choose is your first step in heading toward Heaven or Hell; so choose everything you place in your life wisely. This is why Proverbs 13:20 KJV is my favorite verse. *"He that walks with wise men shall be wise, but a companion of fools shall be destroyed."* So who are you spending your time with; Satan? Fear? Porn? Harry Potter? But what would happen if you spent your time with God? Walking in Faith? Learning to Love? Dedicating yourself to daily Worship? But you say, "I'm not use to those things and so I wouldn't like them.

I know, down through the years you have grown a taste for worldliness, wickedness, off-color jokes, wizards, porn and learning to shoot people in games for fun. Now learn something new, *You Crave What You Eat, and You Eat What You Crave.* Understand? It takes 21 days to learn a new habit. I never used to eat broccoli, but when I started a new habit of eating broccoli I learned to love broccoli? I knew a lady who learned to hate drinking water and men who learned to love whiskey. You can learn anything; good or bad, so start making the right choices. What happens to young boys with no dad in their home who see gang members of 20 years old who sell drugs buying brand new cars and live a life of material wealth? If they continue to watch these gang members, how long will it be before they are selling drugs, concealing their own gun and using it when necessary so they can buy new cars like the role model they saw five years ago?

v7 Be careful whose road you Start.
Watch closely for Satan's Dart.
v8 As he will corrupt your Heart.
Lead you in sin, and tear you Apart.
Dad 11:7, 8

But let's continue understanding these spiritual rules. Now demons that have just entered your body <u>due to regular ongoing sins you've been willing to do</u> are very weak at first at level **1**. Once in you, they have very little power or control over their unsuspecting <u>uneducated</u> naïve host as they sit quietly observing your daily routine and studying your day to day bad habits to see how they can **exploit** your **regular Pet Sins** you still love to do against you for greater control over you. They will always <u>take whatever sins you give them</u> whispering further sins into your mind they hope they can <u>build more sins on</u> and get you into more **regular sins** that will <u>feed them</u> making them stronger. As they stare quietly out from your eyes just watching and observing your every move, they grow all the more powerful inside of you waiting for more sins to increase their control over you the uneducated host. So even while you're in the <u>bathroom</u> they are watching or in your own private <u>shower</u> they go with you staring out from your eyes just watching everything you do. Even while your conscious mind is sleeping and your subconscious mind is available for their wicked input they speak to your mind things like <u>gritting your teeth at night</u> while you're sleeping just to bring you more pain because they hate you. They speak anything and everything directly into your subconscious mind; <u>bad dreams</u>, <u>sinful desires</u>, <u>wild sexual fantasies</u>, whatever they think you will succumb to as they want to increase your sin levels to a controlling higher number of **Demonic Power Levels** of **2** or **3**? From this inside advantage point these thorny things look for a way to **exploit** any sin they see like the liquor cabinet or other weaknesses they might find in your home. That drinking liquor sin you still do regularly is giving your self-control, a fruit of the spirit from God, (Galatians 5:23) over to the dark kingdom if you **even** get a little "tipsy" on a regular bases. Remember habitual sin is all that is needed for demons to gain entrance and greater control over you.

v5 Think Twice:
v6 Why do the Vice?
v7 Why roll the Dice?
v8 Don't look at Entice!
v9 Only Jesus will Suffice.
v10 Let go of Satan's Device!
v11 Why pay their terrible Price?
v12 Stop buying their Merchandise!
v13 God's rewards are worth the Sacrifice.
v14 Then you'll enjoy God's life in Paradise.
Dad 10:5-14

So that **regular sin** of booze you did repeatedly to get **tipsy** could have been their Reason of Sin to Enter **YOU**. These *Twisted* treacherous things will try to coerce you into more sin for more power for more control over **you** steering you into more sin! By this subtle misunderstood method that even most Christians aren't aware of, a newly entered demon quietly and slowly grows stronger inside you taking you over one subtle little sin at a time like a slow growing cancer over much time consuming you one cell at a time and gaining all the more strength over you as you continue to feed them their food which is more daily sins you love.

They'll continue gaining strength in your mind daily **if** you continue **yielding** to their sinful thoughts or obey their suggestions as they whisper thoughts inside your mind. "Have some more wine and enjoy life; after all, you've had a hard day." Yielding to those kinds of thoughts will cause demons to build up their evil power over you as fast as you yield your Pet Sins like lap doggies you love to pet and hold close to you. This day to day process of sin yielding might take demons months and possibly even years to advance you to their next higher level of control depending on how fast you accept their sinful suggestions. This is when the **wise** Christians **repents** or stops sinning confessing their sins **regularly** to God informing Him who they really want running their lives and by repenting or if you quit sinning, you will stop the demon's Legal Right to be in you **IF YOU REPENT** or **quit sinning** and remove the booze and all other sins in your home. Sincere genuine repentance (2 Chronicles 7:14) informs the dark army of your latest change of direction from wanting them to wanting God instead. So it's time to clean house from your sins removing the enemy that comes with your Pet Sins you still love as demons are still gaining more control over you but now those sins you've been doing must go today! And by doing this Cleansing of the House Thing, you have now remove the demon's power they

had built **up** in their Spiritual Bank Account to control you like when you flush a toilet sending the unwanted "stuff." or their

"Legal Rights" or your "sins" you've been doing, away. It's important to understand that spiritual rule of the Spiritual Bank Account. But if we don't confess our sins and get rid of their Legal Right to be inside of us saved sinners or their legal power by God's rules to choose obedience or rebellion like so few Christians truly understand today, then know this, they will continue to rule over you and drag you deeper into more of their sin for more control over you. So when we foolishly **LET** these sins we're still enjoying build **up** inside of us, it's like their Demonic Bank Account in the spirit realm where they can then use those sins we've given them against us foolish uneducated Christians who think a little sin in our life won't matter. This is where demons save up your sinful actions in a Spiritual Bank Account compliant with God's rules of our **freewill to choose** right or wrong. So, these newly entered demons will then wait to spend all these stored-up sins you gave them at a chosen weak moment in your life when they can get the biggest destructive bang for their demonic buck. Waiting patiently for the right time to manifest their trouble at a crucial moment in your life or stir up an argument when you're at your weakest point for maximum discord in your home. Like late at night when you or your spouse are physically tired and had a hard day so they choose then to manifest or act up in you to get the maximum damage as you both argue till 4:00 in the morning with these thorny things whispering destructive words in the minds of both married spouses. With the sins they have collected from the both of you over time stored up in their Spiritual Bank Account (Romans 2:5) you have foolishly given over to them, they will now direct your argument and steer it to your complete destruction. This is why playing with your ongoing "fun" Pet Sins are so dangerous and why you should just <u>get used to living in harmony</u> with God and adjusting your stained darkened mind over to obeying God's rules until you now don't mind living a righteous life with God as you now <u>like that life</u> and <u>used to living that way</u>.

But understand the consequences to rejecting a godly life: "*. . . because of your stubbornness and your unrepentant heart, you are* **_storing up wrath_** *against yourself for the day of God's wrath*." Romans 2:5. Assuming you don't want God's judgment or His ". . .**_wrath_** *against yourself for the day of God's wrath*" you need to make this adjustment of walking in your sin, to walking in God's will for your life. So, **Regular <u>confession</u>** and <u>repentance</u> is very wise for these play-around sin-enjoying Christians who have sinned as the demons are gaining strength daily and adding up their stronger control over you daily. As you are <u>willing to give them greater power</u>, they'll advance you to the next level of **2** or **3** to <u>their control</u> over <u>their new **slave**</u> toward <u>their goal of total takeover</u>! So if you don't repent and foolishly decide to keep your **<u>favorite Pet Sins</u>** going, you will be feeding these dark spirits <u>their food</u>, which is <u>daily ongoing sin</u>. Just like feeding a new puppy and watching it grow bigger and stronger to a full grown dog, this is the <u>normal speed of growth</u> as these demons are always looking to increase your sin level so their stronghold control over you grows while advancing you to higher **Demonic Power Levels** of **2** and **3** as your life will surly start to spiral out of control. And with each new sin you do and how many times you have done it, the demons will increase their strength or their Legal Right within God's rules <u>to stay in you</u> because by your willingness to enjoy your favorite <u>Pet Sin</u> you are telling the demons and God <u>who you really love and who you truly want</u> dominating <u>in</u> your life.

Sometimes truth can be a scary place. So, the demons you continue to feed will eventually take over your troubled uneasy life with most people even Christians oblivious to their presence. Understand: Before these evil spirits can advance you to higher levels, they'll try to coerce you into feeding them more daily sins for their more daily power they need to grow stronger control inside you; otherwise you'll remain at **Power Level 1**. Their Spiritual Bank Account will save up your sins you give them compliant with God's rules of everyone has a **Freedom to Choose** right or wrong. We should learn the basics of some spiritual rules. Rule#**1:** Sin lets demons in. Rule#**2:** Only **real** Christian have true **authority** from God to command demons to leave their home. (Mark 6:7 * Mark 16:17 * Mark 6:13 * Mark 9:8 * Matthew 10:1 * Luke 9:1 * 1 Cor. 6:3 * Luke 10:9 * Luke 11:20 * Acts 1:8 * John 20:21). [31] *"Now we know that God heareth not sinners: but if any man be a worshipper of God, and doeth His will, him He heareth."* John 9:31. Consider the Seven Sons of Sceva who were beat up by demons trying to use the powerful name of Jesus but were not truly Born Again. Acts 19:13-16. The only prayer God will hear from the unsaved person is, "I want to be saved, Born Again and have Jesus my Savoir live in my heart; please come into me and help me live a godly life." But then the HARD part comes; you have to make **every effort** to walk the Christian righteous **walk** as Andy did with active faith not just talk the Christian righteous **talk** like Billy only spoke. Christianity was **never easy** and it's still not made for lukewarm Christians! That's what separates the real men from the little boys who still love their fleshly sins and are Christians only if it's easy! Rule#**3:** You cannot command the demon spirits of Lust or any other fallen angel to leave your house **if** someone in the house still wants these dirty demons there by their sinful actions they're still doing willingly. God will not honor hypocrisy or fake christians. That physical porn paraphernalia and all the other sinful actions someone in your family is still doing is what gives these evil spirits their much needed "**Legal Right**" **compliant** with God's rules of choosing sin **they need** to **stay in** your home? So, remove all physical sin paraphernalia, magazines, DVDs, mental desires for sins you still **want**, et cetera, before you attempt to cast out any demons from your home otherwise it will not work. Jas 1:8.

Rule#**4:** If any hidden sins are left, this will give these demons power to feed their Legal Right to stay and fight you back with. All sinners need to confess to God the Father in the name of Jesus that they're sorry for what they did **out loud** so the demons and fallen angels can hear your new decision stating to God they will never go back to that old sin again. Also, the Head of the House needs to hear everyone's true repentance to be sure before starting to cast them out so he's sure there's no Legal Right or power left.

Rule#**5:** Then ask God the Father to forgive your sins and so cleanse each family member placing all sin under the blood of Jesus so God does not hold those sins against you anymore.

Rule#**6:** Now if your family has completed the first five rules, and if you're truly saved, you can NOW command these Hell-bound hindering demons or fallen angels to leave your home so you can have spiritual peace and have them stop leading your family into constant sin followed by God's judgment you surly don't want.

Rule#**9:** How often should I command these demons to leave my house? As often as you, the sinner, or your sinful family sins and lets those dastardly demons back in your home. How often should you say you're sorry for wrong doing? As often as you do the wrong; make sense?   But remember there are no shortcuts with God, you must go through all of the repenting rules and clean your house spiritually all over again as you did the first time before attempting to cast them out for the second time. (Rules 1-6). Demons never stop trying to corrupt you and your family, and we Christians never stop trying to walk a godly walk with Jesus helping us every inch of the way if we're truly trying. This is why Christianity is a spiritual ongoing **WAR** not a cheap "**Religion**" but it's always a loving **Relationship** with our **Savior Lord Jesus**.

Rule#**11:** Demons often attach themselves to ongoing emotions like; **Fear** they bond to making them **stronger** and you weaker.

Others like **Sadness, Depression Discouragement** also feeds them strengthening them while it destroys you making you weaker and easier to take over and then yielding to those negative emotions invites in more demons for their growing power over you as you fall yielding to them getting spiritually weaker.

Rule#**14:** If you continue doing the same sin, you're authority to throw these demons out of your home will wane as your ongoing sinful actions will trump and overpower your weaker words you are not following of telling them you want these demons to leave your home. Hypocrites have no authority. So it's back to Rules 1-6.

Rule#**18:** Long standing Pet Sins can cause the sinner **regular physical sicknesses.** At first demons can cause headaches, anxiety that leads to fearfulness, their greater control, hives, sudden muscle cramps, shooting pains. It's true those same pains could be a result of a lack of nutrition and consuming to many junk foods as that could also be the source of your ongoing pain as well, but so can regular sins you will not stop doing as your pains are more likely a combination of both junk foods and sins you still do. There are many verses to back up this phenomenon of <u>Sin and Sickness</u> but we don't have that kind of time to get into them all now.

Rule#**24:**   When things go wrong in your life and you think it might be the enemy's disruption, just say, "If this is the enemy stop!"   <u>If</u> you ask in <u>faith</u>, your guardian angel will back you up and stop this demon unless they have a Legal Right to cause this disturbance.   Then you might <u>get a thought</u> reminding you of your <u>Pet Sin</u> you still have not repented of yet.   But if your home is spiritually clean and all your sins are repented of, you will be amazed how many times the demonic trouble will actually stop.

Rule#**29:**   Fallen angels or Demons <u>hate all lov</u>ing relationships, kindness, friendship, giving, especially <u>acts of selflessness</u> where you help others showing this cold unsaved world God's love through your loving actions.   This is why I believe the kingdom of darkness hates me so much.   We can't go over every rule now, so let's do one more you should understand about your "friends".

Rule#**54:**   After your sin-filled guest leaves your place, never assume that just because your friends are now gone that their many spirits <u>they brought</u> left with them.   Depending on how many spirits they have, the host <u>spirits</u> will most likely stay with their host because they now have a real <u>body</u> or <u>home</u> inside that possessed person or their host.   However, there are many other <u>spirits that follow along</u> with the host <u>spirits</u> on the outside of them just floating along next to the host that are just **"<u>want-a-bes</u>"**!   Spirits that just <u>want to be</u> **IN** the host but have not yet been <u>legally</u> invited in by the sinner's ongoing Pet Sins to <u>gain more</u> **Legal Rights** or <u>Permission</u> to enter the host by God's laws of our <u>Freedom of Choice</u> to **<u>Choose</u>** right or wrong established by God!   These want-a-be spirits <u>looking for more sin</u> are called, *"Trailing Spirits"* because they trail along or float along outside the host just <u>waiting for more sin to invite them in as well</u>. Right before I got saved, in **June 1980**, I went into a smoky bar to get a six-pack of beer, something I rarely did because even back then I hated the bar scene. I wasn't in there for more than ten minutes, but when I came out, my coat and clothes reeked of smoke! That smoky stench <u>attached itself</u> to my clothes <u>following me home</u> and clung to my black leather jacket for days! That's a perfect example of what these *Trailing Spirits* will do with

you! They will stay with you on the outside just waiting **IF** they think they'll gain a permanent home <u>in you</u> as their prospective new host. So, <u>if you're saved</u> and you forget to take authority over these *Trailing Spirits* left over from your "party" expelling them from your

house, they might just stay seeking a permanent home in you <u>when you sin asking them in</u> without knowing what you are doing! Remember, Christian, your ignorance is the devil's best friend! These **"want-a-be"** *Trailing Spirits* make their decisions based on

what sins they see you doing or what sins they see stacked up in your home. They can see how many sins or <u>decisions for sins</u> you have already stacked up and racked up on your shelves in your home! Like your Harry Potter movies <u>and the like</u>. Your wild sinful music selections, your <u>violent video games</u> you choose to play as you are unaware of this spirit world and the spiritual war you are already in daily. So let's not forget to repent and <u>confess these sins</u> we still do like an overloaded toilet <u>that simply needs to be flushed</u>. As you can see if we keep on going with these spiritual rules, the 40 pages we just read could easily go on for another 400 pages; but I don't have time <u>in this book</u> to continue explaining the seemingly endless rules of the spirit world that my heavenly Father revealed to me, so we're just going to move on with my testimony.

Tenth Anniversary

We were all in the auditorium when a JES Cruises lady came out on stage early even before Kay did as they wanted to help her celebrate her tenth anniversary by playing a surprise fun trick on her. So they handed out these party whistles while Kay was not there that roll out and blasted loud every time you blew into them and so we were all instructed to blow them every time Kay mentioned her "<u>Tenth Anniversary</u>". Now the fun trick JES Cruises wanted to play on Kay was all set up with the audience ready to participate and a few minutes later Kay did come out right on time unaware of their fun. She welcomed us all to her tenth anniversary and sure enough we all blew those party whistles right on cue as instructed. I'm pretty sure Kay did not catch on right away to the joke the first time but after she continued to mention her tenth anniversary again I think she said with a curious smile something like, "Where did you all get those?" Watching those fans in the front rows I saw some of them closest to Kay told her the trick from JES Cruises and informed her of their celebration. That's when Kay smiled looking back stage at them as they were grinning like the cat that swallowed the canary with a guilty look on their face and so she got the joke they were playing.

So where was I when all this was happening? I was sitting up in the balcony as everyone came early and the seating arrangement was first come first serve. This being my first time, there was a very long line to wait behind that I was not aware of and so by the time I came to the line only an hour early I was somewhere in the middle of the queue. Therefore, when they opened the doors, all the front row seats were taken quickly and almost half the auditorium was filled up by then and so I thought me being a person who <u>learns more by vision</u> and appreciates beauty more than most, that the balcony might be the best place to view Kay and drink in all of her incredible gorgeous good-looks.

You know as I'm writing these thoughts out for the first time in 15 year, my memory of these events are starting to surface and blossom again as the Lord is reminding me and I'm slowly remembering some of the old nostalgia details so I will try to the best of my ability to explain them as best as I can recall. This first ship I was on was smaller than the other four that came after it and so it would rock you to sleep at night do to the effect of the <u>waves</u> on that smaller ship and the <u>speed</u> they were traveling which then got into a <u>rhythmic motion</u> on the ocean causing this reciprocating back and forth rocking action. Now some of the passengers got queasy and so to settle their upset stomachs the crew put out these little green apples available in baskets all over the ship to settle their nauseous digestive tracts.

But I believe it was early in the week at one of Kay's shows on the ship that another artist Kay requested for this week in the Bahama Sun as they were up to perform next singing their famous songs that most of the fans already knew. This auditorium as best as I can recall had little tables with individual chairs around them and small candles in the middle of these tables like a night club. They also had short couch-like seats <u>on the sides</u> fastened to the floor that fit just three people where I was sitting **by myself** because even though I was now educated on standing in line 90 minutes early, other fans got to the door even earlier than I did. Therefore, they enter the auditorium first to see Kay and so these three person side seats were all that was left in the front row. But I was the only one sitting on this short couch-like seat and that left two seats available for "some couple" <u>to sit next to me</u>.

After Kay announced her singing artist on stage that was preforming that night and they took over the show preforming, she would then sit in the audience somewhere herself and watch the show as well. Now the place was packed and every seat was taken except maybe the very back balcony on the upper tier and of course the two seats beside me and so not long after that I was approached by Kay's best friend; at least that's the way I remember hearing her title and name following her announcement on stage. So while I was watching the show a woman I couldn't see in this very dim lighting standing in the aisle from beside and behind me bent over to whisper a few words. Since the lights were down low and she was basically behind me I did not know who she was at the moment while she whispered very discreetly and softly asking, "Could you move over two seats and then I can sit by you and -------- could sit by me." Notice her carefully worded statement? Kay's best friend made sure Kay was available for light conversation if this new guy wanted to meet her, but Kay was not trying to make this move look like she was trying to meet or connect to anyone. Professionals like Kay have to be very careful how they come across to the <u>unknown public</u>. So I whispered back quickly, "Sure." I moved over two seats and they both sat down next to me as we are all now looking at the performer on stage. Now I got a thought and noticed the hand of God as to what He was doing and what He just did. This seating arrangement was orchestrated by the Lord as every seat was taken but the two beside me. Heaven playing the age old game of cupid was trying to sit single hand-picked girl next to single hand-picked boy and make a heavenly love connection available. So now Kay the one God sent me down here to meet and strike up a conversation with to start our loving relationship toward a future Holy marriage someday is now very conveniently only two seats away. Was this God's planning that I got that three person seat couch and no one else sat next to me making this whole cupid scene possible?

Was this Kay's way of making herself available for light conversation if I so desired to <u>initiate the start</u> of our relationship in this darken auditorium as is commonly done in these nightclub atmospheres? Once again God did His job in setting me up but as He told me earlier I <u>had to</u> take the Promise Land, which was Kay, by His **faith**, not by the enemy's **fear**! Just like God told me, [8] *"Behold, I have set the land* (Kay) *before you: go in and possess the land . . ."* Deuteronomy 1:8. So it's now my turn to be **bold** in **faith** to "<u>take</u>" the <u>Promised Land</u> by faith as God informed me!

Now try to understand Kay's romantic heart; this is her once in a year opportunity to meet someone she has been praying to God for years to meet and fall in love and hopefully get married to some sweet man she could lavish all her many years of stored up love on. After all if you look in all of her books she wrote and song lyrics she sung, the fact that she would like sweet love in a godly man to make a romantic marriage was certainly not a secret to anyone. Someone she might fall in love with and be happy for the rest of her life was her regular prayer to the God of Love 1 John 4:8. And then I also remember Kay saying something on stage one time to the effect of, "I really wasn't planning on being the poster child for singlehood" in one of her talks while preforming. And so who knows, this man right here, just two seats away, might just be that mystery man she's been waiting and praying to finally meet <u>for decades</u>. She won't find out who this new man is until she tries to connect with him and then he might just be the one God truly chose for her or maybe not unless she speaks up to fine out.

The show went on and nothing was said. Should I have interrupted this show while she was enjoying it? Or try to lean over her friend which might seem awkward to her and try to say a word to Kay that she might not even hear; remember the music is loud? Is this really the right time to speak up, right in the middle of this show? What if Kay wants to watch this artist and hear their music and sees me as an annoyance interrupting her pleasant night. Do I want to seem as an irritating or pushy person? Certainly not.

But the enemy saw us two and he must have thought we were <u>way to close</u> for his comfort because he poured on the <u>worthless talk</u> and started condemning me with, "Who are you to be talking to the star?" "You're nothing but a lowly common contractor who freezes up when you had your <u>once in a life time</u> chance." "She could get a million men better than you." The enemy continued hammering the condemnation until I was chopped down to the size of a toothpick and by the end of that show I just wanted to go home and crawl under a rock in the dark and die quietly. Kay sat there through the whole show giving me every opportunity to speak up to her but even after the show was over and <u>the lights were on</u> with everyone talking and having light conversation there was then ample time for me to talk to her. There was no reason left for my ongoing silence as I still said nothing feeling completely condemned and **worthless** as she waited patiently in expectation that this man is hopefully the one.

When the show was over and the lights came on it's customary to start the procedure of filling out and heading toward the exit doors to get on with our lives. But Kay did not do this common routine. She stood there just one person away from me and only four feet between us having an intermittent conversation with her best friend as there were long gaps in their sporadic chat and some unusual looking around as if she were <u>waiting for something to happen</u>? Or maybe wanting some<u>one</u> to <u>speak up and talk to her</u>? It was the unusual uncommon waiting I saw as I felt she was waiting especially for me to pipe up and say something; anything!!! But I was overwhelmed with the enemy's crushing feeling of **worthlessness** as I was still in their spiritual **PRISON** <u>unable to speak</u> because I was still unknowingly and uneducated on this particular spiritual rule and so I was still yielding to their stronghold of intimidation keeping me in their **PRISON**. The enemy spoke that condemnation over me for hours on end just after *The Moment* or ever since I froze up the first time in the auditorium shaking her hand but saying nothing.

But I didn't leave this seating location by the stage where she was either as I didn't want her to feel I was rejecting her by my quick exit, so I hung around but <u>could not say a single word</u> like "*Zechariah*" Luke 1:<u>20</u>. NIV. I was paralyzed, swimming in the enemy's condemnation and drowning in their lie that I was completely worthless and unworthy to speak to the star. So finally after several minutes of awkward standing around and waiting while most of the people had already left, Kay and her best friend also finally left as I'm sure Kay felt greatly disappointed. This is now the second time the enemy <u>Disrupted</u> and <u>Stopped</u> our meeting and then these demons blamed that whole awkward scene that just happened on me as they convinced me it was me that blew it a second time and so the condemnation from the enemy only increased and I just wanted to go home and hide in the dark under a large rock and die. I have to say this feeling of worthlessness is not normally a daily thing for me in my regular life, but then our enemy tends to <u>exploit our weaknesses</u> at <u>opportune time</u> when it really counts for them. They tried to destroy our loving relationship before it even got started on the very night we were supposed to meet like Satan destroyed all of mankind in the Garden of Eden before mankind even got started. Genesis 3:4-13.

Now it's true Kay could have spoken up to me first to open this conversation if that's what she wanted to do. But think about it, any man would respond positively to Kay if she were the initiator and took the aggressive lead and that would have told her absolutely nothing about my intentions and am I God's choice for her or not. Remember, she's trying to wait on God's leading **so she will know** this is the man God has chosen specifically for her and custom made for her marriage of Oneness and her lifetime of bliss. She doesn't just want any man who she is able to activate with her outstanding looks thus ending up years later in divorce court because she impatiently chose the wrong man herself and did not wait on Heaven's lead. **She needed to know** if this man is really God's choice for her so she doesn't make any lifetime mistakes. She doesn't want just any single man that she could easily stimulate his interest by her exceptional good looks on her own. Think about it, if she sparks the interest in a man God has not chosen for her and two months after she's married things aren't going so well and then she sees the right man when it's too late for a lifetime relationship, how bad is she going to feel at that point? So it was imperative that she waits on God's leading through the man He has truly chosen and so it was all up to **me**, as God already told me before; [8] "*Behold, I have set the land* (Kay) *before you: go in and possess the land . . .*" (Deuteronomy 1:8) by faith!

After I floundered in the first auditorium just hours ago I remembered prayed, "Lord send another man better than me for Kay as she should have someone to love and not go lonely." The man is normally the initiator in any relationship and so God typically works through the man first in any couple. Besides, if I am going to take this Promised Land, the Lord already told me it will only be taken by God's **FAITH** not Satan's **FEAR**. If you can't believe anything by God's **faith**, then you are domed to a life dominating by doubt and Satan's controlling **fear**. The enemy is well aware of God's mandatory procedure of ✝faith✝ as His $payment$ and not ☠fear☠. So the enemy knew his worthlessness they got me to **Believe** in to take this Promised Land would surely fail. That's why the enemy blasted me with endless condemnation at the most crucial times of these few moments of our initial connections. What if Miss America would talk to any man, would the average man show an interest in her beauty and then respond positively? Of course he would, beauty like Kay's doesn't come along like that but once in a life time if at all in any one's life.

So I have to assume she must have come to the obvious conclusion, "If this man was truly interested in talking with me he would of said something by now. But since he never made an attempt, I guess he's just not interested and "supposedly" not God's man for me at all." This meant she had to wait another year before she would get another shot at God's choice for her highly desired Love. And maybe worse than that, this year was her last chance to be married as a woman still in her forties as she was 49 years old headed for her fifties at that disappointing sad moment.

I have something to tell you Kay I heard the following day after that second disappointment that may or may not be true. The next day on the ship after this incident with you only two seats away, a man found out and then told me that Kay was crying all morning in her cabin till noon as someone had badly disappointed her. When I heard this I immediately looked up to Heaven and wondered if that was true and did I have anything to do with her falling ♦tears♦? I think God was sending me a clear serious message telling me I missed yet another golden opportunity that He and His heavenly angels set up for us both. I also got another thought that Kay asked God if she could meet her future husband before she was out of her forties. Well she did meet her future husband as she was still 49 when we met in the first auditorium with just over three months left before her fiftieth birthday as our love-hating enemy did everything he could to <u>Disrupt</u> and <u>Stop</u> our joining of two souls into one deep ♥ heart of romance.

So after my first meeting did not go as I had hoped, and then I missed God's second golden opportunity, I spent the rest of the week **by myself** living in condemnation. <u>I finally accepted the enemy's lies</u> that I was completely worthless and not worthy of Kay and so I was not even looking for another chance to talk to her. I even started to avoid her after that when I saw her because I knew <u>I blew it twice</u> and now it was even more <u>embarrassing</u>.

If you have spiritual eyes to see and know the spiritual rules as I do <u>today</u>, you can easily see the enemy building his separating wall to keep us hand-picked by God Christians apart. As I already said in my opening statement in the last chapter, **Understanding Spiritual Rules**, <u>Step Two</u>: demons try to bring <u>hurt</u> that last a lifetime or in our case 15 long years now so they can continue using this <u>hurt</u> against us like the shame of <u>embarrassment</u>. That <u>hurt</u> or shame and <u>embarrassments</u> that followed came on strong after *The Moment* when they started as their ongoing condemnation followed for my past mistakes of me <u>being afraid</u> and freezing up while trying to talk to a nice kind beautiful lady I was too shy to talk to and intimidated by her looks.

Many times we see people's actions and since we don't understand the spirit world very well and not being privy to their inside strategy or the enemies actions they did on the other person we then come to wrong conclusions. Then we <u>miss interpret once in a lifetime opportunities</u> we did not understand correctly. Like when Kay assuming Craig was just not interested in her at all. So it turns out we were both lied too by the deceiving enemy working their evil behind the invisible scenes to <u>Disrupt</u> and <u>Stop</u> anything God is doing; like answering their years of prayers and joining two Christian in Holy matrimony they prayed for years to come into their lives. So I may have been shy about talking to good looking girls, but on this trip I had a lot more than just shyness to overcome as the enemy **<u>exploited</u>** my weakness and <u>Disrupted</u> and <u>Stopped</u> God's work. As I said before, demons can't create anything but they can **<u>exploit</u>** any weakness in us or sin we might have like shyness <u>which is a mild fear</u> when talking to girls or being intimidated by beautiful ladies. Then the enemy <u>exploits</u> your weaknesses into strongholds placing you into their spiritual **<u>PRISON</u>** as you don't understand the spiritual rules very well.

So sure the sand was white and warm as I dug my toes into it; and yes the water was clear and the most beautiful blue-teal color I ever saw before. The Sun was bright and the temperature was perfect. In fact the whole trip was great; only one thing was missing, <u>someone</u> to share all this fabulous atmosphere with; but our enemy had wicked work to do and weaknesses to **<u>exploit</u>**. I love the beach more than any other place on Earth but I never did regain my damaged confidence that week to approach ♩ <u>My Special Angel</u> ♩ (the Vogues) again and so the week ended with me taking my lonely humbled heart home to spend the rest of my days with just me and my four walls to hide behind and <u>live in regret</u>.

Conversing with God

Once I was home I ask the Lord with a hurt pathos, "Since You can see the future, then You knew I would fall like a house of cards; so what was the whole point of me going down to see Kay all about?" The Lord spoke thoughts to my mind. "Yes I do know the future. But you both pleaded many times in prayer for years asking for the right godly spouse to show up in your lives and the golden bowl was finally filled by both praying saints; so the earthly part of the prayer request was completed. Once both your parts were done, I moved forward with My original plan of placing you two together. Heaven will not be guilty of dropping the ball on My children's prayers of that you can be sure. But if you two get together or not that part is not chiseled in stone like the Ten Commandment are and I will not be the One guilty of keeping you two apart, especially when I initiated this whole merging of your two souls into your beautiful Oneness which I still want. As I said before Craig, I will move Heaven and Earth to complete My will for you both, but your actual marriage into Oneness will be left up to you two. I cannot interfere with matters of the heart and my children's personal choices and then force that merger I want without violating the both of you and your own free wills that I have given My word to all of mankind to exercise as they see fit."

I understood all that the Lord impressed on my mind and so I knew He did His very best for me and so the blame was on me. I also believe Kay went as far as she could, waiting for me to speak up even after the lights were on without her being the initiator and then possibly prompting someone who might not even be God's choice. So now I felt I must live the rest of my life in regret of the one and only chance I had with that loving heart God tried to give me that could have been mine to lavish all my love on and honor her with my servant's heart I long to serve some<u>one</u> with. But maybe that's <u>T</u>he Chance Love Take<u>s</u>? Then the Lord impressed upon me, "You can try again next year. She has these cruises every year and next year attempt to bond to your True Love." But the enemy did not stop condemning me and since I failed badly at *The Moment* of our meeting, the dark army was still "helping"

me think and so I replied, "NO Lord! I'm all done with that! <u>I'll</u> <u>never</u> do that <u>embarrassment</u> again!" I remembered some of those lines in that song the Lord gave me at the start of writing this book; <u>On My Own</u> as it is stirring me today; **"Losing you it cuts like a knife. Hey, <u>I</u> walked out and their went my life. I . . . "<u>This wasn't how it was supposed to end</u>." I wish that we could do it all again.** I felt the loss but my broken heart and strong will was made up at that time so I never heard Lord Jesus reply again that day; that is until next year came around and the Lord's golden bowl was still full with our names on it and over flowing in disappointed fallen ◆tears.◆◆◆

v14 Facing your fears
is like approaching a Paper Tiger.
v15 Once you confront it,
you understand the Truth.
v16 Satan has been lying
to you all along.

Dad 5:14-16

_{V17}Be **BOLD!**
_{V18}Take what is yours!
_{V19}You have approval from <u>Above</u>.
_{V20}Shrink back,
and you'll miss out on <u>Love</u>.
Dad 5:17-20

So I gathered up my courage and dared to try again; only this time I had a different strategy. Now not willing to talk to Kay directly about our being chosen by God to fall in love with each other and then get married I decided to sidestep that difficult conversation and tried a new approach I thought up by asking Kay if she would write the forward for my first novel. You remember, "My Plan" to fine a wife? Where I figured she might read my first book of romance and then want to look for the romantic author and so we would then finally meet and hopefully <u>live happily ever after</u>. That Walt Disney, "Happily ever after" plan was always my love-longing strategy, but God had other ideas and so here I am asking Kay if she'll write the forward to my first book. I thought to do that she'll have to read the book I wrote of romance and then maybe she'll get to know the loving author and maybe that way we'll get together. But because I went about our merger that way I'm guessing the enemy must have told her I was only interested in her for the financial angle and her endorsement fame so I could make lots of money in this evil world "<u>using her</u>" to make a grand profit off her already established fame. But that thought was never truth; the only reason I even wrote that book in the first place or the sequel that came after that was too fine a loving heart to have and to hold and then live together happily ever after. Truth is I would have gladly burned that whole book in a heartbeat just to get her looking one time in my direction. In my opinion, money is only valuable in this cold wicked world where Satan is in charge and we would all do better if we could convert this temporary earthly money we have control of for such a short time into heavenly building block where we can then enjoy it forever in Heaven. You know what the Bible says, *"For where your treasure is, there will your heart be also."* Matthew 6:21. KJV. I believe every word in the Bible, (Luke 6:38) so I've given more money away to people in need and godly ministries than most people make in a year. In my mind, earthly money has little value and is only good in this world to do God's work and help other people with while we are still here for such a very short time. I was only ever interested in <u>Love</u> which I believe has <u>great value</u> as I see love as the real prize to have while we're here for such a few short years. James 4:<u>14</u>. Since God told me Kay was my future Wife, I simply wanted to get started trading our highly desired love back and forth every day. My problem was, despite having a girlfriend every year I was in school I never had any experience asking any woman out on a date. They always noticed me first and then found a way to get my attention and so I never had to work up the courage to ask anyone out or face that natural fear of rejection. Some girl my senior year in school was cruising around with my older sister Lynn and asked, "See if Craig will go out with me?" Do you see how she avoided asking me directly? Lynn responded surprised, "You want to go out with my brother?" She replied, "Yeah, he has great legs." That was back in 1976 when everyone was wearing those really short shorts. So I never had to approach a girl and face that fear of rejection and ask out anyone.

The Alaska Trip

The third year I was hesitant to even go this time but my Lord prompted me many times to **try again** and see Kay another time and so the following year I tried again to connect with my future bride and that time her fans and I went with Kay to Alaska but something different happened this time as <u>Hope's Alive</u>. Looking back I believe it was the second show and I was wiser this time. So if you came two hours early to stand in line at the ship's auditorium doors where Kay's show would start, you could be assured to be the first one in line to get that highly coveted front row seat. But if you showed up only 90 minutes early there would already be a dozen or so highly excited fans there. Yet if you came only an hour early you would not get the first row seating at all as the queue would be very long by then. So by the second day I was sitting in the front row as I wanted to have a good view of Kay's beauty but maybe even more important was the fact that I knew Kay was looking for a soulmate and I wanted to send her my shy version of a visual message by me sitting in the front row.

What I wasn't remembering at that time was this was not only a once a year opportunity for me, but also Kay's once a year chance as well; and it seemed this year she was determined not to miss out on her remaining life of Love she still had left at age 51. So fifteen minutes early they open the big double doors for the fans and we all file in getting as close to the stage as we could. I got my highly desired front row seat and almost perfect center by only two seats. After that hurry scurry to scramble for the best seat was over, there's light conversation between the fans themselves and so this is what we were all doing while waiting for this highly anticipated show to begin and hopefully Kay would notice me.

Now again you might need to know the inside scoop on the two hopeful hearts to understand this next part. Even though Kay was strikingly lovely and could easily attract any man's attention, she was still single and <u>maybe by God's design</u>, but she would have rather been married to a sweet man she could lavish all of her years of stored up love on. It's <u>as if she was set aside by our God</u> ¹⁴ "<u>. . . *for such a time as this*</u>." Esther 4:14. ᴇꜱᴠ. ¹⁴ "*For if you remain silent at this time, relief and deliverance for the Jews will arise from another place, but you and your father's family will perish. And who knows but that you have come to your royal position for such a time as this?*" Now listen Kay to the scriptures for God's reason for waiting so long in your life, ¹ "*As Jesus went along, He saw a man blind from birth. ² His disciples asked Him, 'Rabbi, who sinned, this man or his parents, that he was born blind?' ³ Neither this man nor his parents sinned,' said Jesus, 'but this happened **so that the work of God might be displayed in his life**.*" John 9:1-3. ɴɪᴠ. Being Jews ✡ and knowing the Law, the disciples were well familiar with the law and especially The Ten Commandments or Exodus 20:5 about the sins of the fathers that visit the children to the third and fourth generation, and so they were <u>trying to learn the spiritual rules</u> about who sinned to understand this curse on the blind man like I was curious and hungry to learn all those spiritual rules I was writing in my first novel. However, in this case, Jesus taught them something different saying, ³ "*. . . Neither this man nor his parents sinned,' said Jesus, 'but this happened **so that the work of God might be displayed in his life**.*" So you might ask why was Kay not married after all these many years of praying and waiting and wanting to be married and yet it never happened. And then also, as pretty as she is, you would have thought she would be the first one all men would seek after and the last one to be left standing all alone at the end of her single life and so you might be wondering, what is the secret to this puzzling mystery? But consider this verse Jesus just spoke: What if God designed her to be single all these many years [14] "*for such a time as this?*" or what if [3] ". . . *this happened* **so that the <u>work of God</u> might be displayed in <u>her</u> life**" for God's special **amazing** purpose <u>between us both</u> waiting for this end time surprise <u>grand finale</u>? For as you and I may know God works in mysterious ways and He sees His entire plan at the <u>end</u> before He even starts the puzzling <u>beginning</u> we Christians often times don't understand. [10] "*Declaring the <u>end</u> from the <u>beginning</u>, and from ancient times the things that are <u>not</u> <u>yet done</u>, saying, <u>My counsel shall stand</u>, and <u>I will do all My pleasure</u>:*" Isaiah. 46:10. Get ready Kay; because God's plan <u>for us</u> is coming.

So anyway, while I was sitting in the front row with my right ankle resting on my left knee and looking to my right while listening to another fan sharing her thoughts with me I heard a voice speaking up a little louder than the other gentle voices around me coming from this very large room. And so I wondered was this voice actually talking to me; so "*I turned around to see the voice that was speaking to me . . .*" Revelation 1:12. Then much to my chagrin looking up I saw Kay <u>close up</u> standing just five feet in front of me and she was making <u>direct eye contact</u> with her <u>beaming beauty</u> as she had just <u>asked me a question</u>, "Are you Nick?" At first I was startled to see Kay <u>beauty</u> <u>so close</u> and <u>looking directly at me</u> and also surprisingly <u>asking me a question</u> as well as I was not prepared for that <u>four-way</u> <u>close up</u> <u>surprise</u> at all. Now Kay's staff gave us fans all name tags on day one but I was under the impression that Kay already knew who I was so I took my name tag off so not to appear as a novice to her shows. Still looking at Kay I heard what she said, but I paused as I was somewhat puzzled at her question. After all this was now my third trip to see her and the second day and we have talked before about my book back then on the other trips. So while looking at her I was thinking of how to answer such an unusual question and she seeing me looking back at her and my few seconds of delay, repeated that very same question a second time very distinctly. "Are - you - <u>Nick</u>?" Now that she asked that question twice I had somewhat of a guilty look on my face like I had done something wrong and then I simply responded, "No. My name is Craig. Someone else is Nick." Then I started reaching for my name tag that I peeled off and put in my pocket thinking at first she already knows me when I sat down but now I'm thinking maybe I shouldn't have taken it off at all.

V1 **The first bite in a Subway sandwich is often only bread and not that tasty.** V2 **But like relationships <u>the really good stuff</u> comes after you get passed the awkward beginning.**

Dad 3:1, 2

Forgive my visual analogies; but sometimes God speaks to me in pictures.

I could tell by her facial expression my answer was not what she was hoping for and so I figured somehow I must have messed up our magic moment meeting again and then this unusual conversation came to a halt. After a few minutes the show started up and when it was over that was the end of that short experience leaving me wondering, "What was that question all about? ? But months later when I was home watching an old 1957 movie on TCM starring Cary Grant as Nickie Ferrante and Deborah Karr as Terry McKay called **An Affair To Remember** and when I heard Terry call Cary Grant Nickie in that movie that's when I got this clarifying thought while sitting on the couch. "Now you know who **Nick** is. It's just Kay putting out another fleece of wool on the threshing floor (Judges 6:37) and then she'll know if you are the right one for her or not." Isn't it disheartening to find out years later all our efforts did us more harm than the good we planned on for love.

But now back on that same Alaska trip the next day I figured since I apparently messed up this year again there's no sense trying to connect with Kay after that last embarrassing misstep I didn't understand, so I went into the dining gallery at about 1:00 PM. I decided to drown my sorrows in my novel writing work and so I started reading and while listening to my Lord speak wisdom about these spiritual rules I was making corrections on my book as was my regular custom when I'm at home. Working with my Lord on my laptop was my regular soothing therapy I enjoyed or what made my heart happy like comfort food to a person on a starving diet and right now I needed to be comforted or happy about something. So reading scriptures and talking with God I felt a lot better and so now on this third ship the ocean liner was much larger than the first one and the waves did not rock us all to sleep, nor was there any need for those little green apples for some passengers who got nauseous.

Now this year's dining hall was also greater in size or 200 feet long and at least 100 feet wide. The lunch crowd was just now over so this enormous room was almost empty as I took my choice of any seat I wanted in this titanic-size room. I selected the top spot in the back of this enormous room where I thought I could

HIDE from my <u>latest embarrassing flounder</u>. Psalm 139:<u>7-10</u>. That decision turned out to be a big half round multi-seat booth that was somewhat difficult to get into the middle as you had to slowly lift and slide your way along little at a time to the center of it for the straight on view of these giant wall-size windows to see Alaska's glorious grandeur of mammoth glacier ice and falling snow.

Have you ever wondered why the glacier ice seems to be blue? It turns out that glacier ice is blue because the red long wavelengths of white light is absorbed by ice leaving the shorter wavelengths of blue in light to be transmitted and scattered in the ice giving it a blue cast. The longer the path light travels in ice and the bigger the ice is, the more blue shows up as we see it. Forgive the trivia; these are some of the curious questions I long to know.

Anyway I wanted some peace and quiet time to hear my Dad's wise input as usual to increase my knowledge on God. "... *that you may be filled with the knowledge of His will in all spiritual wisdom and understand.*" Colossians 1:9 NIV. These multiple huge room-size windows went the length of this immense area on the ship directly in front of me and so I first gazed at the Lord's beautiful icy creation before starting up my battery operated laptop and reading my novel for editing and any of my Lord's new input as usual. The ship then turned and went into a very large naturel bay in Alaska where the land and the mountains were visible close up and you could see nearby blue/white glaciers on the icy jagged coastline. I took a good long look for a while and then started reading my novel. But then every 30 minutes or so <u>my pattern</u> was to stop typing my book and just look up at those same wall-size windows that went the length of this incredibly large room to view out at this amazing icy landscape directly in front of me as I thought I might as well soak in these amazing sight while I'm here.

After a while of drinking in all this spectacular view I would return to my book and continue writing with my Lord's insight helping me to improve it as was my normal custom. Hours later with this looking first and then writing in my book pattern second I had relaxed and was very involved and happy in all my creative work. But then still engrossed in my thoughts I could hear a large assembly of people coming in as the dinner crowd was now starting up and choosing seats to dine but I did not take my eyes off my creative writing because my Lord was speaking His regular grand insight and hidden secrets to me. Those people were now sitting right in front of me just 12 feet away; right where I would regularly look out to see Alaska in all of its Sun glittering icy beauty. But I already just looked right before they came in so I just continued quite happily with my Best Friend speaking and all my creative juices working synergistically with the Holy Spirit leading me as He always spoke His wisdom and illuminating ideas to my mind. Once again God was working behind the scenes to set me up for success so I could finally meet Kay and start up our loving relationship this year to complete the very reason God sent me down here and not go home depressed again as usual. After another half hour went by of typing God's principles, I thought I should look up one last time before getting ready for the upcoming evening show on Kay's itinerary not long from now.

So I stopped typing and looked up and <u>right in front of me looking directly at me was Kay</u> making perfect eye to eye contact. How long did she look over at me just waiting for me to finally look up and catch my eyes looking back at her; I don't know? If she put that kind of effort and determination into hoping to make our connection happen, then what might that reveal to me about her inner hidden heart I can't see clearly? Once our eyes met and locked in, she smiled that infectious heart-capturing smile that flashed in my eyes and pierced right through me like cupid's arrow and all the way into my lonely love-hopping soul. Obviously Kay was still interested in this hopeful new man she really didn't know and not wanting to miss this year's p<u>ossible</u> future husband as he seems to keep coming back year after year <u>for ?some? reason</u>.

Now if that eye-pleasing moment wasn't obvious enough, she then waved to me with one of those finger waves where they flip their fingers up and down sweetly <u>definitely trying to get your attention</u>. So Craig: If ever someone was trying to arouse your interest, those can't-miss actions you just saw <u>was certainly it!!!</u> So this is your set-up moment **again** Craig by God's creative hand, therefore please don't mess it up! So I returned her sweet smile with one of my own but then the enemy reminded me of my past <u>embarrassing</u> history of falling short in front of her in the past. Also they spoke the fact that, "You're not this Nick fellow she wants;" as I did not find out till months later at home watching an old 1957 movie. So dominating me through their chief weapon of fear of a pretty face their stronghold, or **PRISON**, (Romans 7:23) stopped me once again; I couldn't bring myself to get up out of that center spot in the half round booth that was so awkward to get into. Then I would have had to walk over boldly to meet her and then strike up a <u>confident</u> conversation with someone as dazzling and impressive as Kay and <u>with all her friends watching me</u>. How easy would it be for you to just walk up to JFK back in the 1960s while he was sitting with all <u>his cabinet members</u> with <u>the Secret Service agents</u> there <u>guarding him</u> and then carry on a relaxed casual conversation like he was just common regular folk and nothing special? And if JFK doesn't stir up your nervousness than who does? The Queen of England? Dean Martin? T<u>ony Bennet</u>?

> ## <u>As</u> the kayaker <u>must</u> <u>push through</u>
> ## the rough waves at the
> ## shoreline to enter a calm
> ## and stable <u>sea</u>,
> ## <u>so</u> new lovers must push through
> ## their nervous awkwardness to enter
> ## their calm and stable relationship
> ## before they, 👁 <u>see</u> 👁.
> Who they missed / Dad 2:20

Remember I don't normally 👁see👁 and converse with this caliber of upper tier famous people in my day to day construction life. I am use to seeing <u>regular standard people</u> in my A to Z home improvement remodeling business and I talk quite confidently and comfortably with all of the <u>common working public.</u> Even with the good looking women I'm able to talk to them <u>if</u> <u>they don't get to close</u> because <u>we were talking business</u> or I was dominating the conversation with **<u>my</u>** <u>subjects</u> like the <u>Bible</u> or the <u>future New World Order events.</u> I spoke about those subjects quite often to my many customs, or other well-known subject I'm familiar with like <u>nutrition</u> and <u>minerals</u> most people know so little or even nothing about. But conversing with the <u>best</u> super model who could win the Miss World contest without even trying hard and telling her God sent me down here to marry her was certainly not my relaxed norm. Forgive me for my <u>superlative</u>[9] colloquialisms[10]

---

[9] <u>Superlative</u>: Describing a thing or a person at the highest level; <u>best</u>, greatest.
[10] Colloquialisms: Colloquialisms are exaggeration statements to stress a point the speaker or writer is trying to get across; such as, "He's as old as the hills" or "Dead as a doornail". However, Kay really could be a super model <u>with ease</u>.

but some things need to be emphasized to get the point across. It's not that easy to look into the face of an angel and then have a spontaneous relaxing conversation after God told you who she is to me. Just ask any of those biblical people in the Bible who were afraid being in the angel's presence. That's why the phrase "fear not" appears in the Bible 365 times. Yet, the enemy's demonic attack and my hesitation on the Alaska trip in my overwhelmed heart being intimidated as I was, cost me dearly because that magical moment God offered me again melted away quickly like Frosty the Snowmen warming himself by the fire as all that was left of me was a melted puddle of disappointment. Decades of constant condemnation crushed my confidence paralyzed me as the kingdom of darkness continued stating you're just "**worthless**".

With every opportunity the Lord lined up for us both, it seemed Satan was right there to <u>Disrupt</u> and <u>Stop</u> every magical moment with the same stronghold and keep me in his **PRISON**. Assuming I messed up our meeting again I decided not to dwell on the Kay connection disappointment that just happened so I agreed to meet a couple of new friends I just met yesterday for dinner as they were looking for a friend and some dinner conversation that night in <u>one of the two very large formal dining halls</u>. While I was waiting there at the ship's double dining hall doors <u>on time as always</u> in my rented black tuxedo I was secretly hoping to see Kay tonight even from a distance so I could enjoy her view still hoping for our future life together somehow. After an hour these two married ladies were late as I wondered if they were coming at all. Yet being patient, little did I know the Lord's guardian angel who was watching over me was still hard at work planning our next opportunity like God instructed him to do that I knew nothing about as the golden bowls were still filled and now overflowing with our pleading falling ◆tears◆. The two ladies finally showed up all gussied up for this formal night, so we proceeded to look for three seats that might be left in this humungous dinning gallery. While walking almost the length of this floating city ship and looking for three seats, I was also keeping an eye out for where Kay might be seated. Now at the end of the large hall and finding nothing we turned left across the width of this immense room then turned again proceeding down the other long last side as well. Still nothing was available as we came too late and this place was completely packed. But seeing the head waiter I asked, "Are we too late? There're no more seats available? That's when my guardian angel's plan kicked in to answer my latest prayer. The head waiter decided to open up the center seating he was preserving for the following day and we three late comers were seated in the forbidden center no one was supposed to be in. I saw to it that the ladies were seated first and then sat opposite them for our night of light dinner conversation as we were given our menus.

While making my dinner selection I tipped my menu down just enough to see the two ladies I came with but actually in truth I was still looking for where Kay might be seated and decided to start looking right in front of me. Surprisingly I noticed right between these two ladies I just met yesterday was Kay having dinner only 20 feet away with her regular entourage of friends and maybe some distant family members. The distance God chose was absolutely perfect for looking. I wasn't so far away that I couldn't get a good view, but I also wasn't so close that she might see me looking at her. I tell you I couldn't have planned it any better if I were God Almighty with many angels in Heaven to assist me. Then while looking over my menu and seeing Kay right between the two ladies I came with, a timely thought came to my mind,

"There she is. You wanted to view her from a distance." Heaven had set me up with the perfect scenario I had longed for. I knew where Kay was and if I wanted to step out in faith and go over there and talk to her to start up our relationship I could, or most likely I'll just sit here where it's safe and enjoy the view like I wanted to do that was much easier. This was just another God planned set up for me to walk in faith if I dared to with her friends watching me, but like always my intimidation of Kay's beauty and my fear of talking to girls proved to be too much for me. Heaven hadn't given up on us being one together like I had despite my numerous embarrassing moments of blundering our meetings in the past years. She had her dark frame lower half 𝒢𝓸 reading glasses on I had never seen before while reading her menu as her table was already at the dessert stage of their meal. It was then I remember a love song growing up in 1975 sung by Frankie Valli,

♩ **"My eyes adored you. Though I never laid a hand on you, my eyes adored you. Like a million miles away from me you couldn't see how I adored you. So close, so close and yet so far."** ♩ After all the missteps in the past I didn't have the courage to excuse myself from these two ladies, boldly walk over there in confidence as she would then see me coming. Then I'd have to interrupt Kay's dinner conversation and awkwardly stand there like an intruder and talk to her with her friends watching me which would add to the pressure. Satan knew as inexperienced as I was talking to girls, I had but one chance of walking in faith and courage and he **Disrupted** and **Stopped** our only connection back at *The Moment* we first met as it was downhill from there on in.

Other Kay Encounters

Yet another time Kay and I had a close encounter was either the fourth or fifth time that I came to see her and we had a different venue on that ship where there was no actual physical stage in this smaller/big room but just an area on the same floor as the audience designated as the stage and things got a lot tighter. Again I came over 90 minutes early to stand in line to get a good seat to view Kay and by doing so continue sending her that ongoing message that I was still interested in seeing her. So I was sitting in the front row with my right ankle resting on my left knee as usual and just like before I was listening to some other fan to my right when Kay came along in front of me which I did not notice and that's when Kay touched my ankle with her finger possibly trying to get my attention. When I felt that touch I thought before I looked that my foot must be sticking out too far into the aisle as there was only three feet to get by in this tight room before you would be tripping over microphone stands and floor monitors on this pretend not physical stage area.

But when I turned to see, "*Who touched me*", (Luke 8:45-47) I saw Kay bending over slightly to touch my sock and then she smiled at me and said something I did not hear as it happened fast. The room was filled with hundreds of people all talking in this big room that sounded like the dull loud roar of a large cafeteria crowd and so I really didn't catch her comment at all and so could not respond to her. That's another round the enemy won and one more missed opportunity for the two hopeful hearts like ships passing in the night that accidently bumped into each other catching a slight glimpse of the one smiling at the other but made no connection.

Another time Key and I almost connected I was unusually sitting back in the seventh row somewhat depressed not connecting with Kay at the end of the week and unable to fulfill my Mission of Love my Lord sent me down here to accomplish. As another performer was on stage entertaining for that night, I repeatedly looked down four rows to my left to see Kay sitting in her seat with her friends watching the show. But one of Kay's friends noticed me glancing and informed Kay I was viewing her as Kay then looked back to see me and our eyes met briefly. This familiar back and forth sneak peeking with her friends looking to inform Kay I was periodically looking at her, reminded me of my school years where this shy behavior commonly took place as this was the common method of letting a fellow student know you liked them. But the enemy also caught that moment with me glancing and then I got his thought, "She probably thinks you're a strange stalker and someone she should fear." When that thought came it swayed my decision to stop looking as I didn't want to come off as some strange stalker; and so that moment ended. But only a day later as another performer was on stage singing and I was in the sixth row and Kay was just three rows ahead of me to my right and at the end of that performance Kay stood and turned around almost facing me some eight feet away. When I believe it was Kays friend E---- who spoke up talking very honoring about Kay to the crowd and today the only line I can still remember she finished with was, ". . . and isn't she beautiful?" When I heard that, I was about ready to blurt out the truth, "I'll say!", as a trumpet like those rocks that can't be silenced, 40 ". . . if I should hold My peace, the stones would immediately cry out the truth." Luke 19:40. NIV. But again the enemy timed his negative "stalker" comment perfectly and so I decided to hold my tongue and just say nothing.

Another time I was in the middle of the ship in this big wide open well-lit area that resembled Las Vegas with all of the bright colored lights surrounding us with food shops, souvenirs stores and as I looked up several stories high I could see people in their cabins looking out on either side over the balconies down on us passengers walking along slowly. Still **by myself** I had just bought an ice-cream cone to pick up my somber mood and then I brightened up glancing through the crowd when I saw Kay's iconic face about 60 feet ahead of me walking slowly by herself which was **very rare** as she normally is within her entourage of staff and rarely ever goes anywhere by herself. But this time in the center of this huge illuminated recreation vicinity right in front of me she was walking **alone** slowly and looking like she wanted to meet or talk to someone. I knew the Lord was trying to set me up again for our umpteenth time or my opportunity with her as you could look for days to find someone on these gargantuan ships like searching for a needle in a very large haystack and never find them at all.

I knew the time to connect with Kay was running short as this week and this year's chances were slipping by quickly so this time I needed to be bold or go home defeated again. But as usual the Lord could not tell me what to say but He did give me a little time to think of something as Kay was still 40 feet away and slowly casually walking toward me in this crowded sea of people. With me also **boldly** lining up to meet her and walking slowly toward her the distance was closing in quickly and so the pressure was mounting up with every step I took. Then in this crowd our eyes finally made contact and in a few more steps it's customary for one of us to speak up and say something when this happens. Kay was smiling and looking at me but waiting in hope to hear my opening comment before just naturally joining in the conversation.

I believe the Lord wanted me to **S**pe**a**k first in **faith** (Hebrews 11:6) as this is God's $currency$ in Heaven to receive anything we Christians want or ask for by prayer. I finally did sp**ea**k as I used my ice-cream cone as a supporting visual prop when I looked her in the eyes and said, "I thought I'd get an ice-cream cone since I'm on vacation. It's pretty good.", as I kept on walking. But since I waited till the very last second to sp**ea**k and turned sideways while I was talked to her, I actually passed her by while talking and then after I was finished speaking sideways to her and slightly backwards I turned back toward the front again where I kept right on walking **as if** I wanted to cut the conversation off. So it must have appeared to Kay that I really didn't want to talk to her at all as when I finished speaking, I turned toward the front where I continued walking forward which cut the eye contact and then the conversation itself was cut off. So, ----- -------- really never had a proper moment to respond as I slowly walked away because I was overwhelmed being that close to her intoxicating face and I was just plain **afraid** to face my **fear** of talking to a pretty sweet girl like her. I believe God wanted me to stand up to my fears and talk to Kay face to face in **faith** which I almost but never really did. If I would have done that, I would have won the battle over my fear and the enemy's Legal Right (fear) and that stronghold the enemy had over me would then have been **broken**. After that the fear that held me captive or in their **PRISON** would be destroyed thus freeing me from the enemy's stronghold.

All the condemnation the enemy placed in me during my growing up years, became an establish habit in me that the enemy could then access that stronghold in me and **exploit** that fear at any time during key moments **Disrupting** and **Stopping** our imprint bonding that the kingdom of Heaven was trying to accomplish. By doing this repeatedly the dark kingdom could keep us apart indefinitely <u>as long as I continued to</u> **believe their lies** that I was **worthless.** This became <u>their Legal Right</u> or their reason for their <u>stronghold</u> of holding me in fear or holding me in their spiritual **PRISON** like I explained in the title **Understanding Spiritual Rules**. Remember: The word "*strong*" is #3794 **ochyroma**: in the Greek. Translated into our English, that definition is (**Stronghold, fortress**; or **PRISON**). But when <u>I stopped believing</u> their lie about being **worthless** just recently in November 2022 the enemy's Legal Right or their stronghold was <u>severed</u>✂ as their power was <u>cut</u>✂ and so their hold over me was dissolved at that moment, that's why I believe God prompted me with that song **On My Own**. Then since our golden bowls in Heaven were still full some 15 years ago and over flowing, there was then nothing left to keep us apart at that moment thus <u>the spiritual door for us to try our relationship again was suddenly</u> **opened** by those lyrics of Patti LaBelle and Michael McDonald. "**My heart is saying that <u>it's time</u> again**"

[17] "*. . . He will joy over thee with singing.*" Zephaniah 3:17. NKJV.

The Lord just spoke <u>the answer</u> to me <u>Right Now</u> as to <u>what triggered that song</u> **On My Own** by Patti LaBelle and Michael McDonald, on 11-11-2022 that started me writing this whole book to reconnect to Kay after all these many 15 years. So now watch the secret God just revealed to my mind. Here I am on March 17th 2023 making corrections on this very book you are reading so it can be approved by Westbow and then sent out to the public, when the <u>Holy Spirit reveals the answer</u> as to what started this whole book idea <u>or Love Letter</u> depending on who's reading it and what started my hope for our reconnection again after 15 long years. Remember I said in this book 12 lines right before the title **The Alaska Trip,** "My problem was despite having a girlfriend every year I was in school I never had any experience asking any woman out on a date. They always noticed me first and then found a way to get my attention and so I never had to work up the courage to ask anyone out or face that natural fear of rejection. This **fear** of **rejection** and the **lie** I was **worthless** and **talking** to a **pretty face** were the three-way demonic power "Legal Right" the enemy had for their stronghold they needed over me to keep me in their spiritual **PRISON** or in their strong grip or their "stronghold" the enemy needed for my bondage to hinder me for the last 15 years. So as long as I held on to that lie I was worthless and held on to that fear of rejection, and afraid to talk to a pretty face, that three-way stronghold the enemy had over me would continue to **Disrupt** and **Stop** me as they held me in their spiritual **PRISON** compliant with God's spiritual rules. Why? Because all humans have a freewill to choice wrong over right or even walking in **fear** as opposed to living in **faith** as the righteous are commanded to do. Romans 1:17 * Galatians 3:11 * Hebrews 10:38. And so as I chose fear instead of faith when I was intimidated with Kay's beauty just inside the auditorium's doors, the dark kingdom had the "Legal Right" by that pressured key time at *The Moment*

to keep me from **Spea**king up and being bold enough to talk to Kay face to face while holding her hand.

So now you ask, "Okay I understand the spiritual insight the Holy Spirit just revealed to you and your corresponding physical problem (not able to speak) you had in real life, but then what <u>changed in you spiritually</u> so the enemy could no longer hold you in their three-way stronghold any longer. And what got you over this fear and the enemy's ability they had to hold these "Legal Right<u>s</u>" and their bondage holding you in this spiritual **<u>PRISON</u>**? Here's <u>the secret</u> the Holy Spirit just revealed to my mind.

Three or four months before I got that song, **On My Own** by Patti LaBelle and Michael McDonald, on 11-11-2022 I was helping my very poor niece fix up her new house as it was very old and needed absolutely everything. But to get into their new house to fix it up all those months I had to call up the real estate lady and get her to unlock the front door first because my niece's loan was not approved yet and the prior owners still owned the house. Well months went by in the summer of me fixing up her new house as this real estate lady and I had short business conversations about unlocking the door and how long it would take her to get over there at that property to unlock the client's house. After I was done helping my niece in the summer, later in early November 2022 I was again all **<u>by myself</u>** sitting at home in the evening watching a romantic Hallmark movie as usual and so I <u>got a</u> **<u>BOLD</u>** <u>new thought</u> to call up this real estate woman and for the first time in my entire life be **<u>bold</u>** and <u>ask her out on a date</u>.

As usual I was super nervous like always as you would have thought I was calling up the Queen of England while I rehearsed my thoughts several times before calling her. Nevertheless, I did call her and after <u>my entire life of never asking a woman out on a date</u>, I did not talk to her about business anymore but asked her if she wanted to just get together sometime and talk socially like friends. But she responded she already had a boyfriend she was seeing and so I replied, "Well if you already have someone you're happy with than I'll just bow out gracefully and leave you two to enjoy each other. She thanked me for my courtesy and respecting her wishes and then we ended the phone call and that blind God made miracle I didn't understand was over.

I didn't realize at that time **what I just did** until just now when God revealed to me the hidden secret. The Holy Spirit said, "That phone call you made to the real estate woman back then as you finally **faced** your **fear** of asking out a woman as you then realized you're not **worthless** any longer finally broke the enemy's stronghold. Since the enemy tricked you into their trap (Genesis 3:4, 5) on your first trip 15 years ago to the Bahamas that's when your lifetime stronghold was then used against you. So the stronghold to you both getting together again without the enemy's **fears** and lie of **worthlessness** hindering you was then destroyed when you faced your fears asking out that real estate lady." The enemy shut the spiritual door back at *The Moment* using that stronghold in the auditorium when it was convenient for them to have me meet Kay up close without slowly getting used to her beaming beauty like the Lord told me in the Hot Tub parable. That's when they **exploited** my shy weakness of never asking out a girl that paralyzed me with their **FEAR** as I could not even remember my own name at that time while the enemy **Disrupted** and **Stopped** our merging of two souls in one heart of Oneness. The Lord warned me very specifically I had to take the Promise Land, which was **Kay,** by FAITH and not by **fear** as the Israelites did or I would end up as they did wondering in the wilderness for 40 years! But when I dove into the Hot Tub all at once seeing Kay's beaming beauty right in front of me up close and me thinking I had no value, that sharp contrast was like the moon trying to date the Sun shining in all of its strength, (Revelation 1:16 KJV) as I panicked with beauty overload! But remember this . . .

You cannot have courage
or a courageous man
without a <u>great fear</u> to first overcome.

Dad 9:13

And so the enemy had their "Legal Right" over me of a fearful worthless stronghold and <u>God saw no faith in me</u> to take the Promise Land, <u>Ka</u>y. I had failed the spiritual <u>test</u> (Gen. 22:10-12 * Ex. 15:<u>25</u> * Job 2:<u>10</u> * 23:<u>10</u> * Ps 66:<u>10</u> * Pro 3:<u>26</u> * 17:<u>3</u> * Matt 4:<u>1</u> * Luke 4:<u>1</u>, <u>2</u> * 12:<u>20</u>, <u>21</u> * John 6:<u>6</u> * 1 Cor. 2:3-<u>5</u> * 10:<u>13</u> * 2 Cor. 5:<u>7</u> * Philip. 4:<u>6</u>, <u>7</u> * 1 Tim. 3:<u>10</u> * Heb. 12:<u>4-11</u> * James 1:<u>2-4</u>, * <u>12</u> * 1 Peter 1:<u>6</u>, <u>7</u> * 4:<u>12-19</u> * 5:<u>10</u>) under a pressured moment of <u>take the Promise Land</u> by **FAITH**.

Are you starting to see how the spirit world works and are you learning <u>some</u> of these <u>Spiritual Rules</u> and how God will not accept the **Cheaper Fear** for the **Deeper Faith** required to take the **godly gift** God is offering me? Remember this rule in your future. God was offering me a godly gift 🎁 which was <u>Ka</u>y. But to receive God's <u>gift</u>, I needed to take this <u>gift</u> (**Kay**) using God's $<u>currency</u>$, ✝**FAITH**✝ and not Satan's ☠**currency**☠, **Fear** which did not work at all. Our enemy knew about these spiritual rules much better than I did as he has been twisting them against us humans for 6,000 years now. He knew I would fold up like an accordion and fall like a house of cards if I faced **Kay**'s beauty <u>all at once</u> and <u>up close</u>. The Lord knew a shy guy like me needed the whole week to slowly get used to her level of beauty and seeing her <u>close up</u> like the Hot Tub parable the Lord spoke to me. So the enemy <u>exploited</u> my zeal to see you Kay and gave me that thought to meet you right away at the very beginning after I found my cabin on our first trip. His, "**Go now**! **Don't wait**!", strategy the enemy launched in the first few minutes I was aboard the ship worked to their evil destructive advantage as they had hoped and planned as I was excited to meet my future wife but then turned petrified like the Tin Man without his oil can standing in the field of red Poppies while gazing at the glittering Emerald City. Understanding how the spirit realm works and all of God's rules has always been a deep passion for me since I started writing my first book back in 2005. Now listen to the Lord's powerful words He first gave me back when I started writing my first novel.

_{V7} You cannot offer God
the **cheaper** for the <u>deeper</u>.

"everything that does not come from <u>faith</u> is <u>sin</u>." Romans 14:23.

_{V8} God will not compromise

His $p**a**yment**s**$ of <u>faith</u>
for <u>blessings</u> you don't earn!

Dad 1:7, 8

So not **S**pe**a**king up in <u>faith</u> cost me everything! I lived with regret thinking about ----- --------- or **Kay** for the last ten years as I even quit listening to her music and stopped visiting her website as all I ever did after the fifth trip was cry every time I recalled her sweet face listening to her CDs knowing I blew the best <u>gift</u> God ever gave me. I even had to find different worship music to honor my Lord every morning as I could not sing to her first seven songs or <u>Kay's</u> worship CD, <u>Draw Me Close</u> any longer

I originally got off the TV as they reminded me of the beautiful godly wife God told me was mine. So after that third trip failure in Alaska and the two years of worshiping to her music, I had to find something else to worship my Lord with. The memories of the past five trips and how the Lord set me up for success with His very best angel troubled me for ten long years after the fifth trip was over as I knew I missed that *Magical Moment?*

v17 The road to victory
leads through a humble Heart.

Moses was the most humble man on the Earth. Numbers 12:3.

v18 Don't let the enemy keep us Apart,
when he shoots his Dart.
v19 We need to be Smart,
so our love can finally Start.
v20 Always remember,
humble is your Best Friend.

"God gives grace to the humble." Proverbs 3:34.
Dad 3:17-20

As a small pin prick,
in a pressured balloon quickly
deflates all that supports it inside,
so does a mustard seed of ☠doubt☠,
it quickly deflates the size and
strength of our faith!

Dad 5:6

Why Does God Call Humble People?
Numbers 12:3

Gideon is often considered the poster boy for **fear** in the Bible as I was also walking in fear trying to take the Promise Land which was Kay and establish our future marriage of Oneness like God told me, "Go down and see her." When God first commanded Gideon to lead the Israelites, he was hiding by a winepress in fear to escape being seen by his enemies the Midianites. Judges 6:11. I was also greatly intimidated when I saw Kay's beauty and thought I was unworthy as those sharp tongued people condemned me in the past and so they convinced me over decades I had no value.

Throughout Gideon's entire story in history, did he not demonstrate fear, anxiety and doubt just as I did when trying to talk to Kay those five trips down to see her. Yet God used a lowly man like Gideon anyway who was not full of faith but fearful just as He used a humble man like me back in 2008. I was not full of faith either at the beginning as I still believed back then I was **worthless** and not good enough for Kay. But God did use Gideon despite his lack of faith and now God is also working through me to establish His faith as He is building me up again to do the task he called me to do like the faith I'm walking in today while writing this book believing Kay will respond positively.

Gideon constantly tested God by asking him to **perform signs** because his faith was weak. First, he had God consume an offering of food he presented to an angel. Judges 6:20-21. Then Gideon **needed** dew on the fleece and dry ground all around as his faith was still weak because his **Faith** needed to be strengthened. Then Gideon needed the fleece to be dry and the ground all around to be wet with dew to again bolster up his weak faith and prove or increase his lagging **Trust** that <u>God was truly calling him</u> to do the leadership position Gideon was finally willing to **Believe** <u>in and do</u> as <u>God was still building up His man</u> to do His will and so complete the job he was led by God to do.

But was I not like Gideon questioning God numerous times with rebuttals because of my <u>weak faith</u> that God was truly <u>calling me to be the future husband of this incredibly beautiful and famous lady</u>? Was I not casting doubt on God's many promptings telling me to <u>go down and see Kay</u> while God did many miracles to prove to me He was truly calling me to bolster up my <u>weak faith</u>? Like paving the way with Dr. Gary Smalley VHS tapes in a cardboard box on the upper shelf in a back dark hallway I would have never found without His divine leading in a library I've never been in my entire life? Or God's split second timing on a TV remote my dad was clicking one click per second to choose the right channel the very night before I would be watching so the channel would end up on the only Christian station on TV? Or my dad that just happened to be at the doctors that day when I needed the only TV with a very old VHS player that still worked out of the four TVs mom and dad had? Or I just happened to catch a Christian show with Kay on it who I never saw in my entire life that day on a TV I hadn't watched in six years? Or God gave me the largest commercial Job in my entire life to pay for all my taxes, all my winter bills for months and even enough to pay for this expensive Bahama trip just to get me down to see this one Christian woman? Or finding luggage <u>just when I needed it</u> after I've never seen luggage anywhere before in any store in my entire life? Or airline tickets I could not secure and then my sister Chris and her husband Louis show up <u>the next day</u> from California to visit mom and this only happens <u>once every two years</u>? Or the money God provided every year for all five trips after that first year God continued to provide the money I needed to go down and see Kay if I was willing for those five years in a row until I decided not to try any more to connect with Kay and then the money God provided every year also stopped.

Gideon was called by God to lead the Israelites just as I was called by God to go down on a cruise ship and take the Promised Land to start our loving relationship in Oneness as well?

So if Gideon was hesitant to be God's leader and I was hesitant or shy to go down and face Kay's beauty and just talk to her casually face to face, how did Gideon and I both overcome our fear and finally do God's job He called us to do?

Gideon was familiar with the grace of God working step by patient step through his food offering and going along with his weak faith as he tested God by the due on the fleece and then on the ground he requested twice. I was also familiar with God's grace of working patiently through my low self-esteem while God patiently waited and allowed me to question His leading me down to see Kay on an ocean cruise ship several times back in the title **The Lord Rebukes the "Worthless" Man.**

But Gideon was truly just scared to follow the courageous calling God called him to do as I also was greatly intimidated to follow through with God's calling me to go down and see Kay close up and talk to her beautiful face without being overwhelmed.

God was patient and took Gideon at the speed of Gideon's weak faith in himself to lead God's people while enduring his doubt and hesitation to **Trust**, **Believe** and have **Faith** through his offerings of food to the angel and again with the "fleece" twice as he tested God to be sure God was truly calling him. God reassured Gideon He was calling him by bolstering his weak faith as Gideon was feeling he was <u>not good enough</u> for this lofty and high position of leading God's people into battle believing for a victory.

But did God not take Craig at the speed of my weak hesitant faith (2 Corinthians 5:7) to romance a beautiful lady while God endured my doubt and uncertainty through my resistance and rebuttals twice stating, <u>who am I</u> to be Kay's equal and questioning <u>am I good enough</u> for this stunning godly lady who sings to millions. I challenged God <u>to be sure</u> He was truly calling me and God reassured me by miracle after miracle bolstering up my weak faith as I did not feel I was <u>valuable</u> enough for that high and lofty love Oneness calling me to be Kay's loving husband.

Gideon was scared to do the job God was calling him to do. Just as I was intimidated to do the job God was calling me to do. But after each time Gideon tested God, God strengthened Gideon step by step with His gradual enduring <u>grace</u> until Gideon's frightened will was <u>built up</u> to do the job God called him to do as he was then <u>resting in confidence</u> and ready to be Israel's leader and be the man <u>God saw from the start</u> that <u>Gideon did not see</u>.

Just like each time I questioned God, God strengthened me step by step with His gradual enduring <u>grace</u> of being patient with me taking me <u>one slow step at a time</u> at my hesitant sluggish speed of progress because of my false belief the enemy bombarded me with that I was **unworthy**. God patiently worked with me until my will was built up to be the man God called me to be while <u>surrendering my hesitant fears one by one</u> and then finally resting in God's assurance I was then ready to go down to see Kay in my new <u>zeal</u> and <u>confidence</u> that <u>God saw from the start</u> <u>that I didn't</u>.

In short: God searched for soulmates for us both praying Christians and saw the good in me as I loved to work for hours with Him as writing my novel and chase the very <u>Core of God's</u>

Heart in scriptures for years on end and so He saw I would be a good fit for Kay's deep loving biblical heart teaching others. But God had to find a way to get me over my shyness and the unending condemnation the enemy place in me for decades. So my loving Lord was patient with me like the *Kintsugi* Japanese pottery master craftsmen carefully picking up each broken "**worthless**" piece and carefully refitting me back together like the Scarecrow torn all apart and thrown everywhere with His loving patient care. God took the time I needed to transform broken "**worthless**" piece after broken "**worthless**" piece as He changed the **Fool** the dark kingdom tried to make after all these painful decades the sharp tongues were willing to cut down and destroy, into the **King** inside of me that God knew was always available that only God took the time to build up. My Lord converted the unfit shame from the enemy like the golden Japanese pottery master craftsmen undoing the broken pottery to make **a more valuable vessel** when Satan was done for God's divine use to love one of His best Earth Angels. After God helped me passed the many years of past pain the dark kingdom saddled me with, God built me back up to a place of excited confidence to then go down and see Kay while walking in great faith with excitement, zeal and enthusiasm.

But when I entered the ship to start God's week of slowly completing the Lord's love-bonding process after all these many months of miracles and His patient preparations, the dark kingdom saw I was walking in faith and excitement to see Kay now and not hesitant any more so the enemy knew they must now devise a sabotaging plan before this love connection about to actually happen gets started. The enemy needed to act quickly and if they didn't do something fast; God's two praying Christians would merge their combined godliness into one <u>greater powerful force of Oneness</u>. Then their shared powerful passion<u>s</u> and creative godly gift<u>s</u> would soon be a whole new authoritative influential <u>team</u> that would do much greater good for God and damage to the kingdom of darkness than if they had remained separate. Their combined love-Oneness fighting Satan's dark kingdom daily with God's overpowering Holy dominant Word would then cripple the dark kingdom. So they devised a sabotaging quick plan of blending my enthusiasm to see Kay with my weakness of talking to a beautiful lady <u>up close</u>. Then while under that pressure in front of Kay in the auditorium, I froze up seeing a pretty face and so the enemy's stronghold **PRISON** got started again while the dark kingdom condemned me from that moment on every time I tried to connect with Kay because they had the <u>stronghold</u> "Legal Right" back and stronger than ever compliant with God's rules. So, God's plan of Oneness for these two praying Christians He started back in Butler for a Holy marriage was never completed and the enemy's sabotaging plan worked and held on for 15 long lonely years of crushing disappointment as they stole our happiness all that time.

Now even though I went down in enthusiasm to see Kay they countered that <u>build up</u> work God did to get me there by reinstituting a past stronghold and "Legal Right<u>s</u>" to reinstate an old stronghold <u>I had</u> that <u>God got me over</u> to put me back <u>in</u> their spiritual **PRISON** stronger. Therefore, on this first Bahama trip we couldn't connect, nor on the St. Thomas Island second trip as they still had this stronghold and "Legal Right<u>s</u>" reestablished to keep me in their **PRISON**. This stronghold continued on the Alaska trip and so on for all five trips including my last trip down to Belize Central America to see you Kay. But remember, <u>God</u>

sees the **end** of this long history before He even started the **beginning**. ¹⁰ *"Declaring the end from the beginning, and from ancient times the things that are **not yet done**, saying, My counsel shall stand, and I will **do** all My pleasure:"* Isaiah 46:10. KJV. God saw the end result in Gideon's life before He started Gideon's adventure and so now do you think God sees our end result still yet to come? I believe He certainly does. Consider the verse in Luke 22:26 NKJV that tells us, ²⁶ *". . . the greatest among you should be like the youngest, (**Humble**) and the one who rules like the one who serves."* So did God want a humble leader for our future marriage by this long plan of building the humble up to become the bold man walking now in faith that I have become? Was it God's plan all along to outsmart the dark kingdom to ". . . ***do all His*** *pleasure:"* Isaiah 46:10. KJV. And what heavenly job does God have planned for us after we merge our hearts? Hmmm, consider this.

V18 God can take your Mess, and turn it into Your Message.
V19 It could actually Be, if your faith could only ◉See◉.

Dad 2:18, 19 / Genesis **50:20**

Now do you remember my words I wrote under the title, **The Lord Rebukes the "Worthless" Man** when I said, **"**I'm not worthy of her personal company." But the Lord encouraged me. "Lots of famous people have non-famous spouses and they don't sing or sell teaching DVDs either." But the enemy used his chief weapon of fear to lead me in another rebuttal to the Lord's encouraging me, so I reasoned back. "But Lord, who am I?

Exodus 3:11. I'm just a common carpenter in a small town making much less money than her; surely she deserves better than that." But the Lord responded a rebuking thought back into my mind, "**Am I not sending you**; (Judges 6:14) and besides did I not chose Peter, James and John for my bride and how many other regular people for my future wife in Heaven!?" Revelation 19:6-9."

So now look at the words of Moses in Exodus 3:11-12. NIV. **11** "*But Moses said to God, "Who am I that I should go to Pharaoh and bring the Israelites out of Egypt?*" Exodus 3:11. NIV. Moses was the most humble man in all the world (Numbers 12:3) and did not think highly of himself either; just like I did not as well. God said, **12** "*I will be with you* . . ." Exodus 3:12. When God called Moses to leave his shepherding business to confront Pharaoh to release the Israelites or to say, "Let my people go", Moses too was afraid to talk to Pharaoh as I was trying to simply talk with Kay. The ten leaders of Moses who were sent to scout out the Promise Land, were they not also afraid of the giants in the Promise Land they saw? Kay's stardom on the stage and her strikingly lovely looks that I saw were my giants I was afraid of facing. Numbers 13:33.

Then the Holy Spirit spoke the reason to me while making corrections on this book we're reading now how I broke the enemy's stronghold over me when I faced my fears of talking to women by asking out that real-estate lady on a date and that facing of my fears and overcoming them at that moment was what set me **free** from the enemy's stronghold. Like a [7] ". . . *thorn in the flesh, the massager of Satan to buffet me*," (2 Corinthians 12:7 KJV) as Paul was buffeted by these destructive God-hating demons as well. How many times after those five trips down to see Kay did I cry out to God in those 10 years following, (Numbers 14:23) "Lord I feel like the Israelites after failing to take the Promise Land by faith because of their fear of those giants."; and so they spent the next 40 years wondering around in the desert just waiting to die off.

And so I said the same thing as I cried out, "Is that all you have left for me Lord is wondering around in this love-less desert life of mine waiting to die?" Each time I cried out to God I hung my head in regret and hopelessness wishing I had another chance at the loving heart of Kay that I missed back in 2008 and for the next five years in a row. But after those five trips and those 10 years that followed were finally over of suffering **On My Own** for the past sin of fear of talking to a petty face, God gave me another chance at the Promised Land Kay by writing this book. Now that the Holy Spirit clued me in as to how the enemy's stronghold was broken I now know how I got this second chance to reconnect to Kay by facing my fear with the real estate lady and broke their stronghold and that's when God spoke those romantic lyrics to my mind stating, **My heart is saying that it's time again.**

So I started up this book which requires a lot of **faith** as well to believe Kay will see it and respond positively seeking out the man /slash/ future husband she missed back at the age of **49**. One of the ironies of fear is that it takes fear to overcome fear. For instance, Moses was afraid of the Egyptians (Exodus 2:11-13) and, to some extent, his own people because some of them saw him as part of Pharaoh's harsh kingdom to the Hebrews. Yet He had to face an all-powerful God (Exodus 6:3) for Moses to acquire a healthy fear of His God. It was his fear of Jehovah God (Exodus 3:6 * Proverbs 9:10) that gave Moses the courage to face those whom he feared like Pharaoh and Moses had to face his own people and risk rejection that could have cost him his life if they revolted against him. Numbers 16:3. But ironically I too had to face my fear of rejection by calling up that real-estate lady to be set free from the enemy's stronghold. And now I must face my giants once again as Kay is still a **famous singer** who has traveled all over the world and even if James 1:10, 11 (TNLB) say *the little flower droops and falls, and its beauty fades away,* she still looks **beautiful** to me. I believe God has plans for us both in a ministry after we connect as He has shared some of those ideas with me, but I will hold up on explaining those thought until after we connect. Back in 2005 when I first started writing my book seeking a soulmate, one of God's first words He ever spoke to my mind was . . .

If you want a Queen of Hearts, ♥ *you must first stop being the Six of Spades.* ♠
Dad 2:10

Today I have gone full circle as my faith is strong while the stronghold of the enemy has been destroyed as I now know I'm not **worthless** and so the enemy's Legal Right about me being worthless is now gone. At the beginning of this book I said on day one (November 11th 2022) I went to the computer and wrote out the title of this book: *My 20 Miracle Prayers For a Wife,* which by the way took faith, and my last thoughts in a question form. So here are those last few thoughts and that last question I wrote out on day one. You've now read about all the miracles and every detail God did to help me along the way and prepare me for meeting you Kay face to face prior to us being squeezed together between that one three foot wide ship door in the auditorium where

I saw you **alone** for the very first time face to face despite that one million square foot ship we were on. Here's something to think about.

v16 God designs the test He Makes, But <u>we</u> determine <u>**how long**</u> it Takes! v17 If you allow the enemy's <u>Fears</u>, it will cost you <u>Years</u>, of endless ●<u>Tears</u>●●●●

Dad 2:16, 17
Don't I know it!

Yet God woke me up after the last trip and the 10 years of silence that followed when my fears were finally gone while I was watching a romantic Hallmark movie with that song **On My Own** lyrics that said <u>**My heart is saying that it's time again**</u> on 11-11- 2022. God reminded me I missed the "Promise Land" or our own marriage of Oneness which could have been glorious as He was working through the man; but this time I didn't hang my head in regret any more as the Legal Rights the enemy had were **<u>GONE</u>**.   I was then able to discuss that past painful subject without emotional guilt or remorse from the enemy as I was finally able to try our love connection again <u>with **faith**</u> while my Lord was saying, "**<u>It's time</u>** to **<u>try</u>** once more." But you tell me today Kay, <u>W</u>here do you draw the line on lov<u>e</u>? Should I just let these last few romantic love-ambers God stirred up in me flicker out, grow cold and die? And then forget all about us and what we could have had together? <u>Or</u> should I <u>wait in hope</u> (Hope = faith) and **Believe** that you will respond positively and seek out your man you prayed for years to find and have and missed way back on February 25th to March 2nd 2008 at your own 10th anniversary? Waiting in hope…

Money Can't Buy You Love; or Can it?

Today they say money makes the world go round, and I guess in Satan's sinful system that sad statement might be true. But God's love greases the axle and without this lubricant of love, life would truly seize up and stop turning altogether. Money never hugged and kissed me and said those three magic words I still long to hear. Dion Warwick had it right back in 1966 when she sang,

♩ **"What the world, needs now,**
is love, sweet love.
It's the only thing that there's just <u>too little of</u>.
What the world, needs now,
is love, sweet love.
No not just for some, <u>but for everyone</u>." ♩

I hand out kindness most every day and maybe I'm foolish waiting for an echo, but sometimes I get it. I'm retired now Kay, receiving only what the government through Social Security gives me. Despite this low income status I owe no man anything and since I don't do drugs, smoke⊗ or <u>chew</u>, nor run around with girls that <u>do</u>; I have managed to pinch out some money a little bit per monthly deposit and so after many years I saved back, $2,000 dollars. Which may not sound like a lot to most working people, but this is <u>way more</u> than I get per month to live on. So right before the 2022 mid-term election, while I was watching a slow moving football game, I was having a conversation with the Lord who's the only one in my loneliness I can talk to when He asked, "What are you going to do with your $2,000 you've saved up?"

Even though we all need money for the basics of life to live in this world, I don't have much interest in money at all and have never touched that $2,000 for years now. Luke 16:10. I never did dream about lots of money in my life as earthly money can only buy you earthly things of <u>little temporary value</u>. Luke 12:15. Like brand new <u>bold baubles</u> the world thinks we all need, or <u>traditional trinkets</u> earthly people seem to treasure, and maybe even some <u>goofy gadgets</u> I never desired or had any interest in. These worldly items and the latest new thrills the world advertises saying we all need I really don't care for at all. But ever since I was nine, I only ever really longed for <u>one glorious thing</u>. Lots of people have many things on their <u>Bucket List</u> they want to do before their life is over. Parachute out of a plane, go hang gliding, parasailing, climb a mountain, whatever they've always wanted to do but never had the time or the chance in their life to do.

But all my life I only had <u>one thing</u> on my Bucket List; **Love.** I thought to myself, "<u>What has more value than love</u>? Nothing, I reasoned. *"Many waters cannot quench **love**; rivers cannot wash it away."* Song of Solomon 8:7a. I was lucky enough to be in love quite a few times in my early life when I was growing up. I loved those young girls and later a lady or two for a brief year or so, but I guess after some time they fell out of love with me. Maybe you know what that feels like Kay and possibly you're familiar with that emotional heart break? But during that brief time of being in love I have to say, it was the proverbial Heaven on Earth; where <u>E</u>verything Change<u>s</u> or so I thought until they left. As anyone in love will tell you, there's nothing like it in all the world. And they're right; love comes from God, for He is Love, (1 John 4:8) that's why it feels so great when you're in it. Before I get Raptured into Heaven where earthly marriage between a man and a woman never happens any more, (Matthew 22:30) I would really like the glorious privilege of falling in love with a good godly woman and maybe she might even reflect all the love I give her back on me if she understands the <u>Mounting Magic</u> of reciprocating love.

So after the Lord asked me what I was going to buy with this $2,000 dollars I had managed to save up, I said, "There really isn't anything in this <u>loveless world</u> that I truly want. <u>Love is the only thing with any real value, but my $2,000 dollars won't buy me love</u>, so I guess I'll just save up for a new car some day when my 2017 Toyota Camry gives out. Not long after that conversation about what I'm going to do with my $2,000 dollars and the 2022 midterm election was over, on 11-11-2022 I got that song lyric in my head. **<u>My heart is saying that it's time again</u>** from Patti LaBelle and Michael McDonald singing **On My Own**. That one romantic heart-starting song lyric and God prompting me with a question, "Why don't you write about your 20 miracles you had; I'm sure lots of people would like to hear about that"; started me writing this book, *My 20 Miracle Prayers For a Wife*.

But the reason I bring all this up is to inform you Kay, even though I wanted the most powerful gift from God, "Love!" and my $<u>2,000</u> dollar won't buy me that God given gift of love, the price to publish this book was $2,500 which I didn't have; but when I called Westbow, Amber made it $<u>1,999</u> dollars just for me. So now I'm wondering: "Even though money can't buy me love, is this book a tool in God's hands to get me the Oneness love I've always wanted? Hmmm, I wonder? Maybe you could answer that curious question for me Kay. But what can I offer a successful woman like Kay that she doesn't already have? **? Hmmm . . .**

There's Great Power in 𝕺𝖓𝖊𝖓𝖊𝖘𝖘.

Once <u>Oneness</u> is achieved between the ♥ two ♥ hearts
⁶ *"then nothing they plan to do will be impossible for them."*
—Genesis 11:6 NIV

⁸ *"Then the Lord said,*
"Look, I am setting a <u>plumb line</u> among My people."
—Amos 7:8 NIV

Watch the <u>Love Magic</u> and I'll show you <u>God's original</u> <u>plan</u> for evangelizing the whole world through His marriage institution of Oneness. There are three parts to <u>The Power of</u> <u>Oneness</u>, the godly man, the godly woman, and the Holy Spirit who holds them both together in His Holy Oneness by the Almighty God <u>they worship dail</u>y. Genesis 2:22-24. Worshiping God with a **<u>sincere holy heart</u>** <u>is the ke</u>y to the Holy Spirit working out the harmony between the two sinners saved by God's grace in their Holy earthly matrimony. This is why ☹<u>unequally</u>☺_<u>yoked</u> "<u>marriages</u>" never work out well but crash and burn in divorce (Galatians. 5:17) most of the time. 2 Corinthians 6:14-17 * Deuteronomy 7:1-6 * Ezra 9:1, 2, 12, 14 * 10:3, 11, 19 * Nehemiah 13:23-27 * Ephesians 5:7, 11.

<u>**As**</u> Fire Consumes Wood,
leaving only worthless ashes in its wake,
<u>**so**</u> an unequally yoked marriage (Romans 13:14)
will consume the godly Christian forever,
leaving a devoured soul
that only withers and dies! (suicidal thoughts)
Dad 2:9

v13 As the plants need Carbon Dioxide, and expel Oxygen,
and the humans need Oxygen, and expels Carbon Dioxide,
each fulfills the other in God's perfect harmony.

v14 So also the God-filled husband lavishes
his love on his hungry-for-love <u>godly</u> wife.

v15 Yet she in return reflects all her husband gives her and
fulfills his deepest longings with the love he has given her.

v16 Yet she adds an abundance of her own love back on
him making a Majestic Marriage they return on each other
again and again that the world just can't stop watching.

Dad 3:13-16

Those unequally yoked marriages are missing the key Holy love-power from Heaven in the worshiping of God <u>every morning</u> (Psalm 138) that brings the Holy Spirit into their marriage <u>to cover the saved sinners' many flaws</u> as, "*His mercies are new every morning.*" Lamentations 3:22, 23. Finding even one Christian who will <u>chase hard daily after God's Core Holy Heart</u> through regular Holy worship <u>every morning</u> is a rare thing indeed. But to find two humble sinners saved by God's grand grace in one marriage that are willing to pursue <u>daily</u> after their Holy God to bring Him glory every morning (Revelation 4:11) and at the same time serve their spouse <u>above themselves</u> is even rarer to find. Ephesians 5:25. As unique as this is, that Oneness <u>can only happen</u> with an <u>Equally Yoked Marriage</u> as an <u>active</u> working Holy Spirit like Andy had with the prophet in his life as that <u>active working</u> Holy Spirit is required to make the Oneness Marriage truly work. As we step out to <u>do God's selfless work on our spouse</u>, the Holy Spirit working through our working active faith completes our desire to <u>love as He would</u>. And always remember the Holy Spirit in the saved or born again Christians, <u>will never become one</u> with the evil spirits <u>living **in**</u> the unsaved spouse because the Holy Spirit <u>cannot bond to</u>, <u>nor become one with</u> the evil demon spirits in the unsaved souls of the sinners. Read: 1 Samuel 5:1-5 * Exodus 7:12.

In the same way that
rust never sleeps, (Romans 8:5)
so the ☠unequally yoked☠ marriage
never stops corrupting and
☠<u>consuming you</u>☠ like an out of control
Packman <u>until</u> the godly <u>is destroyed</u>!☠

Dad 2:8
Galatians 5:16 * Proverbs 13:20 * (suicidal thoughts)

Listen carefully to the deep nuts and bolts of Oneness and how God intended the male and female <u>godly</u> couple to work synergistically in an ☺<u>Equally Yoked</u>☺ Marriage. A marriage is **<u>God's</u>** institution and is not just another word in the dictionary for today's "<u>woke</u>" *Twisted* government to think up wicked way to dissect, rearrange and change the definition of marriage to suit their <u>now</u> own upside down lust-filled homosexual (Romans 1:26, 27) lesbian ways. This revised *Twisted* perversion of God's original love Oneness was done so Satan could fuel his ongoing rebellion and America's **<u>soon</u>** <u>coming judgment</u> that our enemy wants for us humans he is jealous of and hates. A marriage was, and still is designed by God today for both parties of <u>male</u> and <u>female</u> to be filled with the Holy Spirit first as they [39] ". . . ***must*** *belong to the Lord."* 1 Corinthians 7:39. Then, from their <u>common Holy minds</u> that read God's Holy Word <u>daily</u> they will be transformed and renewed from their old <u>fleshly,</u> (Galatians 6:8) <u>selfishness</u> and <u>sin-chasing</u> desires they continue to <u>die to daily</u>. 1 Corinthians 15:31. Their Holy hearts of <u>Oneness in God</u>, are now **able** to give **sacrificially** to one another (Matthew 20:26-28 * John 13:12-14) as pleasing their spouse ahead of themselves is not something they <u>have to do</u> but something <u>they long to do</u>. As the servant's heart of God leads them, they also have the same servant's heart they long to lavish from God's love on their spouse and this has become their <u>goal</u> and <u>daily delight</u> <u>they love to do</u>. John 15:12. [25] *"Husbands, love your wives,* ***even as*** *Christ also loved the Church, and gave Himself for it;"* Ephesians 5:25. NIV. All this <u>altruistic love</u> is due to their hearts being filled with so much love from their <u>daily morning worship</u> as they seek the <u>very Core Heart</u> of their Holy God <u>every morning</u> <u>for more</u>. Philippians. 1:11 * John 11:40; **Believe.**

Let worship be the fuel
and the driving force
of every Christian's heart
that motivates their life's passions!

Dad 2:1

The Lord just shared a thought with me. Remember the young man who was only 23 years old and already had 150 women by that young age? However, what the young sinful man did not know until I informed him while he was still working on my job was, the Lord keeps track of all our sins in Heaven in these divine celestial books. Revelation 20:12. And for every sin the <u>unsaved humans</u> do, they must then pay for all of those sins by themselves in Hell forever after they die and are still not saved because they <u>didn't want God</u>. So every time he had his trill with another young woman, <u>he plunged himself all the deeper into Hell</u> and then he will <u>burn all the hotter in his very own fire pit in eternal judgment forever in the molten magma</u> we humans on the surface of Earth call **lava** at roughly 4,000 degrees Fahrenheit. Kind of makes you wonder why they don't want to get saved; doesn't it? But I'm sure they just don't Understand the Spiritual Rules yet. Sorry for the interruption; now let's get back to the <u>Oneness in a Holy marriage</u>.

Once this **base** of love-power is established in your soul (Galatians 6:2) from your morning worship, it just naturally spills out on your spouse <u>first</u> and then everyone else around the love couple <u>second</u> and so they have plenty (John 10:10) to lavish on others and <u>never go dry or empty</u> of God's love. Jesus walking on this Earth showed us Christians this same heavenly <u>Holy secret</u> every time he went up in the mountains to be alone with His Holy Father's love-power to pray and **fill up** (Luke 5:16 * 6:12 * Matthew 14:23 * Mark 6:46 * John 6:15) to reconnect with Heaven and to **drink in** God's Holy love-power <u>for helping others</u>; (2 Corinthians 9:8, 9) something <u>we all should follow and be doing His example</u> for us and our fellow man. Jesus came back down from the mountain, (Ephesians 3:20, 21) or <u>His source</u> of love power and His time with God **soaking up** more of God's love as the Holy Spirit would draw those in need of God's loving touch from Jesus so His Father could receive His much deserved glory. And His children on Earth could receive a touch from their God <u>by this method</u> like the woman with an issue of blood for 12 years stating, [21] "*If I may but touch His garment I shall be whole.*" Matthew 9:21. KJV. Now watch for the transfer of God's Holy love-power. [46] "*But Jesus said, "Someone deliberately touched Me, for I felt healing power **go out** from Me.*" Luke 8:46. NIV. Do you see the **taking in** of God's love-power Jesus gained up in the mountains when He lingered all night with His Father as Jesus **filled up** in His quiet time spent alone with God the Father? And then that same love-power Jesus filled up on will then ***go out*** of the One who is chasing hard after God's holiness?

Do you see that same Holy power transferring **out of Jesus** and then **into** the hurting woman with the issue of blood for 12 years? Is this not what I'm saying the godly couple <u>is to be doing every morning in regular worship</u> as they **fill up** on God's Holy love so they can **pour out** that same Holy love on their own loving spouse <u>first</u>? And then that same Holy love can be **poured out** on the love-empty world <u>second</u> as we just naturally do God's Holy work wherever we go with the love we **received from God** in our morning worship? Galatians 6:10.

This **drinking in** of God's love (James 1:17, 18) and then **pouring out** that same Holy love on others as we, "*draw near to God and He will draw near to you,*" (James 4:8) with our spouse or family <u>first</u> ♩ **so this, is what makes life, divine** ♩ and catches the sinner's attention with God's love, "*By <u>this</u> (love) **everyone will know** that y<u>ou</u> are My disciples, **if** you **love one another**.*" (John 13:35) because their hearts are <u>devoid</u> of God's love. Then the cold world we walk through will receive that same badly needed warm love <u>second</u> like cold people walking in the dark will just naturally seek out the <u>light</u> and the <u>warm</u> campfire when they see it burning nearby. If you were in the dark and saw <u>light</u>, would you walk toward <u>it</u> to be <u>warmed up</u>? This is God's secret today lavishing love and His original master method of spreading the <u>LOVE gospel</u> to a hurting and dying world. Luke 6:45. The power of the Holy Spirit working **in** and **through** His devoted children <u>displaying God's very selfless lavishing nature</u> on each other first is God's goal for the godly couple to replicate more marriages God's loving way. Psalm 72:19. Once the desperate-for-love world sees this level of love-beauty they will desire it with open arms.

Have you ever wondered why even bugs are just naturally drawn to the <u>light</u> whenever they ◉see◉ it? *"For we know that all creation has been <u>groaning</u> as in the <u>pains</u> of childbirth right up to the present time."* Romans 8:22. NLT. The animals suffer right alongside us humans as we suffer through our earthly journey of <u>choosing sin</u>, but Paul reminds us, this world is not our permanent home. <u>1 Peter 2:11</u> * <u>Hebrews 11:13</u>. Awaiting us Christians is a glorious kingdom the God of Love and Light created for us to be His <u>glorious bride</u> where death is defeated, and tears♦♦♦ of sorrow, pain, and grief will all be *"wiped away"*. <u>Revelation 21:4</u>. When we firmly understand our glorious future and lay hold of this celestial promise from God we find in our daily reading of the scriptures, we can then begin to view our current troubles, big or small as light and momentary compared to the far greater eternal weight of glory we will live in come our glory in Heaven. <u>2 Corinthians 4:17</u>.

So when this dry and empty love-starved world sees <u>this level</u> of very desirable love they've been longing for all their lives, will they not question the godly couple they see asking them, "Where did you two get this infectious magnanimous love I ◉see◉ you lavishing on each another? My husband and I would gladly give our right arms to have what you two are displaying daily to each other as we all 👁 see 👁 your <u>true love</u>."

Do you see God's <u>evangelizing **Revival** starting up</u> on this empty love-starved world bound for Hell who lives in this cold, calloused, unsympathetic worldly system that <u>God so badly longs to SAVE</u>? As God is [9] "*. . . not willing that any should perish, but that **all should** come to repentance*." 2 Peter 3:9. ᴋᴊᴠ. Like the people in the dark who see the <u>warm</u> camp fire <u>light</u>, they just naturally walk toward. But you ask, "Why would this spiritually dead world, blinded by Satan's darkness who shuns all goodness ask about this glorious love the godly couple is displaying in plain sight to everyone? Because God's incredible love is highly contagious and His anointing will be on us as we were all created by God to <u>Crave and Want this level of love</u> for ourselves! This is why young girls <u>not loved</u> by their earthly fathers who never have time for them seek out boyfriends for sex because they think sex and love are the same and they're still starving for loving affection they never got from their dads who never had time for them.

Children need Love!
Children spell love T-I-M-E.
Dad 1:3 Wise up dad.

Spend time with your children. The spiritually dead world is empty and devoid of love or **ripe for the picking** for a loving God and His love-filled couples to witness this level of love to this calloused world as most of this world have convinced themselves that God does not even exist. But God is saying today in these evil <u>Communist seeking times</u> we are all living in, its **Harvest Time** and God needs reapers to gather in the love-starved souls by the millions. So this daily worship method gives us Jesus' example to follow (1 Peter 3:7 * 5:1-4 * 1 Corinthians 10:6) in our marriages as we start placing our spouse first (Matthew 25:45) and of greater importance than ourselves. 2 Corinthians 5:15-17. Ask God for a servant's heart and learn to lavish love on others first and watch them stand up and take notice. Put these two words, "Longs" and "Love" in your daily prayer with **deep fervency**. "Oh Lord, help me to have a heart that "Longs" to "Love" others and serve them daily above myself; (1 Peter 4:10, 11) starting with my own spouse. Please Lord change me into Your servant You can work through! I beg You Lord change my selfish nature to reflect Your loving Core Heart of selfless love." Make this your daily prayer and watch the power of God's Love beam through your soul into others around you that sit up and take notice.

Therefore, this contagious Revival of salvation by God's love displayed by His Christian couples can finally begin to start the last Revival before Lord Jesus Raptures us Christians off this corrupted Earth and takes us all home to His Heaven. John 14:3. But every Holy fire that ever started on Earth, began with a simple initiating Holy **SPARK**; are you that willing spark that God can use to begin this last worldwide blaze of salvation across our home land and then proliferate around the entire globe? Will your rewards in Heaven reflect your decision you make today about you begging God in Daily Prayer to have a servant's heart (Isaiah 1:16-20 * Proverbs 19:17) and love your own family first? God is watching and recording your reaction to this question. If today's Christians are not agreeable to this infectious altruistic marriage I described, then this might reveal why we have so many lukewarm marriages that end in painful divorce for lack of love just like the unsaved.

Divorcees say, "I've already tried Love in a marriage and it doesn't work!" But no you haven't! You did the world's idea of a "marriage" where each participant gave only <u>their half and no more</u> in a 50/50 percent of <u>their so-called method</u> of a "marriage". The word marriage means "<u>Oneness</u>" between the two to bring our Lord glory; and a <u>self-centered</u> unequally yoked so-called "marriage", will fail and not bring God any glory at all. 1 Corinthians 10:31. God's main goal in a marriage of Oneness or in anything we do here on Earth for the <u>very few more years we might still have left</u> is to bring God <u>glory</u>! Isaiah 43:<u>7</u> * 1.Corinthians 6:<u>20</u> * Matthew 5:<u>16</u>. But you ask, "Where do I get all this love to lavish on my spouse and others. <u>From God</u> in your <u>morning worship to Him</u>! **Fill Up** like Jesus did in the mountains and then **Pour Out** the love He gives you every morning and then lavish that love on others.

v2 Love longs to lavish,
<u>it's love's grandest desire</u>
and love's greatest reward.
v3 While running in this <u>Race</u>
it's the joy love seeks
written on their spouse's <u>Face</u>.
Dad 4:2, 3

Since Christ also has given Himself up **willingly** ✝ (John 10:18 * John 15:13) for the Church and placed His Bride also as more important than His own Holy Self, <u>so</u> the earthly husband, <u>like Christ</u>, and the wife, <u>like the Church</u>, are to follow His <u>selfless</u> loving sacrificial example of favoring each other ahead of themselves. 1 John 3:16. It is this incredibly high loving level of selfless giving and lavishing their loving hearts upon one another that brings the equally yoked married couples closer to the same level of Oneness the Trinity themselves enjoys! Once God is allowed to have a free hand by the godly couples serving each other, this heavenly overflowing love-power they display to one another is quickly noticed by everyone else around them as they love what they see and then long to try this selfless love in their own marriage to have the same level of joy we have. So because the saved people allow God to work through them, God now has physical ☻eyes☻ to love through and see your married spouse first to love while demonstrating His kindness through you and then seeing the cold-hearted world second He can demonstrate His Love to help the hurting and lonely in their love-empty lives.

Now that you walk in God's love, He also has physical 𝒟 ears 𝒟 as well through this loving couple's willingness to hear the **greatest desires** of their spouse first, and then the cries of this hurting cold world screaming for help that permeates through to the love couple's physical ♥hearts♥ second as we long to help like God. God also has a physical mind to be compassionate with through you **if** we're willing to move in compassion on our spouse first, then overflow the same powerful passion to the lonely empty world second. God will then use our physical ✋hands✋ in which to demonstrate tender gentle loving caresses to our spouse first, then reach out to demonstrate compassionate kindness to the hurting overworked cold-hearted world second! God now has a physical 🛉🛉🛉 body to work His love through as these kinds of Christians are willing to do His loving work to help others while their ♥hearts♥ are now reflecting His love. I'm unraveling the very **<u>Core of God's Heart</u>**, and I'm being very rapacious so you'll understand <u>God's Loving Nature</u> working in a Holy marriage and I hope you'll see His beautiful loving ways of <u>helping other</u> who are blind sitting in the dark not knowing about God's Love. <u>This is God's original design for evangelizing this whole world through this kind of Holy Majestic Marriage or His marriage institution</u>. Listen for God's Holy heart in this verse, [34] *"A new commandment I give you, <u>love one another</u>.* ***As I have loved you****, so you <u>**must** love one another</u>.* [35] *By this <u>all men will know</u> that you are My disciples, <u>**if**</u> you have love one for another."* John 13:34, 35. NIV.

v16 Life is hard and cold like <u>Ice</u>,
but it starts to melt when we're <u>Nice</u>.
v17 Love has a <u>Way</u>, to soften stubborn <u>Clay</u>.
v18 It may take all <u>Day</u>, if you're willing <u>Kay</u>.
v19 It's God's <u>Way</u>, if you can hear me <u>Say</u>?
v20 Don't <u>Delay</u>, or our time will slip <u>Away</u>.

Dad 9:16-20

v4 When you are away from your heart, ♥
a day seems like forever!
v5 But when you are with your heart: ♥
Forever seems like, only a day.
v6 That's the power of <u>Oneness</u>!!!

Dad 4:4-6

Can you see this incredible beauty in a <u>Majestic Marriage</u> and why God says [33] "*. . . seek ye first the kingdom of God* (or the very <u>Core of God's loving Heart</u>) *and His righteousness* (1 Kings 2:<u>3</u>, <u>4</u>) *and* (**then**) *all these thing will be added unto you."*? Matthew 6:33. KJV.

God knows our greatest desire. ". . . *your Father knows what you need before you ask Him.*" Matthew 6:8. So if we please Him by doing His will first, will He not please us and lavish anything and everything on us second? Deuteronomy 7:9-16. God will shower His love upon you (Psalm 85:10-13) for doing His top number one **will** in all this world; evangelizing the lost with His abundant love-power. [11] ". . . *no good thing will He withhold from them that walk uprightly.*" Psalm 84:11. KJV. So you tell me, is this life of endless altruistic love I just described anything you want? This grand loving life style is available to all who seek hard after God's loving Core with a servant's heart (Jeremiah 29:11-13) looking to serve others (Mark 10:45) with no desire to be paid anything in return and always ready to serve their spouse **AS** God Himself would serve if He were physically on this Earth today and married to you. You would then be engulfed in His love and eventually consumed with time in worship with His humble loving nature. Look at mankind's selfish soul and at the same time notice the Holy heart of God in Lord Jesus in these scripture from Luke. [24] "*Now there was also a dispute among them, as to which of them should be considered the greatest.* (all 12 disciples selfishly arguing I am the greatest with a selfish greedy mo first, you last soul) [25] *And Jesus said to them, "The kings of the Gentiles* (unsaved rulers) *exercise lordship* (their earthly authority) *over them,* (or me-first you last heart because they think they are so much better than you, the lowly "worthless" people that the proud hearts step on as they exalt themselves above the lowly worthless little people with their selfish me-first you last souls) *and those* (the proud rulers who think they are so much better) *who exercise authority over them* (the lowly "worthless" little people) *are called 'benefactors.'* [26] *But **not so among you;*** (This is a commandment from Jesus who is hoping His disciples will follow His **altruistic loving ways** and not their own selfish me-first you last worldly way like the world does) *on the contrary,* (or totally opposite) *he who is greatest among you,* (the saved) *let him be* (do it!) *as the younger,* (**Humble** ready to serve others with the you first and me last) *and he who governs* (rulers: like the head of the house or the husbands) as he who serves. **Humble!** Your wife is to be valued more than Philippians 2:3-8) **you** by your daily actions of servanthood and when she sees your selfless actions she will then reflect or echo back on you the very same love you have lavished on her). Learn God's loving Core Heart in daily worship while sitting still, quiet before His Holy throne conversing with God. Psalm 37:7. Learn how God lavishes as He does on us Christians His bride to be in Heaven and study His in-depth level of altruistic love so your wife can reflect back on you what you lavish on her every day. Jesus continues to educate His disciples, ²⁷ *"For who is greater, he who sits at the table, or he who serves? Is it not he who sits at the table? Yet I am among you as the One who serves."* Luke 22:24-27. NKJV. So I say to the Christians today, should we who claim to be godly people not follow God's **Humble example?** Should this not be **all** of our goals as we chase hard after God especially in all of our equally yoked Holy marriages? If we Christians learn to live this selfless way on Earth, loving **as God loves**, will we not have a great life here on Earth for the short time we have left and also in eternal Heaven forever as well? ? Watch what God will do for those who follow this type of selfless love in their marriage: ¹⁷ *"And He said unto him, Well done, thou good and faithful servant: because thou hast been faithful in a very little, have thou authority over **ten cities**."* Luke 19:17. NKJV. You'll be rewarded greatly for your loving actions.

What do you think we will be doing after the Rapture when we Christians are wed to Lord Jesus at the marriage supper of the Lamb? ⁶ *"And I heard as it were the voice of a great multitude,* (all the Christians past and present) *and as the voice of many waters, and as the voice of mighty thunderings, saying, Alleluia: for the Lord God omnipotent* (All-Powerful) *reigneth.* ⁷ *Let us be glad and rejoice, and give honor to Him: for **the marriage of the Lamb** is come, and His wife* (after the Rapture all us Christians in Heaven) *hath made herself ready.* (are you ready to be Lord Jesus' Holy bride?) ⁸ *And to her* (us, the spiritual wife of Lord Jesus) *was granted that she should be arrayed in fine linen, clean and white:* (**Shekinah Glory** reflecting our level of righteous life or our earthly decisions we made) *for the fine linen is the righteousness of saints.* (That "... *fine linen* ..." will reflect our selfless actions we did on Earth. What will your heavenly wedding garment look like; bright white glowing in God's Holy glory because you helped others and loved His hurting people, or dull, dismal, drab, cloudy in color? Because you were selfish like everybody else? Sparkling white bringing you personal glory for our earthly decisions; or dim and dull as everyone will see your wedding garment you are wearing and know your lazy past for an eternity?) ⁹*And he saith unto me,* (John the revelator) *Write, Blessed are they which are called unto the **marriage supper of the Lamb**. And he saith unto me, "These are the true sayings of God."* Revelation 19:6-9. NIV.

To the degree we lay down our personal desires for our <u>Wife</u>, is the same degree of happiness we obtain in our <u>Life</u>!

Dad 4:1
³⁸ "*Give, and it shall be given ...*" Luke 6:38. KJV.

Once you <u>see</u> and <u>experience</u> the beauty of this kind of selfless relationship, like few Christians ever do, you will also want a marriage like theirs for yourself as you seek out a soul mate who thinks the same humble selfless serving way as you do.

Now that we are **filled up** to the height of ecstasy by what we **Pour Out** on each other daily, this same intoxicating love we can no longer contain for our spouse, will then quite fortuitously[11] be splashed on to the love-starved cold hurting world second. This is how the Lord intended us Christians to witness His loving heart to the world through this kind of love-marriage to evangelize the unsaved calloused hard-hearted world. Your selfish nature or greediness for more earthly money might seem very appealing to the cold-hearted souls who knows nothing about God's love, but once they see God's Holy Core Heart in you as you help them wanting nothing in return, will their cold hearts not melt into God's hands as He reshapes it to love others like you're doing?

However, Satan steered mankind early on to take a selfish sinful turn in the Garden of Eden when we humans through Adam obeyed Satan rather than God and so we now have far too many selfish people seeking a 50/50 percent marriage as Satan has taught us to be stingy with God's love he hates. This earthly love-dead☠ so-called "marriage" is where the other spouse is expected to keep up their full half of the marriage as neither of them are willing to go beyond their required 50% half to please their mate who better keep up their 50% half or the flimsy made deal designed by Satan is off and they will quit their 50% half as divorce is now looming!

What kind of half-hearted sad commitment is that? How long can any "marriage" last today with that kind of poor pitiful pledge promise? However when this unsaved world begins to see God's level of joy and breathtaking beauty in this level of altruistic Christian couple who give and lavish 100% on each other all the time demanding absolutely nothing in return as they are not

---

[11] Fortuitously: Happening not on purpose but conveniently by accident.

insecure of any love, those cold souls will long for the very same love we have. Why? Because their hearts <u>are so dry and empty</u> and devoid of love they'll long for and crave the love they now see and badly want. So when the unsaved sees God's intoxicated love demonstrated every day to this love-starved world they will seek out the same precious love we have and display before them. God is seeking those who long to <u>worship Him daily</u> to **<u>fill up</u>** on His abundance of love and then **<u>Pour it Out</u>** on the hurting; <u>is that you?</u> [37] *"Then saith He unto His disciples, The harvest truly is plenteous, but **<u>the labourers are few</u>**;* [38] ***Pray ye** therefore the Lord of the harvest, that He will <u>send forth labourers into His harvest</u>."* Matthew 9:37, 38. KJV. Again I ask you, <u>is this you</u>? Can God count on you to work His love on your <u>spouse first</u> and then spill the abundant extras out on this hurting, love-starved <u>world second</u> as you cannot keep all this love from your daily worship God pours in you to yourself. Ask God to turn you into one of <u>His Lavishers</u>.

v3 <u>As</u> a Potter, making pottery,
and molds a lump of raw clay
into something He needs,
v4 <u>so</u> God is the Master Potter,
who molds me and you
v5 the raw <u>stiff</u> and <u>stubborn</u> clay,
into some useful vessel
or an article He needs,
v6 like a Mighty Man <u>worthy</u> and
capable of loving a Wonderful Woman
God's <u>selfless</u> and <u>sacrificial</u> way.

Dad 11:3-6

This incredible lofty love level is so fulfilling to you and others that God is longing for all marriages to experience it and at the same time witness this infectious selfless love to the lonely God-purpose<u>less</u> people to save and fill their souls like the Christian couple I have just described. But God needs <u>soft pliable humble hearts</u> that are willing vessels in which to work <u>His Loving Core Heart</u> through. So what about you? Are you willing to be that soft loving heart whose personality is intoxicating to everyone around you because they see God's love shinning in you? This duel blessing, one for the married love couple and the other for God and His salvation to the unsaved world, is very contagious to other marriages and equally powerful for evangelistic purposes! However, some will see this level of longing love and choose to be jealous, envious and even spiteful in their response rather than humble and hungry to copy this level of love they see and truly need. The sacrificial love couple is what God is hoping the <u>love thirst</u>y empty world will notice in this kind of holy matrimony He's asking you to display before the cold world to see and want.

Then God is hoping the world will desire to <u>reproduce</u> what they see in the altruistic love couple. Therefore, <u>they will replicate similar selfless Majestic Marriages</u> to the unsaved and <u>duplicate</u> God's grand love across the land the **way God originally planned it** to take hold bringing other unsaved people to saving grace and create their own selfless breathtaking Majestic Marriage as it then spreads out like wild fire across the face of this whole Earth. God only needs <u>a willing **spark**</u> in you to start setting the whole world ablaze with His greatest weapon to win this world; <u>Love</u>. Then every marriage engulfed in His Holy fire with this kind of selfless serving love Oneness we're all living before the cold world will be such a stark different to their 50/50 marriage, that <u>the lion's share</u>

of the world will be hungry to join God's Majestic Marriage. <u>Are you that willing **Spark**</u> that God can count on to start this whole <u>Worldwide Revival</u> as you start placing your God first in daily worship and then pouring out on your spouse second while finally naturally witnessing to everyone everywhere you go to save them?

"Delight yourself in the Lord and He will give you the desires of your heart."
Psalm 37:4

V10 The speed of the leader, determines the rate of the pack!

King David conquered Goliath and is mentioned in the O. T. more than anyone.

V11 Who's leading your family  a **King** or a **Fool** ?

The love of **King** Lord Jesus or Satan and his band of following **Fools**

V12 "Curses Chase the Wicked!

"The Lord's curse is on the house of the wicked." Proverbs 3:33a
* Deuteronomy 31:17

V13 While Blessings Chase the Righteous!

"God blesses the home of the righteous." Proverbs 3:33b * Psalm 84:11

V14 So . . . . What's Chasing You?"

✝ **?** ☠

Halos? or Horns?

Dad 4:10-14

This is also what God has in store for everyone seeking a soulmate _if they can see_ this kind of infectious beauty I'm elaborating on and if they are _willing_ to **chase hard** after it _every_ _morning_ _with a Whole Heart for God_. **IF** you will p_lace God first_ in your life, (Matthew 6:33) and your spouse second ahead of yourself, (Ephesians 5:25) you can experience this type of Holy Majestic Matrimony and the overwhelming joy from Heaven that comes with it. Yes there is work involved, but anything worth having is worth the work to get it; just like when you go to work and get paid at the end of the week and this lofty goal of incredible love I believe is worth all the sacrificing work to receive it. Romans 8:18. What do you think? Matthew 6:20, 21. Worship God every morning.

Thus, you also will infect the world around you with more of the same selfless intoxicating love-Oneness God displays through your own love-filled heart and Majestic Marriage! Like having Jesus multiplied ten million times! What might that do to change this "_crooked and depraved generation?_" Philippians 2:15. NIV. Sound like anything you want to participate in? But you must first **pay the price** as _real_ salvation is required first; remember Andy and the prophet and how he put his _talking_ faith into _walking working_ faith. Then make our God Lord Jesus truly Lord of your life second where everything we do _revolves around pleasing Him_. Eph. 5:10. So, it is essential that you fill up on the _Source of Love first_; Lord Jesus and His holiness from Heaven and then the joy unspeakable _that will surely come_ to all _who chase hard_ after God with _all their heart_! Jeremiah 29:13. Do you understand the Holy order and are you aware of the _very short time_ we Christians have left before we all get Raptured up to Heaven? After you seek God _first,_ He will _then_ see your willing to serve heart and deep desire to please Him and **then** He'll find you your soulmate to match your level of selfless love you are already displaying. And do you think the price you must pay to God first is worth all the work to get this incredible love-prize that you will cherish and treasure forever even into eternal Heaven? But consider this: A six of Spades gets another six of Spades and a Queen of Hearts gets her King's Heart for God. Now don't forget, your source of love-power is the God of Love. 1 John 4:8. So willing servant, fine your knees in prayer daily and make them work for you as you start Begging and Pleading every day to your Holy Father of Love that you need to have kindness in your soul like Lord Jesus had for the people He loved on Earth and willingly laid down His life for. John 10:17, 18. Plead with your heavenly Father that you **must have** the patience of Job (Psalm 46:10 37:7) and please Lord help me **not to complain about everything!** Numbers 11:1 * 14:27-29 * Philippians 2:14. Help me Father not to think it strange concerning the fiery trials which You are testing me with as though some strange thing were happening to me. 1 Peter 4:12. May I pass your test Lord You are testing me with daily, (Genesis 22:9-12 * Exodus 15:25) with flying colors and help me be the godly servant You need me to be to love the unlovable people starting with my own spouse first.

Help me Lord to rejoice, inasmuch as I am a partaker of Christ's sufferings; that I am counted worthy to suffer with Him, (Acts 5:41) and that when His glory shall be revealed, (Rapture) I will be glad with the other Christian servants with exceeding great joy at Your coming Lord. Luke 6:23 * Revelation 19:7 * 22:12 * Hebrews 9:28. And Father please **change my selfish nature** (Philippians 2:3-5 * 1 Corinthians 10:24 * 3:18 * Acts 10:24 * Mark 8:34) to emulate your altruistic sweet loving nature as I do not want to be my old selfish nature anymore. And Lord please take all my bad habits away so I can love the world as You already do. Father I **must have** this new loving nature in my heart and in my life and be a part of Your Holy laborers to reap in the heavenly harvest before we Christian all go up home in this Rapture that is coming very soon as we real Christians will be taken up to Your glorious Heaven.

Father I am chasing **HARD** after this kind of Majestic Marriage of Oneness and I **must have** it! Cry to your heavenly Father and tell Him how you're not going to stop Begging and Pleading until He changes your selfish nature into His loving sweet altruistic ways! Genesis 32:24-28. *"O God of my life, I'm lovesick for You in this weary wilderness. I thirst with the deepest longings to love You more, with cravings in my heart that can't be described. Such yearning grips my soul for You, my God! I'm energized every time I enter your heavenly sanctuary to seek more of Your power and **drink in** more of Your glory. For your tender mercies mean more to me than life itself. How I love and praise You, God! Daily I will worship You passionately and with all my heart. My arms will wave to You like banners of praise."* Psalm 63:1-4. TPT. Beg and Plead with all your heart telling this God of Love what you truly want and don't forget to add the ♦tears♦♦♦♦♦♦ of fervency you learned about in Our Prayers in Golden Bowls to speed up your new loving results that your spouse will absolutely love. It's like God told me 18 years ago . . .

"If you want a Queen of Hearts, ♥ you must first stop being the Six of Spades." ♠
Dad 2:10

The Magic of Prayer

But there's a <u>secret</u> in **HOW** to change your old ways that you should know. So you go to prayer and ask God to change your old selfish ways and Lord help me not to complain about everything and help me not to be so impatient with people and all the trials that come my way every day. Now that God heard your prayer, do you really think He has a <u>magic wand</u> and surly God will just wave His magic wand over the serious praying Christian and say magic words like Abracadabra Presto Change-o you're suddenly changed into the very thing you have been asking Him for like some Genie and the Magic Lamp you saw on a Disney movie? Well I'm sorry to have to tell you Hopeful Heart; prayer doesn't work like that at all. God wants you to be <u>very involved</u> in your new heart of change and your new kind nature <u>you say you want</u>. Talking is easy as it does not require much effort on your part; but putting your easy to say words into much harder to **DO** <u>actions</u> requires a lot of <u>death</u> on your part to obtain your goal. Not that you have the power within your own strength to change your own sinful nature by your own power or ability, but we all must rely on our all-powerful God to transform our old sinful nature. Like God's Word says, *"This is the Word of the LORD to Zerubbabel: <u>Not by</u> <u>might</u>, nor by <u>power</u>, but <u>by My Spirit</u>, says the LORD of hosts"* Zechariah 4:6, ESV. Both in the Old and New Testament, God's people are called to <u>shine the light</u> of God's glory into all the world. (Isaiah 60:1–3 * Matthew 5:14–16). It is the great commission of every believer. Matthew 28:19–20. Just as Zerubbabel would need to depend on the Spirit of the Lord to accomplish the work he needed to do, so do Christians today <u>need to depend on God's Holy Spirit</u>

to help them make godly changes in their lives so they can shine the light of God's love to a hurting and love-starved world. God's people have no ability in themselves to shine the light of God's truth to those walking in darkness so the Holy Spirit must do the work in us willing to pray with all our hearts, and die to our old sin nature as much as we can on our own knowing we still need God to do the Holy work we are not able to do on our own for true change to occur. We Christians may be saved, but we are still sinners saved by God's grace and led by the Holy Spirit **IF** we yield to Him. So if you find your knees and plead in prayer and beg God to transform your old worldly sinful character daily **with** your **struggling effort** to die to your old bad habits, God will see your true trying ways to change and then He will do the Holy work that He knows you cannot complete on your own. But rest assured, your **daily dying efforts are required** if your sinful ways are to be change. So when you see these many Opportunities in that area you have ask God to change in your old nature, recognize this is your answer to prayer and **try to die to it** with all your heart.

So as you get these multiple opportunities to change your old ways, and we all hate to die to our old fleshly nature, you **MUST** participate in the **Dying Process** to your old sin nature suffering like Christ suffered and died as He did on the old rugged cross. Look what the scriptures tell us. [13] "*But **rejoice** that you participate in the sufferings of Christ,* (Acts 5:41) *so that you may be overjoyed when His glory is revealed."* 1 Peter 4:13. NIV. If we want to share in Heaven's glory, we **must** participate in His sufferings; understand? This is what separates the real men from the fake pretenders that only want change if there's **no work** involved. Remember, God can only bless what you **do**. So do a little, and change a little. Do a lot, and God will change you a lot as you die.

A Parable between the Sun ☀ and the Moon ☾

A parable is an earthly story you do know containing a heavenly truth you don't know as Jesus is teaching you about Heaven and His Holy ways so you'll know how to change your ways and then be blessed. So listen to this homemade parable for deeper understanding. The Husband Parallels the Sun: Since God commands the man to be the head of the house; it is his duty to initiate or seek out the Holy source, God, for wisdom and love. Therefore, As the Sun beams out sunlight, so the husband beams out God's wisdom from His Holy Word to fill his wife up first and then his children second as [35] *"Wisdom is vindicated by all her children."* Luke 7:35. As the Sun also **initiates** heat to the whole Earth enabling all the people to live in warmth, **so** the husband chases hard after God to get His love through obedience and daily worship to fill his wife's heart with love first that spills over to their children second who follows the parent's love for obedience. This heavenly method creates blessings from God to witness to the sinful world true happiness can be yours if you follow God's ways.

Joy is not the absence of suffering,
but the presence of God.
Find a heart filled with obedience,
and you'll actually find Joy in Dying.
Then experience Joy Unspeakable
that floods and fills your Obedient
Happy Soul for an Eternity.

Dad 4:7

The Wife Mimics the Moon ☾

Now the Moon's job having no light of its own in this powerful parable is to reflect what the Sun gives it. So the wife's job is to **reflect** like a **mirror** all that her husband gives her. If he speaks love, his wife will reflect back to him love. If he speaks negative words or sin, she will reflect negatively right back to him the very sin he spoke. So good love reflects back good love. Bad attitude or sin returns the same bad attitude or sin right back at him so he's always receiving what he's handing out <u>in normal</u> **saved** <u>conditions,</u> as demons won't cooperate with God's obedience. So, husbands who worship daily, beam out <u>God</u>'s love like a flashlight shines light from <u>its source</u> the <u>battery</u>. God designed wives to typically reflect back exactly what their husbands do like mirrors reflects back exactly what is looking at it. **If** they both follow this heavenly pattern God has designed from the beginning of time, their <u>natural love</u> they pass <u>back and forth</u> to bolster up each other will witness to this world with over whelming love and then bring God the glory He's seeking through this love-power evangelism the love couple is displaying to all. That's when the love couple will feel like they're in Heaven and they will also be just naturally witnessing through their normal life to everyone! It works by the Husband <u>first</u> <u>chasing hard after God</u> through his morning worship <u>with a whole heart</u> to God and then initiating God's sacrificial love to his wife <u>second</u>. She then **reflects** all he gives her <u>adding her own selfless love she got from God</u> in her worship time to this potent powerful mix sending it right back to her Husband. So like a reciprocating ( ) tennis match of constant back and forth, the selfless lavishing love the husband initially got from God is endlessly passed back and forth between them both building up their marriage daily into a life of happiness that witnesses to all.

If this process is done every day, the love-couple is in utter ecstasy and the honeymoon **NEVER** has to end as there is always a fresh supply of love extracted from God's Holy heart daily! The endless love permeating between them both will constantly build up their love-Oneness and flood any troubles or pressures the enemy can throw at the Love-Soaked Couple. So as soon as a hindrance occurs, this Love-Marinated Couple consumes that new problem quickly because of their abundant love they're constantly living in while that trouble never stand for long as love conquers all in record time. Since both their love-needs are more than met, they don't Demand anything anymore as **selfishness**, the root of every sin, is now a thing of the past. Nor do they major on the miner issues in a pedantic way letting little unimportant things go making them easy to get along with as they're now filled with God's love to the max overflowing with love to hand out to others.

So I ask you, what is there to argue about? Here you are swimming neck deep in God's love every day and you're going to strike up an argument because he left a few hairs in the sink? When you are that engulfed in love, you can overlook just about anything and happiness rules over your life in great abundance.

The best leader for you, is the one who knows how to follow Jesus with a whole heart!
Dad 5:3

So what problem can arise that you are willing to toss this lofty level of love aside for like some old worthless bubble gum wrapper having no value at all to get him to clean up those pesky hairs in the sink? Even if he or she does something big like wrecks the car, you both still have this abundant love to swim in while it's being repaired. So **if** you focus on eternal love in Heaven and keep temporary sinful Earth in its proper place, your Majestic Marriage will be like superman totally impervious to sadness, selfishness, petty silly stupid arguments about whose turn it is to bath up the dog or, "I made the bed last time so it's your turn to do it!" These trivial ten cent quarrels that happen with other worldly flesh-driven so-called 50/50 present "marriages" are a distant memory from years gone by that you saw in the world's married couples that don't ever happen in your new Majestic Marriage. Why, because every day you and your Love receive a fresh supply of lavishing love from God Almighty to live on. So those issues are minimized and troubles dissolve quickly as they are totally consumed because you have this incredible love-base to live on that makes you happy that carries you both through just about anything! Philippians 4:13.

This was the original plan Adam and Eve were supposed to live like but as always Satan **Disrupts** and **Stops** what good God is doing that make us all happy. That lavishing love plan God started out doing, the dark prince was jealous of as he wanted to be the center of attention receiving all the glory for himself. So Satan hindered Oneness in the Garden of Eden and ours today as well. If Adam and Eve had not been scammed into disobedience and chose sin first, God's original plan would have spread across the whole face of the Earth and we would all be globally populated today with these selfless love-couples displaying God's most powerful weapon to this world; Love! And so our enemy today still longs to **Disrupt** and **Stop** this original evangelizing power from taking root as he replaced it with our Greedy Selfish me-first you-last sin-chasing soul. Now there's always a doubter who says, how do you know God's willing to do this Majestic Marriage? Look to the scriptures; [10] *"The thief* (Satan) *comes only to steal, kill and destroy. But I came that they may have __life__ and have it __more abundantly__."* John 10:10. KJV. So do you want **life** and **love more abundantly** or is mediocrity and daily petty silly arguing good enough for you?

V11 Like a game of chess God waits, sometimes for years!
V12 Why so long?
Because it's still your move!
Dad 2:11, 12

V13 Isn't it nice to find out, when we finally do make our move years later, we discover, God's on both sides of the same chess board helping us on our side too!
Dad 2:13

The Lord just spoke another word to me as I am making corrections on my book. Or is it His book? Hmmm, I wonder? Anyway, the Lord would like to share a word for all the people with troubled marriages who need His help. It's entitled . . .

Stan the Man Beware of Dan

Listen, Stan: God here. I have a helpful word for you. Proverbs 5:1, 2. Do you know that what you give your wife is what she'll offer right back to you? If you give her a smile, she'll smile back at you. If you give her a nasty attitude, she'll give that very same nasty attitude right back in your face. To the degree you <u>love</u> or <u>abuse</u> your own wife, Stan, is the same degree I designed her to <u>reflect</u> what you give right back on you <u>So you Get what you Give</u>.

So lend Me your ears Stan and I'll teach you a lesson you can use to fix your failing troubled marriage, and to make your dying romance jump into overdrive with happiness. I designed women to be like <u>Mirrors</u> reflecting their husband's leadings, and I designed men like <u>Flashlights</u> beaming God's love and <u>Setting the Pace</u> in a Holy Majestic Marriage of love as every husband should shine My love and that will <u>sets the mood</u> of romance in your marriage Stan! Therefore, what you shine, Stan, is what your wife will surely reflect back on you. She will match you step for step, word for word, attitude for attitude, and kindness for kindness. So, Stan, what kind of a wife do you like? **Sweet or bitter**?

Loving or nasty? Remember Stan, you're the one <u>Setting the Pace</u> in your marriage as your wife and children are watching your every move and <u>stand ready to reflect your lead</u>! Whatever you shine, Stan, your wife will quickly reflect back on you like a clean Mirror beaming Sunlight! But I've heard you say before Stan, "My wife never speaks anything nice to me! She's never kind or friendly! All she ever does is buy new clothes and eat comfort foods and gets fat! I tell you God I need a new wife!"

I agree with you Stan; you do need a new wife. But it's up to you to <u>build</u> and <u>create</u> this new wife you want. Let me share another hidden secret with you, Stan. The reason your wife buys new clothes all the time is so she'll feel good about herself. Lonely women buy clothes to <u>fill the empty void</u> in their lonely hearts because "<u>someone</u>" is not loving or even talking sweetly to them anymore; you know what I mean, Stan? Wives sometimes also eat comfort <u>foods</u> because they're <u>trying to fill the empty void</u> (Genesis 3:7) <u>where love once was</u> in their lonely empty hearts because "**someone**" is not sweet-talking them or spending any real quality time with them anymore. Do you know who that might be Stan? So, Stan, the size of your fat wife might very well depict the size of her lonely <u>loveless</u> empty heart. Now Stan if only there were "**someone**", to talk sweetly to her and start filling up her <u>lonely empty heart</u>; her NEED for buying new clothes and eating satisfying fat comfort foods might quickly diminish. Am I reaching you, Stan? You know what I mean; jellybean. I made all husbands to be the initiators in a marriage and so what you <u>GIVE</u> to your wife or <u>withhold</u> from her daily is what you will surely get in return, Stan. So the good news is Stan, <u>you're in charge</u>! You can have a new sweet wife just as soon as you want her to show up.

One last thought Stan, before we end today's lesson. Proverbs 5:7. If you haven't given your wife any kind or loving words in quite some time, she might be tempted to just hoard your new kind sweet loving spirit for quite a long while never giving you anything or returning any of your kindness back on you! But don't stop Stan. She might stock-pile your NEW sweet loving nature for months before she <u>finally fills up</u> and learns you are really for real; and she can now trust you that this new love you're now giving her is really here to stay. So keep chasing her heart, Stan. When she can't receive any more of your loving sweet kindness and her heart is full to overflowing, she will **THEN** have to give all that overflowing sweetness you've been giving her to "**someone**"! Remember, Stan, your wife is still a Mirror, and you are still a Flashlight! She will always reflect what you shine at her. Therefore, your future is grand, Stan. So now Stan, I give you a new commandment, "**Go For It**!" But if you do not, consider this hard retaliation rule for love empty hearts Stan. If "**someone**" else is kind and sweet to her only lonely empty love-starved heart first, she might just give her lonely empty hungry-for-love heart to that "**someone**". Do you understand, Stan? Then, Stan, her new man, might just be, sweet talking Dan?

"*Husbands love your wives . . .*"
Ephesians 5:25

Prayer is the key that unlocks every resource in Heaven so God's power can be unleashed on our planet we humans are to manage for God Almighty in righteousness (Psalm 115:16 * 9:8) that pushes back the fallen angels or demons evil spirits as the Kingdom of Darkness will then lose more ground. So have you prayed today? Start pushing the darkness back so God's light can rule our world. "Father, I come before your Holy throne in the name of Jesus to repent first and then war against the forces of evil while fighting on my knees against . . .

Now that I've got you started, continue speaking against our enemy to bring about the Last Revival of God before we leave.

Endless Spiritual Battles to
<u>Disrupt</u> **or** <u>Stop</u> **our Connection**

Have you noticed every time God points me toward Kay, the enemy tries to <u>Disrupt</u> or <u>Stop</u> me? If God encourages me to write a book of Oneness to connect with Kay the furnace first mysteriously breaks down the same day; and not just once, but after four days of delay and I forget all about writing the book and then God reminds me a second time, it happens again for another four day before it could be fixed to <u>Disrupt</u> my thinking and <u>Stop</u> this book from even being started. Then the Lord encourages me to start a third time and I finally do, but then the hot water heater suddenly doesn't work for four to five more days to steer my attention away from continuing this book I just got started. Then the hot water heater starts working all on its own and I haven't had a problem with it since; how mysterious is that? Ever since I started writing this book to reconnect with the lady I lost back 15 years ago it's been one weird phenomenon right after the other. One day while writing this book my computer shut down and would not even start; but I got passed that problem with the Lord's help. Another day the dark army had some oversea hacker lock up my computer leaving me a phone number to call and then wouldn't let me use my own computer unless I paid him several hundreds of dollars. That sly guy or slick demon never got a dime!

But that's beside the point; isn't it obvious the enemy doesn't want this book written? But what is the reason; just to keep two people from getting together? Don't men and women get together all the time? Yet the enemy is trying unusually hard to keep us apart like he did repeatedly 15 years ago? Everyone has lost power before as we've all sat in the dark sometimes for hours just waiting for the lights to come back on. But in all my years I've never sat in the dark for 24 hours with no heat wearing four sets of clothes to stay warm and no hot water for a shower as well. I tell you I felt like a troglodyte; but then I've always been a bit of a Luddite[12] anyway. But always remember . . .

V16 Satan may attack us to keep us <u>Low</u>,
yet all this <u>Woe</u>, helps make us a <u>Pro</u>.
V17 Trials are good, they help us <u>Grow</u>,
they teach us all what we need to <u>Know</u>.
V18 Trouble from <u>Below</u>, may seem like a <u>Foe</u>,
but once in Heaven, you'll surely <u>Glow</u>.
V19 Jesus is our best <u>Friend</u>, even to the <u>End</u>.
V20 Converting bad to good is His secret <u>Blend</u>.

Dad 10:16-20 / Genesis **50:20**

A fault finding man stated to Thomas Edison, "You failed 10,000 times trying to discover how to make a lightbulb." Thomas Edison replied, "I have not failed, I just found 10,000 ways that won't work" before he took us all out of darkness and into the modern world of lights. Failure is a big part of life that may happen 10,000 times that builds our strong character like it did in my life. I've probably made more mistakes than any man alive, yet God applauds the fact that I just keep right on trying to win to please Him. Even Paul said, ". . . *I am a nobody.*" 2 Corinthians 12:11. ESV. <u>Do you now understand the secret perseverance to success</u>?

So without all this Pain, how can we Gain?
Dad 11:1

---

[12] Luddite: Someone who is not very tech savvy. Not educated on technology.

Now keep in mind prior to starting this book none of these strange phenomenon ever happened before; but once God gave me the green light to write this book thus reconnect to Kay, it was one unusual sabotage right after the other. So are these phenomenons just standard life experiences that everyone receives in their lives at some point, or are there dark angels afoot trying to **Disrupt** or **Stop** our merging and **Stop** or **Disrupt** our love Oneness from happening like they did back on the cruise ship 15 years ago? But why go to all this trouble to keep these two praying Christians apart? Don't even Christians get married all the time? Does the Lord have something specially planned for us that goes way beyond just a simple marriage? Can the dark angels see something in the spirit realm that tips them off like a Worldwide Revival and that's why all this unusual negative activity? I believe God does have a special plan that goes way beyond a simple wedding.

Back in 2007 the enemy tried to Disrupt or Stop me when I was sitting down in my dad's man cave and the Lord said, "What about her?" But then the enemy started casting doubts in my mind at that moment as usual when God speaks of anything good and so then my next thoughts were, "No way. Why would someone that beautiful want anything to do with an average nobody like me? I'm not famous; . . . . . No, . . . I'll just end up getting my heart broke again." So once again the enemy Disrupted or Stopped whatever the Lord was doing and anything God starts, the enemy kept us from getting together and today it's the same thing all over.

Then walking upstairs after the lesson with Kay I got a thought in my head as God encouraged me again about seeing Kay, and this time with a long list of rebuking encouraging thoughts. Then the enemy attacked again and brought up all the financial pressures and convinced me I can't go for lack of money and winter bills or taxes in the Spring I don't yet have money for. But God counters that attack from Satan by giving me the largest job I ever had in my entire life to keep me going in His planned direction to see some woman who I don't even know and in so doing answered our many years of prayers for a loving spouse.

Then it was all that paper work I don't know how to do and I had no time to get it done by normal snail mail; but then God helps me with that faster than normal strategy and shows me how to save time by driving to New Castle and paying extra to get my passport quicker to beat the 90 day usual return. Then the enemy tries to convince me the future wife God is sending me down to see, already has a boyfriend through her video when I saw Kay supposedly kissing that other man who turned out to be a hired prop for her video. But God sent my daughter who rarely comes over to see me <u>the very next day</u> and quenches that lie from the enemy to keep me going in the same God appointed direction.

Do you see the endless back and forth battle between halos and horns as God's kingdom is going out of His way to overpower the dark enemy who continually tries to thwart me at every turn as God just continues to steer me down to Fort Lauderdale to see Kay on a cruise liner ship? And at the same time the kingdom of darkness is doing everything it can to **Disrupt** or **Stop** us from connecting our hearts again and again by one slick trick after the other? But then the airline ticket stopped me cold so I can't go until the only family member who knows how to properly secure an airline ticket comes over **the very next day** at just the right time and despite the tight time-window to get this ticket and our past hard political words between Louis and I, he is all too glad to help me and he only comes 3,000 miles from California across the country <u>once every two years</u>; so how rare is that move from God?

So I have to ask myself, "If the enemy is trying this hard to **Disrupt** or **Stop** us from being together and the kingdom of God is trying this hard to make this connection happen through multiple miracles one after the other, then what plan is God trying to accomplish, and what is the dark kingdom trying to prevent? Just a simple Christian marriage? Or is there something God wants to do through us after we wed that they don't like? [28] *"And we know that all things work together for good to them that love God, to them who are the called according to His purpose."* Romans 8:28. KJV. [11] *"For I know the plans I have for you,"* *declares the LORD,* *"plans to prosper you and not to harm you, plans to give you hope and a future."* Jeramiah 29:11. NIV. [20] *"You intended to harm me, but God intended it for good to accomplish what is now being done, the saving of many lives."* Genesis 50:20. NIV. You mean like an End Time Revival that might save ". . . *many lives.*" through a Majestic Marriage before the Rapture occurs that's coming soon? Hmmm . . .

Yes the enemy tried to Disrupt and Stop me every step of the way back then in 2007 from ever meeting Kay as he tried to crush my thinking with his ongoing intimidation of Kay's outstanding good looks and the fear that followed and Stopped our connection even while writing this book in 2022 and into 2023 as well. There was another major surprise computer problem that erased the whole book and with my sad tech ability I almost couldn't get it back at all. That satanic move almost stopped this book from being completed as well. From the very beginning with the furnace not working twice and then the hot water tank not working for days and even stopping the computer itself that would not even turn on or the hacker who locked up my computer so I could not finish the book at all. Or the power going out for 24 hours which never happened before in my entire life. All of this within a few months while I'm working on this book to meet you Kay when I got that line while watching a romantic movie on TV, "**My heart is saying that it's time again**". So I have to ask myself, why is all this spiritual energy being spent on stopping this one Christian man from connecting to this one Christian woman? So Kay, you tell me, what do you **see** after hearing my account in 2007 and today? But keep in mind . . .

v14 **The same Sun that hardens clay can also soften butter.**
v15**The cold souls see trailer trash**
Matthew 6:22 * 13:13 * Luke 10:24.

but through the Lord's ☻ eyes ☻ some see truckloads of true treasure.
Dad 2:14, 15 / 2 Corinthians 2:16

So Kay tell me, <u>what do you **see** in all this unusual spiritual activity</u>? At first God stirred me up to write this book by speaking that romantic 1986 song **On My Own**. But after the enemy's many diversions I was on the verge of dismissing this whole book

idea <u>or Love Letter</u> ✉ <u>depending on who's reading it</u> while the enemy gave me a discouraging thought, "Don't bother with this book it won't work out you'll just lose all your years of saved up money with their startup cost." So for days enduring the time the furnace did not work and then the hot water tank distractions I decided against writing this book at all as I thought I will probably just lose all my saved up money on their startup cost. That's when the Lord stirred me up again with a **second song** to motivate me to continue with this idea to write this book again.

So I went to You Tube to look up that <u>second song</u> and accidently stumbled on to a <u>third song</u> that really spoke to my situation with you Kay 15 years ago and that motivation from God prompted me <u>to finally write this book again</u> for the final time. So here's how it all happened: That night when I turned on the TV I saw an old odd song I never heard before from an old movie. I found out later after going on You Tube and punching in those lyrics it was called, Eee-O Eleven. Some of those unusual lyrics caught my attention about my short experiences I had on those five <u>ships</u> we were both on as we never joined and <u>my dream for the Majestic Marriage went dead</u>. "Show me a man <u>without a dream</u>, and I'll show you a man that's <u>dead; real dead</u>. Once I had me <u>a dream</u>, but that dream <u>got kicked in the head. Dream dead</u>." I couldn't help but think how those song lyrics and my original dream of the Majestic Marriage at age nine <u>got kicked in the head</u> and how God spoke those exact lyrics I longed for and then that lifetime dream of mine was dead; <u>Dream dead</u>." That original <u>dream of a Majestic Marriage</u> started, but after the five trips of me going down to see you Kay, that <u>Majestic Dream Marriage</u> went **dead** because I could not get released from the enemy's spiritual **PRISON** to <u>step out in faith</u> and connect with you. However, God knows us very well and He can work through <u>what moves us</u>; like for me, music moves my heart and that's why I put Zephaniah 3:17 at the beginning of that first song **On My Own**. So when I went to look up this odd old song I never heard before, Eee-O Eleven on You Tube, the Lord took me in a different direction that same night before I wrote anything and this time God's motivation to write this book came to me in the form of another new song <u>I never heard before</u> by Lily Meola's original song "<u>Daydream</u>" on America's got Talent.

But the strange thing about that is, I never watch America's got Talent; **ever**! My sister Lynn watches it, lots of other people must be watching it or it wouldn't be so popular, but I've never decided to actually watch it myself. Yet there's a God in Heaven who will move Heaven and Earth to make miracles happen 20 times a day if He needs to get something through to His servants like <u>us</u>. So again quite serendipitously I stumbled on to this final third song <u>when I was ready to quit the whole book writing project</u> and so I want to show you Kay what I found on You Tube. So while I was looking up that second song, Eee-O Eleven, it motivated me to write ✍ this book. But those lyrics from Lily Meola who wrote and sang her own song <u>Daydream</u> spoke deeper into my heart about this whole 15 yearlong saga, <u>Quest for a Queen rebirth</u> that started back on 11-11-2022.

On You Tube I remember seeing Lily Meola on stage who described the theme to her song and said how it all came about. We start out as young children growing up <u>who have great faith</u> believing we will become an astronaut and go to the moon, or be a famous rock star singer and tour the world. But after we're in our teens we're told by our well-meaning parents we need to **stop dreaming** and just get a job and start being responsible. So we **give up** our grandest Daydream so we can wait on tables and make minimum wage and have some ratty apartment. But she felt this was wrong and we should never give up on our <u>God directed Daydreams</u> but <u>pursue them to their conclusion</u>. After all, where would you be Kay if you gave up on your dream of singing and did not step out in faith to sing as God had designed you to do with the grand gift He gave you? Lily said, how many people give up their Daydreams God gave them to wait on table and squeak out a sad minimum wage insistence rather than <u>living God's real Daydream</u>.

Now in this entire book I have spoken of a mysterious singer/teacher lady that I have kept anonymous out of respect with the pseudonym name of "Kay". And so now I am asking you, "Kay", listen to this song and then you tell me at this time in your life, "What do you want to do?" <u>P</u>laying it Saf<u>e</u>, <u>G</u>uarding your Hear<u>t</u> and remain single for the little bit of time we both have left; (James 4:14 * Psalm 39:4b); or <u>T</u>ake Your Heart Off the Shel<u>f</u>, plug it in to real love, and start living your Daydream to see if there's any romance still left in you that your endorphins[13] might really enjoy.

v8 An over flux of endorphin emotions all occurring in the same place.

---

[13]Endorphins: \-en-ˈdòr-fins\ Are chemical hormones in the Pituitary Gland located in the brain or a type of neurotransmitters that are released into the body when we feel pain causing an analgesic or euphoric effect when threatened with extreme pain. God's natural painkiller is 200 times more potent than morphine. (Science News). There are more than 20 different types of endorphins as the more we study God the more amazing we see He really is. So if we are stressed God has made them to be a comfort messenger to our bodies to relieve and reduce that stressful moment. They can even improve our mood during meaningful touch or if our emotions are deeply touched by <u>that certain someone</u> giving you that floating on air effect or a soothing peaceful and secure sense of well-being or a very happy feeling telling that person <u>they are now **in love**</u>. How can you release these pleasure endorphins? One way is by exercising to reduce stress by moving the blood faster and so remove light stress pains; I do this when I go to the gym six days a week. Also eating comfort foods brings positive thoughts to our minds making us happy <u>for the moment</u>. Or getting a positive message like, "I love you." from someone you love releasing these endorphins as well. Even having sex can increase these pleasure endorphins in your body not to be confused with Oxytocin and Dopamine often called the happy hormones that is released during an orgasm and if done correctly can create feelings of euphoria and ecstasy and finally followed by relaxation and deep satisfying peace.

v9 Now what's the technical term for that?
Oh yeah, now I remember,

Love.

Dad 4:8, 9

by Lily Meola
Some of her lyrics are . . .

♩ Darlin', don't quit your daydream
It's your life that you're making
It ain't big enough
if it doesn't <u>scare the H--- out of you</u>.
If it makes you <u>nervous</u>
It's probably <u>worth it</u>
Why save it for sleep
when <u>you could be living your daydream?</u> ♩

So Kay, should we step out of our doubt and start walking in Faith and then begin <u>living **our**</u> Daydream? It's <u>our</u> life that we're making. Are you scared or excited? Remember: It ain't big enough **if it doesn't <u>scare the H--- out of you</u>.** If it makes you <u>nervous</u> it's probably <u>worth it</u>. Why save it for sleep when <u>you could be living your Daydream?</u>

V15 <u>Join me K</u>ay; no regrets.
<u>D</u>on't sit the dance ou<u>t</u>!

*"My lover spoke and said to me, 'Arise my darling, my beautiful one, and **come with me**."* Song of Solomon 2:10. NIV

V16 Listen to the Lord's leadings
and <u>Y</u>ou'll get the most of a<u>ll</u>.
V17 Consider your Daydream.
Your Dream <u>Team</u>.
V18 Your long sought after <u>love</u>
that God sent you from <u>above</u>.

Dad 4:15-18

". . . show me your face, let me hear your voice; for y<u>our voice is sweet and your face is lovely</u>." Song of Solomon 2:14b. NIV.

But remember:

V5 Hearing from God is <u>Par</u>
God can't steer a parked <u>Car</u>!
V6 Step out of your <u>loneliness</u>.
Don't doubt, or you'll miss love to <u>excess</u>.
Consider your future of a
Life of <u>Oneness</u>!

Dad 2:5, 6

The Secret to Happiness

We humans start out in life selfish like every sinner does chasing happiness <u>for ourselves</u> and for a short time it seems to work, or so we think. But after chasing our own ☠selfishness☠ we always get bored. So what's the long term answer for sustainable happiness? What can we do to have happiness last us a lifetime? I asked my heavenly Father that question one time in prayer and so now listen to the secret my heavenly Dad educated me with as I now share His answer with you because friend, it really does work.

<u>Find someone else to make ha</u>ppy; a niece, a poor customer with a leaky roof, a new contractor starting out in business you help through the cold winter month, even if it's a total stranger like a single mon with six kids who needed help on her tattered house after her husband left. But it's always best to start with your own spouse first asking them, "What do they really want in their life or what would make them super ecstatic"; and then strive to get them that dream of their life or the one thing they have always wanted. After presenting it, or doing that service they've always longed for, wait for their response and watch their face closely as their heart will light up with joy and you will see <u>their heart's joy</u> <u>right on their face</u>. If you did your homework well and searched for that one special thing to touch their heart, you will see their hidden heart y<u>ou can't see</u>, <u>light up on their face in their smile y</u>ou can see as their hidden heart is clearly seen in their smile on their face.

That's how the Lord taught me and that is now where I get my happiness from as helping other people and making them happy while watching their happy hearts light up on their faces is very rewarding to your soul. And even after the sweaty job is done there is a real sense of deep satisfaction in your soul as the Lord will let you know, "Well done My son; I am exceedingly pleased with you." Now watch carefully; if both spouses have this kind of helping lavishing heart, and both do the same thing chasing after each other's happiness, that couple's ☺joy☺ will shoot through the roof and your marriage will be something the world won't be able to stop watching as you both have captivated all who see you. So try to outdo the other spouse on pleasing your soulmate more. I've had people who wanted to pay me for helping them and I just think the same way Daniel does . . . ¹⁷ *"Then Daniel answered the king, "You may keep your gifts for yourself and give your rewards to someone else."* Daniel 5:17. NIV. (Philippians 2:3-5 * 1 Corinthians 10:24)

There's so little time before we leave this Earth to help our follow man who is hurting so badly. They have more bills than paycheck to pay them all with and this evil world is killing our economy on purpose making it even harder on the poor people struggling just to survive. They have children to fed, clothe, and raise up with good morals *"in a crooked and depraved generation in which you shine like stars in the universe"*. Philippians 2:15. Our country is sinking ever deeper into Communism and selfishness is absolutely everywhere in every self-centered soul as they only think about themselves. 1 John 3:10. Some working poor souls have to work three jobs just to make ends meet as I did one time to live and still they're short on the basics of life. Far too many people are uncaring and will not give anyone a helping hand unless they are paid for their services as selfishness today is the standard. Then the Lord comes along working through you as you see their needs, you step out of your comfort zone and help them with your time, sweat, and kindness they've never seen before. After you're done, tired and all sweaty, he looked at me and honestly asked with a puzzled look on his face, "Why are you replacing my roof for free." Then you tell him, "Because the rain is pouring in on your living room. You're stretched to the end of your rope and it's obvious someone needs to step in and help you out." Then he continued to stare at me for a few more seconds as he's never seen this type of person before and wondered suspiciously, "What's his angle?" Then while he looked still trying to understand the words I just spoke to him, he asked the very same question with a more puzzling look. "Yeah, but, why are you doing this?" That's when Everything Changes as you know he's never seen the love of God working in his life before and he truly is perplexed and stumped. This is when God gets a foot hold into their life to bring them to salvation if you're willing to speak up for Lord Jesus and lead them in their salvation and Heaven's eternal happiness. Listen to the Word of God tell you, *"Dear children, let us not love with words or tongue but with **actions** and in truth."* 1 John 3:18.

v1 God is not a secret to be kept, but the greatest message to be Told. v2 Speak the gospel of God as His love is pure Gold
Dad 10:1, 2

They look at you like your from another planet, and you are; planet Heaven. Zachariah 6:1. These badly hurting over worked people need to see God's love displayed in their life so they know there really is a God of Love in Heaven who wants to love them as they see His love displayed in your selfless actions. So I say to you, more than praying for God to do a miracle for those hurting people, why not let God use you to **be the miracle** in someone's life. Find the hurting, look for the overburdened, the worn out, the single mom with six kids working trying to feed, clothe and raise up her children in a godly way as the world sinks deeper into their Communist control every day. **Be the miracle** in their life today before time runs out and you live with regret for an **eternity** wishing you had helped those hurting people when you had the chance but didn't because you didn't want to get all sweaty.

". . . *through love, **serve** one another.*" Galatians 5:13. If we all do our helping part, we can make a difference in this selfish (me-first, you last) world sinking faster into their New World Order as God is directing our very footsteps. [23] *"The steps of a good man are ordered by the LORD, and **He delights** in his way."* Psalm 37:23. KJV. And maybe with prayer even some of the politicians will be touched and start to follow our loving lead to help others in need. Now is not a time for lining our own greedy pockets for more new gadgets, baubles and trivial trinkets so we can live a few more selfish days here on Earth to get our own fun and enjoyment before Jesus takes us real Christians home to Heaven to reward us after the Rapture. But now is the time to pray for God's leading, to show us Lavishers, "Who we can help today Lord?" So "*as we have **opportunity**, let us do good to all people.*" Galatians 6:10. NIV.

Remember, [21]"*For where your treasure is, there will your heart be also.*" Matthew 6:21. KJV. And what about these words you have always long to hear. [21] *"Well done, thou good and faithful servant: thou hast been faithful over a few things, I will make thee ruler over many things: enter thou into the joy of thy Lord."* Matthew 25:21. KJV. Is this anything you want to hear when you stand before Lord Jesus in all of His shimmering glorious splendor? **Hmmm?** So, like some singer once said, Go Light Your World with God's altruistic love and step out to be **someone's miracle**.

You now have *The Secret to Happiness*; *"go and do likewise."*
Luke 10:37 * Prodigal Son

A <u>word of hope</u> for all those who struggle in life to make ends meet.

v3 Always remember: Life is hard, but it's harder when you give up. v4 Don't quit on You, look to Jesus and He'll pull you Through.
Dad 10:3, 4

Just remember, if you want Love, <u>L</u>ove Has a Nam<u>e</u>, <u>Jesus</u>. *"Let us not become weary in doing good, for at the **proper time** we will reap a harvest if we do not give up. So then, as we have **opportunity**, <u>let us do good</u> <u>to every</u>one, and especially to those who are of the household of faith."* Galatians 6:9, 10. I remember an unusual song name back in 1966 during my early growing up years called, **"<u>Alfie</u>"** sung by **Dion Warwick**. I feel it might be applicable at this moment with those that are struggling to make ends meet and need help as some have lost their spouse. Listen to this song Kay and tell me if you see that connection? Keep in mind they only allow eight lines on any one song quoted in a book.

♩ **What's it all about, Alfie?**
<u>Is it just for the moment we live</u>?
What's it all about, when you sort it out, Alfie?
Are we meant to <u>take more than we give</u>?
Or <u>are we meant to be kind</u>?
I believe in love, Alfie.
Without <u>true love</u> <u>we just exist</u>, Alfie. ♩
♩ Until you <u>find the love you've missed</u>
you're nothing, Alfie. ♩ Find <u>**Jesus**</u> and <u>learn to love others</u>.

I remember even earlier back in 1964 a song sung by **Peter** and **Gordon** called, **A World Without Love**. The only line today that I can recall is, **I don't care what they say, I won't stay in a world without love**; of which I whole heartily agree. For instance, *"If I give all I possess to the poor and surrender my body to the flames, <u>but have not love</u>, I gain nothing."* 1 Corinthians 13:3. *"For whoever wants to save their life* (live for sin and greedy money) *will lose it, but whoever loses their life for Me* (Jesus: <u>stand up</u> <u>for God</u> and <u>live for Him</u>) *and for the gospel will save it."* Mark 8:35. NIV. In life there're <u>Takers</u> and <u>Givers</u>. When it comes to love I'm more of a **Lavisher** as I tend to believe <u>you get what you give</u>. 2 Cor. 9:6. Later growing up in 1969 I recall an all-girl group as they had a song about love that I really liked called . . .

Love Can Make You Happy by Mercy

♩ Love . . . can make you happy,
<u>if</u> <u>you fine</u> some<u>one</u> who cares
to give, a lifetime to you
and who has a love to share . . .
If you think you've found someone
you'll love for evermore.
Then it's worth the price you'll have to pay . . .
To have, to hold's important when,
<u>forever</u>, is the phrase.
That means the love you've found is going to
<u>stay.</u>
Love . . . can make you happy,
if you find someone who cares
to give, a <u>lifetime</u> to you
and who has a love to share. ♩

Find me Kay so we can start **a lifetime of love** together. . . .

The Core of God's Heart

My goal and dream is to have <u>God's Core Heart</u> ruling in my life.

Would you like to have the <u>Core of God's Heart</u> in you? The <u>Core Heart of God</u> in a nut shell is, "<u>Love</u>". Lavishing kindness, gifts, blessings and pouring happiness out on those it meets as thinking up ways to make others happy is part of the very Core of God's Heart. So let's learn about God's Core Heart. <u>Love</u> is patient with all your mistakes and short comings while always seeking for the good in you and overlooking any faults Love might find in your imperfect character. <u>Love</u> is kind, longing to lavish kindness on others to see your heart light up with joy generated by Love's generous efforts. <u>Love</u> does not envy as Love is so full of God's joy it is satisfied and content with God's Love alone and is only looking for someone else to lavish that abundant love on they received from God and pour it on others. <u>Love</u> does not boast as it is not self focusing and neither is it insecure but complete in God and so knows nothing of ☠<u>selfishness</u>☠ but longs to seek someone else to lavish all their stored up love on. <u>Love</u> is not proud having ☺abandoned☺ all ☠<u>selfishness</u>☠ but lives in a world of humble satisfaction and contentment having plenty of room to lavish its love on others. <u>Love</u> is not rude or self-seeking as God's kindness is over flowingly in Love's ♥heart and so they long to lavish all God's abundant love they have on ☺others☺ who are love-starved as their heart goes out to the hurting☹. <u>Love</u> is not easily angered as their emotions are full of love and <u>well satisfied</u>. Anger is a derivative of ☠<u>selfishness</u>☠ that rules the angry <u>unsatisfied soul</u> as they focus <u>inwardly</u> on how y<u>ou hurt them</u>. But love focuses <u>externally</u> on how <u>they</u> can **<u>lavish</u>** and forgive <u>others</u>.

Love is so preoccupied with lavishing on others that love is quick to overlook almost any hurt you may have caused them so they can continue lavishing their love on you. Love keeps no record of wrongs in your life as revenge does not interest them while repaying wrong for wrong is rooted in ☠**selfishness**☠ and is not even a normal part of Love's Lavishing Nature. Love does not delight in evil, because evil is completely foreign to Love as evil is always hurting others and thinking of its own ☠**selfish**☠ inward desires. Love always rejoices with the truth which is why I enjoy watching the FIVE. Truth is required to build the Core of God's Heart. It's a close cousin of Love as those that love truth gravitate to shows lavishing truth. Love always protects the one it loves as love will gladly lay down its life for the one it loves. Love always trust, as it's always thinking the best about you assuming nothing negative because there's no cynical heart inside of love. Love always hopes for your best as love wants you to succeed and be your happiest. Love always perseveres because Love doesn't ever cease loving as love seeks the very Core of God's Heart in daily worship and so will never stop loving you with God's abundant kindness. Love never fails because Love's source is resting deep in the Core of God's Heart of love. Would you like to start down this road of Love as I have described it? Would you like to be the very Core of God's Heart and love just as He does? Then let's get you started by listening and following the God of Love's scriptures directing you to the Core of God's Heart through His Holy Word.

If you choose to be **Saved** from God's wrath and not burn in Hell for an eternity or choose to be Born Again like John 3:3, or verse 7 tells us sinners to do, *"You must be Born Again"*. Look what encouragement you will get from just one of the books in the Bible; Ephesians. Now we the saved Christians in Ephesians 1:1

". . . *are faithful* . . ." because we <u>Believe</u> the blood of Lord Jesus covers our many sins from His Holy righteous work on the cross. Verse 1:3 says <u>we are blessed in Christ</u> with <u>Every Spiritual Blessing</u> in Heavenly places. Verse 1:4 says we are <u>Chosen</u> in Christ before the foundation of the world and we are <u>Holy</u> and <u>Blameless</u> before God **if** <u>we choose to Believe in Jesus our Lord</u> as our Savior to cover our many sins. Verse 1:5 says we are also <u>Adopted</u> children of God <u>through Jesus Christ</u> our Savior. Verse 1:6 says Jesus loves us giving us saved sinners <u>His Glorious Grace</u> to cover our endless sins we do. Verse 1:7 says we are <u>Forgiven</u> of our sins and <u>Redeemed</u> through His blood. (Redeemed means: <u>Bought back from Satan's control who had the Legal Right to demand our souls into eternal Hell</u> who used to hold our sins over us sinners because of our first father Adam's failure in the Garden of Eden. That is until Jesus came from Heaven to give us condemned sinners a **choice** <u>to be saved</u> and so go to Heaven). When was our salvation available you ask? At the cross when <u>Jesus died for us</u>. And when did we sinners get Born Again? When we sinners **chose** to <u>recognize our sins</u> and then **chose** Lord Jesus as our Savior to cover our sins if we **choose**. Verse 1:8 says Jesus has <u>Lavished</u> on us saved sinners with all <u>Wisdom</u> and <u>Understanding</u> **IF** <u>we choose to sit at His feet daily and learn while we hunger for more of His Truth</u>. Verse 1:11 says *we have obtained an <u>Inheritance</u>,* and a <u>Purpose</u> in His Kingdom according to His Holy will. Remember Lord Jesus rewards us saved sinners in Heaven with <u>great gifts</u> we did back on Earth; then during the 1,000 year Millennium you might rule over ". . . *ten cities* . . ." or ". . . *five cites* . . ." (Luke 19:11-27) based on what we did on Earth when we were alive and had a chance <u>to serve Jesus by serving others</u> who were poor or those struggling needing someone's help in their time of need. Is this you? Are you living for yourself, or for Jesus as you help others who are overburdened? Jesus is watching your compassion and your level of ☠selfishness☠ as He records your actions in His heavenly books so He can Judge us saved sinners and reward our loving actions we did while on Earth living for Him or ☠ourselves☠. Remember when Jesus is teaching us in the Bible, "*I tell you the truth, whatever you did for one of the least of these brothers of mine, you did for Me.*" Matthew 25:40. So when you see hurting people who need help, those needy people are like Jesus who needs help. Will you use your time left on Earth to help "Jesus"? Verse 1:13 says we Christians are Sealed with the Holy Spirit's Promise. (which means Satan cannot steal you back to be condemned in Hell anymore. You are now destined to enter Heaven for your glorious eternal happiness). Verse 1:18 says our Understanding has been Enlightened that we are aware of our Hope and the glory of His Inheritance to us saints. Verse 1:19 says we have His Exceeding Great Power working toward us saved sinners who choose to be Born Again. This means we have His Authority to lay hands on hurting people and ask in the name of Jesus to *cast out unclean spirits* (or demons) *and to heal all manner of sickness and all manner of disease.*" Matthew 10:1. KJV. Verse 2:4 says we are Greatly Loved by our God of love. Verse 2:8 says we are *Saved through Faith, not of good works lest any man should boast.*" Verse 2:15 says we saved sinners are Reconciled back to God. Verse 2:19, 20 says we saved sinners are Fellow Citizens and Members of the heavenly house of God. Let's look at other verses.

⁴"*Rejoice in the Lord always.* (Worship the God of Love every day in your morning worship to start and **Set** the Pace of every day to be a God Man) *I will say it again: Rejoice!* (Pray throughout the day as you always talk to God about **Everything** you do). ⁵ *Let your gentleness be evident to all.* (Beg and Plead for God to change you into His loving God Man). *The*

Lord is near. ("*Come near to God and He will come near to you.*" James 4:8. NIV. *⁶ Do not be anxious about anything,* (<u>trust God to lead you</u> as you go through your life) *but in <u>every situation,</u> by prayer and petition,* (<u>constantly asking</u> God for <u>His will</u> as you <u>learn to die</u> to your own will) *with thanksgiving, present your requests to God.* (Be thankful in **Everything** you have whether a little or a lot as you know you deserve eternal Hell) *⁷ And the peace of God,* (we have peace with God as we <u>no longer are choosing sin to separate us</u>) *which transcends all understanding,* (the unsaved do not understand this kind of godly walk with God as far too many are <u>blinded</u> by Satan for **Rejecting Truth**) *will guard your hearts and your minds in Christ Jesus.* (if you live righteous, you will make yourself extremely valuable to God and He will work with you to do His Holy will). *⁸ Finally, brothers and sisters, whatever is <u>true</u>, whatever is <u>noble</u>, whatever is <u>right</u>, whatever is <u>pure</u>, whatever is <u>lovely</u>, whatever is <u>admirable</u>—if anything is <u>excellent</u> or <u>praiseworthy</u>—<u>think about such things</u>.*" (These are the things Christians need to be focused on, the <u>true</u>, the <u>pure</u>, or <u>praiseworthy</u>, not marinating our minds in Satan's Hollywood filling up on violence, lust, wizards, spells, and his chief weapon **FEAR**.) Philippians 4:4-9.

Let's learn more about <u>God's Core Heart</u> as we read in the Bible. "*And we pray this in order <u>that you may please God in every way: bearing fruit in every good work,</u> growing in the knowledge of God, ¹¹ being strengthened with all power according to His glorious might so that you may have great endurance and patience, and joyfully ¹² giving thanks to the Father, who has qualified you to share in the inheritance of the saints in the kingdom of light.* (God will grant you <u>Great Gifts in Heaven</u>). *¹³ For Lord Jesus has rescued us from the <u>dominion of darkness</u>* (Satan's system of lies and future pain in Hell) *and brought us into the kingdom of the Son the Father loves,* (truth, and glorious joy in Heaven) *¹⁴ in whom we have redemption,* (God transforms us saved sinners originally going to Hell into saints going to Heaven) *the forgiveness of sins.*" Colossians 1:10-14. [45] "*A good man brings good things out of the good* <u>stored up</u> *in his heart,* (you will be blessed in Heaven for all the good y<u>ou let</u> the Holy Spirit do <u>through you</u> in your life) *and an evil man* (someone <u>who lets</u> the demon spirits or the fallen angels <u>do evil through them</u>) *brings evil things out of the **evil stored up** in his heart.* (the dark army takes the sins you do and **stores them up** <u>like a S</u>piritual Bank Account to spring them on you at your weakest moment to gain more control over you so you'll suffer all the more after your dead either in Hell if you're unsaved or in Heaven if you're saved <u>by</u> <u>your loss of God's rewards</u> as you cannot be rewarded for your sins). *For the mouth speaks what the heart is full of.*" Luke 6:45. So as you read God's Holy Word, or watch trashy TV, what you put in your heart, you will surely speak the very sins you have been <u>feeding your mind on</u>. You've heard a lot of Bible truth and inner spiritual insight as I've explained much spiritual truths to you. So it's time for you to choose whose kingdom you truly want here on Earth to follow and obey and whose kingdom you want to live in forever after your short life is over? So listen to the words of Elijah. "*Elijah went before the people and said, 'How long will you waver between two opinions? If the Lord is God, follow Him; but if Baal is God follow him.*" 1 Kings 18:29. NIV. The so-called god of Baal was just Satan masquerading as a "god" so he could deceive the unsaved people of that day to follow him leading them to eternal Hell when they die. So now <u>it's your turn to choose</u> who you will follow. If you choose to be saved, you'll have to **Believe** in Jesus like Andy did having <u>active faith</u> and not like Billy who said he **Believed** but never put his faith into <u>action</u>. So you must **Believe** that Jesus is the Son of God who died on a Roman cross ✝ to be our Savoir to cover your sin if you choose to **Believe** with actions; then y<u>ield</u> to the Holy Spirit as He will <u>start</u> working through you.

A Question for God

Now I have a question Kay, but this time it's for the Lord. So, tell me Lord, "I know you want us to love You, and a lot of us Christians do, but do our physical bodies not need a physical mate as it was not good for Adam to be alone? Genesis 2:18. What good is this grand gift of Love You have given us in our hearts, if there's no mate here on Earth to lavish it all on? Isaiah 41:21. Does love not need a recipient to love and pour our love on? How can we receive Love if there's never someone in our lives who longs to shower all their love on us? Isn't that why You created us humans so You would have a recipient to love on and return it all back on You as we long to mimic Your loving heart? If a single person has no one, than how can they enjoy Your greatest gift of Deep Love in a physical way? You want us to love You, and your closest saints long to do exactly that; but yet we sit dormant for years still waiting on love to come to our ♥hearts♥. How much **glory** could You receive if your children got together in a Majestic Marriage and displayed that love You gave us before this lost world? Isn't that why You created the marriage institution in the first place?

Tell me Lord; is it our turn to make the next move? Are You all done setting us up for the final last time? Please send me such a godly woman I can lavish all my love on Lord and Your **glory** will increase. Someone who has been storing up all her Love in her heart for decades holding it back for that one soulmate she might still be longing for? Father what good is Your greatest gift, if even your own children can't share in this love of yours?

Dream-Giver, you started this dream of romance in me to answer and complete Kay's prayers and dreams of sweet love in a godly man; now I'm asking You, "Please complete those prayers and deepest dreams in both our ♥hearts♥. Let me finish this Q<u>uest</u> <u>for a Q</u>ueen You started <u>17</u> years ago with the one You have chosen for me. I have so much of Your Love inside of me Lord; I need a godly outlet to lavish all my stored up love on." **14** *"For if* <u>y</u>o<u>u</u> *remain* **silent** <u>at this time</u>, <u>relief</u> *and deliverance for the Jews* <u>will arise from another p</u><u>lace</u>, *but you and your father's family* <u>will</u> <u>p</u><u>erish</u>. *And who knows but that* <u>you have come</u> *to your royal position* <u>*for* **such a time as this**</u>*?"* Esther 4:14. NIV. Remember John 9:1-3? **3** *"... Neither this man nor his parents sinned,' said Jesus, but* <u>this happened</u> *so that the* **work of God might be displayed in his** (<u>your</u>) *life*." Our <u>final time</u> has finally come; so <u>find me</u>. 203

Lord, I have waited all my life since nine years old for sweet love to finally come. Most of the time I'm happy in my life. But looking at these same four walls, <u>s</u>ometimes I fall apar<u>t</u> just wishing I hadn't of missed the chance to love <u>Kay's deep heart</u>. The tears blur my hope and <u>it</u>'s hard to find my love longing hear<u>t</u>. Recalling my sad past on five different ships of intimidation of y<u>ou</u> I h<u>u</u>ng my head as I just felt empty like <u>a</u> little boy lost in the dar<u>k</u>. <u>S</u>ometimes I hear Kay sin<u>g</u>ing in my mind, and suddenly I'm back on the ship in the front row like always <u>hoping at the stage</u> where her sweet voice, heart-capturing face and loving <u>s</u>ong never end<u>s</u>. My chance for sweet love is still out ahead of me and I haven't blown my once in a lifetime chance for the sweetest woman yet. <u>H</u>ope's Aliv<u>e</u> at that h<u>c</u>art hoping moment as joy fills my soul to overflowing and at that time I'm still smiling; but then I open up my eyes and the cold hard reality comes crashing in like a dagger. I cry out to my Lord, help my <u>h</u>eart to find a way to hold the pai<u>n</u>. <u>B</u>ut Love remember<u>s</u> my dream, and <u>L</u>ove still listens when I cr<u>y</u>. <u>W</u>hen I can only feel the hurt, I forget about God's precious Wor<u>d</u>. Lord, <u>I</u> don't know what to say, or what to pray I feel so helples<u>s</u>.

My heart grieves this side of Heaven. But still Lord please let it be. Love remembers with abounding grace to face whatever will be. Almighty Lord I need Your courage, without You there's no hope.

How could I've known, right from the start? The enemies dart would keep us both apart. Leave behind a broken heart. So now tell me Kay: Does Love Remember? Does Love Survive? It's Hard to Hear Forever. Does Love still Listen when I Cry? Can you Hear my Heart and See the Light? Can our Hearts Continue to Find a Way to Hold the Pain? After all these years and underneath all those black ashes of loneliness there's still a spark of romantic hope left. So tell me Kay, what do I do with my leftover burning spark I still have waiting in hope as I need strength; he needs courage abounding grace to face, whatever will be could it happen to me, or should I just let that waiting spark flick out and finish dying slowly alone? And what about all those dreams we dare to dream, **do they really come true?**

v1 I was Told, by a God so Bold,
that you were the one I'd Hold.
v2 Love dearly as we both grow Old.
v3 Lord said, Trust Me and be Bold.
v4 But my courage with you did Fold.
v5 Now Love stands out in the Cold,
as I long for a heart of Gold. Proverbs 31:10
v6 Is my heart now left to Mold?
v7 Has our last chance been Sold?
Craig 1:1-7

I often dreamed, of how we'd live. But is there now no room for all the Love I have to Give? Can you forgive, my shy intimidated heart? I believe we can outlive the time we lost in the past so our day of love we can relive? Is it still possible to try again? So is Hope still Alive? But Maybe that's the Chance Love Takes? Now you tell me Kay? Is it too late for Love? Should I just go back to watching my romantic Hallmark movie on the taped TV **by myself** just me and my four walls and wait for the Rapture to come and consume our last few possible moments of Love? My favorite verse is, [20] *"He that walks with wise men shall be wise, but a companion of fools will be destroyed."* Proverbs 13:20. KJV. As life is all about whom you spend time and eternity with. Who you join to as one, or who you will emulate and reflect back the most. I spend much time with my Lord the King and His Holy Word and so I would like to include you in Our inner circle of two to make three. I also know one of your favorite verses is, [13] *"I can do all things through Christ who strengthens me."* Philippians 4:13. NIV. So Kay, can you find the strength to do all things and find me? Then next Christmas we can enjoy loving songs like An Evening In December by First Call back in 1985 and many other favorites we love. In a 1965 movie I remember The nostalgia Sounds Of Music in a song we should consider at this moment that I heard decades ago called, Climb Every Mountain. Remember this advice given?

♩ **Climb every mountain, search high and low.**
Follow every byway, every path you know.
A dream that will need, all the love you can give,
Every day of your life, for as long as you live.
Climb every mountain, ford every stream.
Follow every rainbow, till you find Your Dream.

My Love Longing Heart
still Hoping ♥☺☺♥
Romans 8:28.

All those trips to the Bahamas and St Thomas Island and Cay "something" <u>beach</u> as I remember, while feeling all that warm white sand on my toes and under my feet and seeing all those clear blue/teal waters and the gentle waves slowly lapping softly on the shoreline with the Sun blazing warm; an earthly paradise to be sure. I remember seeing you coming into the white <u>sandy island</u> on their small transfer boat standing in line on shore as you were going through customs <u>to enter the island</u> as I looked over and saw you waving at me going through customs <u>to leave the island</u> then I waved back happy to see you but still sad we never connected.

Unfortunately I already came through customs and was already in line to leave the island and so we missed our connection that time as well. If only we could have bonded our loving hearts in such a heavenly tropical 🏝 paradise as that, how would our love have blossomed into Heaven's happiness? Romance could have flourished into our blessing of bliss and we could have celebrated our 15 wedding anniversary by now. You made the right call Kay, as the ambient atmosphere was picture perfect while God made that sunny warm day for <u>us</u>; what a beautiful idyllic place to meet your Heart and fall in love and spark our souls into loving overdrive like Romeo and Juliet's love.

It was my fault that we missed our love connection as it was hindered by the enemy; I never should have believed the enemy's lie about being **worthless**. Yet even in those beautiful tropical sunny teal/blue waters, <u>places I long for and love to be</u>

there more than any other place on Earth, yet I could not be happy in that heavenly place as I walked around on the warm white sand all **by myself** forever lonely while other couples in love were enjoying "sweet desire". That's when my romantic heart broke and I decided to leave the white sandy Island as the crushing weight of loneliness got the better of me and only after I passed through customs to leave did I finally see you arrive. I looked as I was exiting through the tightly knit double walled wire fencing some 30 feet keeping us apart as you were coming in through customs and waving at me with a smiling face in line still waiting to be cleared on the other side. Its times like these I still remember that song back in high school that Frankie Valli sung in 1975,

♩ **"My eyes adored you. Though I never laid a hand on you, my eyes adored you. Like a million miles away from me you couldn't see how I adored you. So close, so close and yet so far."** ♩ And later in that same song I remember,

"Still I reminisce, about the girl I miss,
and <u>the love I left behind</u>."

My heart was so close to God's choice after all those months of preparation and yet our souls never did touch and join with a loving embraced while <u>my heart ached</u>. While the Lord and **I Still reminisce, about the girl I missed <u>and the love I left behind</u>** on that warm sunny beach. Vacations were made for being with <u>the one you love</u> so we can <u>**see**</u> the love beaming from our Heart's face and filling up our souls to overflowing with God's romantic love. This is <u>where I get</u> my level of unstoppable happiness from; from making my new sweetheart happy with loving words, and love songs we share together in a sunny paradise like the one we had but then missed.

I have become a servant in these last few years Kay longing to help others who are hurting and need relief as my heavenly Father has showed me deeper levels of love/happiness. And as you know a servant's heart is only happy when he's serving someone; Lumiare especially someone he loves. And who better to serve than your spouse hand-picked by God Himself to be your perfect soulmate for the remainder of time we still might have left. Remember Kay,

We've only just begun to live. A kiss for luck and we're on our way. So many roads to choose. We'll start out walkin' and learn to run. Talking it over just the two of us. Working together day to day. And when the evening comes, we smile, so much of life ahead . . . 1970 The Carpenters.

But my problem is I have no one to love. No one to hold close, speak loving thoughts too while we plan our future together. No one to massage or serve or make laugh and share that laughter and joy with and see a happy heart on her face made by my efforts.

Laughter is the lubricant of life.
Dad 1:2 / Proverbs 17:22

To know in my heart I had something to do with your happy heart shining through your face revealed in your smile. Did you know Kay a smile is the face of your heart letting others know at any time just how your heart is doing as you ware your hidden heart on your face where everyone and anyone can see it glowing?

As the eye is the light of the body, so also is a smile the face of your heart.
Dad 11:2

And even though I can't fall in love until we spend time together, I have to believe that my God made the right choice for me back in 2007 in my dad's man cave watching your DVD. In a marriage two hearts <u>become</u> one. On my Bucket List I still only have <u>one thing</u> listed on it; "Oneness in a loving Majestic Marriage". That is the kind of marriage where ♥two♥ hearts melt together in one loving union of <u>two souls</u> <u>sharing the same heart</u>.

♥ Do you see how earthly $money$ has so little value next to the holiness of God's Love? Earthly money can only buy earthly things of temporary value that will **surely burn** in the Seven Year Tribulation (Revelation 8:7 * 11:5 * 14:9-11 * 16:8 * 17:16 * 18:8, 9, 18 * 19:3) coming up soon after we leave Kay in the Rapture of the saints. But <u>the real prize in this cold calloused world is God's loving-Oneness</u> I still seek that lives on into eternity forever even after our earthly Majestic Marriage is dissolved by our heavenly marriage that will last forever to the King of kings and the Lord of lords. Yet if we start our love today, it will still be going strong a hundred trillion years from now as God wants His bride to still love one another. John 13:34. Earthly things were only designed <u>to enhance</u> a Connubial Bliss Marriage[14] of Oneness through eternity. But the world has it all backwards, where their happiness flows from greedy money and how many temporary earthly things they can acquire (Luke 12:15) rather than how much of God's eternal love

---

[14] Connubial Bliss Marriage: A connubial bliss marriage is where the newlywed couple <u>live a happily ever after marriage of bliss</u>.

we can <u>lavish on each other</u>. Luke 6:38. Maybe that's why I gave so much of my money away and parted with it so easily in troubled times in exchange for God's treasured <u>Peace</u> with customers of ☠greed☠ who love earthly money so much. But are these greedy customers willing to <u>sell all they have</u> for a heavenly Pearl of great price (Jesus: Matthew 13:45, 46) and have treasures in Heaven beyond our wildest dreams forever? Or maybe these greedy people would rather hang on to their meager earthly treasures that will rust and corrode for a little while longer on this failing Earth they seem to value? Matthew 13:45, 46 * 6:21 * 19:23-26. If we could have that deep love of Oneness, earthly rich or poor it just wouldn't matter as earthly money isn't what sparks <u>our romantic hearts</u> for happiness. As much as we all need a certain amount of it to get through this <u>earthly life</u> <u>God is **test**ing us in</u>, yet even the multi hundreds of billions of dollars the billionaires and trillionaire companies have can't buy love like we <u>could have</u>, Kay. Every young heart still wants real heavenly love, until they can't find it in an unsaved mate. Then typically in their 40s when they get desperate, they <u>settle for</u> things that money can buy as a sad "plan B", or their last hope cheap substitute to take the place of unfulfilled love. Being one in a heart of Love is the only value this empty loveless world has to offer; and <u>I still long for it</u>; <u>how about you</u>? If the world was going to end in 15 minutes, I would still look for someone to love; why? Cause even a few minutes of love is worth a lifetime of joy. As you sang in your <u>calling for a soulmate</u> song, so now I'm also calling that same message Kay; <u>T</u>ake your Heart Off the Shelf and <u>Please Come</u>. Why? Cause **Hope's Alive**. ♥☺☺♥

"Seek ye out the diamond in the rough." c.o.w. <u>203</u>

Preface

This book is about my testimony displaying the 20 miracles the Lord did back in 2007 to connect me to my future wife <u>by faith</u> while she also prayed for a soulmate for years as neither one of us knew about each other. The spiritual enemy tried everything to thwart those God-laid romantic plans for sweet love of a future marriage between the two love-hopeful praying souls. You'll see the enemy working through a biblical stronghold (2 Corinthians 10:4) to hinder God's well laid plans as an ongoing battle between halos and horns occurred to <u>Disrupt</u> or <u>Stop</u> our merging together as the spiritual war is explained in great detail. In this book you'll see God's inner workings illuminating every miracle or how He blends multiple miracles revealing behind the scene details we so seldom ever see or spiritually comprehend to a conclusion; as God truly does work in mysterious astonishing ways. Every spiritual detail is explained as the Lord looks to the <u>end</u> of His <u>multi-year plan</u>; as this romantic love-chasing union could actually happen in 2024. There's an additional chapter on Understanding Spiritual Rules you'll not want to miss as I explain spiritual laws that angels and demons must follow. You'll gain great knowledge and extensive insight on how spiritual laws actually work and <u>how you can win the spiritual war for your family</u> most don't know anything about. While this spiritual battle continues, always keep in mind God's method of seeing the <u>end</u> of His complexed <u>perfect plans</u> that we humans can't see, before He ever starts the <u>beginning</u> involving us Christians or His weak humble servants seeking a godly loving marriage. ¹⁰ *"Declaring the <u>end</u> from the <u>beginning</u>, and from ancient times the things that are <u>not yet done</u>, saying, <u>My counsel shall stand</u>, and <u>I will do all My pleasure</u>:"* Isaiah. 46:10. KJV.